Whitewater Rafting

We said there warn't no home like a raft, after all. Other places do seem so cramped up and smothery, but a raft don't. You feel mighty free and easy and comfortable on a raft.

Mark Twain, *The Adventures of Huckleberry Finn*

He learnt to swim and to row, and entered into the joy of running water; and with his ear to the reedstems he caught, at intervals, something of what the wind went whispering so constantly among them.

Kenneth Grahame, *The Wind in the Willows*

'Twas brillig, and the slithy toves did gyre and gimble in the wabe . . .

Lewis Carroll, "Jabberwocky"

Whitewater Rafting

WILLIAM McGINNIS

Illustrated with Drawings by Tom Joyce
and Photographs by
Michael Gill / Dandelet Interlinks

Quadrangle / The New York Times Book Co.

Photos copyright © 1975 by Michael Gill, unless otherwise specified.

Text of article, "The Heaving-Line Rescue," copyright © 1973 by O. K. Goodwin, reproduced with permission.

Excerpt entitled, "Cold Water: Drowning and Hypothermia," from *Whitewater; Quietwater,* copyright © 1973 by Dr. Robert J. Palzer; reprinted with permission of the publisher, Evergreen Paddleways, Two Rivers, Wisconsin.

Illustration and excerpt from *Standard First Aid and Personal Safety,* copyright © 1972 by The American National Red Cross, reproduced with permission.

Article entitled, "Photography on Raft Trips," copyright © 1975 by Richard Norgaard and the American River Touring Association, reprinted with permission.

Article entitled, "Saving Our Last Free Rivers," copyright © 1975 by Bill Painter, printed here for the first time.

Article entitled, "The Art of Dutch Oven Cookery," copyright © 1975 by Bill Center, printed here for the first time.

Library of Congress Cataloging in Publication Data

McGinnis, William, 1947-
    Whitewater rafting.

    Bibliography: p.
    Includes index.
    1. Rafting (Sports)—United States. 2. Rafting (Sports) I. Title.
GV776.A2M32 1975   797   74-24280
ISBN 0-8129-0529-6

Design by Tere LoPrete

To my brother Gregor

Acknowledgments

In the course of writing this book I have had the help of many generous people. I would like to thank Bill Center, Bill Painter, Richard Norgaard, O. K. Goodwin, and Bob and Jody Palzer for contributing articles, and Bob Burrell, Eben Thomas, Tim Lawton, Mike Rettie, Jerry Meral, and the redoubtable Harry Chest for their help with the river guides. I am grateful to Jim Sindelar for his help with the safety code, to Leslie Jones and Dave Demaree for their suggestions, to Michael Zimmerman, Eric Solomon, and Manfred Wolf for their encouragement and assistance in the early stages, to Bob Palzer again for his help with both rivers and proofreading, and to Bob Elliott and David Kay of the American River Touring Association for their aid with proofreading, photos, and permission to reprint certain items. Thanks to the Department of the Interior and the National Park Service for permission to take photographs in the Grand Canyon, and to all of the fine people of the Park Service, the Forest Service, the Bureau of Land Management, the American National Red Cross, and especially the Geological Survey for their truly friendly and efficient assistance.

In a very personal way I would like to thank Mike Gill and Tom Joyce for their extraordinary efforts above and beyond, Doc Thompson for his great generosity in many ways, Jan Schwarz for her expert bibliographic probing, Vince Fernandez and Sally Somerl, fine writers both, for advice on words, and above all

Richard Wright, who risked his own life to save mine.

On an entirely homespun note, I would like to thank my family, especially my brother Gregor, for their encouragement and support, Jon Runnestrand, Kathy Meyer, Sandy Little, and my other river cronies for taking care of me, Don Logan for his off-color humor and neighborly generosity, everyone who helped me in regard to the S.S.S., John O'Hare, Greg Vose, and Marc Crawley for glowing with wit and friendship, Toni Meurlott for her support, Buck Swashbuckler, the shadow of my life, my lovely postmistress Margaret, and my inspiration Patrick Noonan, a man in tune with the universal flow, whose greatness is assured if he will only go after it with the tip of his pen.

W. M.

Contents

Preface

When Bill McGinnis asked me to read the manuscript for this book, I was frankly skeptical. A book of this sort runs the risk of encouraging the reader to venture out, unknowingly, beyond his abilities. I had another question as well. Based on the world of rivers I had come to know, the science of whitewater technique was for me inseparable from a personal philosophy of rivers; the two had grown simultaneously within me over the years. How could anyone explain the fine points of whitewater technique and still impart the subtle spirit of the river itself? Like segmenting a flower in a botany lab, there is always the risk of losing touch with the pure form, entire and growing amidst its natural surroundings.

Reading through this manuscript set my doubts to rest; I was truly impressed. Bill provides in this book a thorough, exceptionally clear, and accurate introduction on *how to run rivers on your own* safely and with polish. Thus he offers the reader far more than just technique; he as much as says, "Take pride in your form and style as well—there's more to rafting than just getting through." Unashamedly, he shares with you his own feelings about rivers and the book is sown throughout with a philosophy inspired by the river and the need to harmonize with its force and being.

When you begin each new river trip, you feel what might best be described as the "commitment of a journey" upon entering the flux and movement of the river . . . calm, excitement, and calm again. You involve yourself totally in what you are doing and you share your involvement closely with your companions. You follow the river's lead, and, when it appears hostile, you approach it with caution. When it is teasing, you are playful. When it is serene, you become one with its peace. Yet moving within this serenity there is Bill's reminder, "Somewhere inside yourself maintain a primitive pocket of fear, a frank, clear perception that what you are doing is dangerous." Isn't that what's at the very heart of adventure?

I think you'll enjoy this book. Be kind to the river . . . and take care.

Bob Elliott
American River Touring Association

Introduction

Your raft slides toward the brink of Jawbone Falls. The long pool above the falls is shallowing, the current is picking up speed. Round stones the size of grapefruit cover the river bottom, like bumps on a toad. The sleek shape of a salmon glides past headed upstream. Granite houseboulders line the banks, and lodgepole pine thickly mount the steep valley walls. The sun, brilliant and reassuring, shimmers on the diamond water. Ahead, the falls appears as a horizon line across the river. Beyond that horizon the river races down a twisting chute and crashes in white, foamy thunder upon a jagged blade of rock—Jawbone Rock. Then, screaming, the water careens left, explodes down a broad, rocky slope, and, finally, leaps through a series of enormous standing waves—each evenly spaced, each slightly smaller than the one before—which gradually diminish into calm. To make it through, you know from your scouting trek, a raft must somehow pass to the left of Jawbone Rock, then thread its way along an intricate but navigable course down the rock-strewn pitch, and, lastly, keep bow pointed into the big waves near the foot.

The edge is very near. You stand to check your position. You pull on the oars to line the raft up with the best point of entry, just left of midstream. Suddenly the entire boiling falls sweeps into view. Just as the raft dips over the lip, you swing the boat to point the bow downstream. Like a shot you're off—spray flying, waves crashing in, rocks gnashing past—off down the narrow chute. You look down along the grain of the current, and dead ahead is Jawbone, tearing the river in two with its ragged edge of teeth. At the right moment you begin pulling left, left, left like a wild man, aiming for that passage, that chance, that prayer. Oar blades plow, fly deep searching for catch and the raft blows, sputters left. Jawbone lunges close—and slashes past on the right. Now, sucked along in the howling, surging foam, the boat makes the turn and enters the broad, steep rock maze. You begin to maneuver this way and that, fighting to keep off the rocks. But Jill, riding in the bow, has lost her grip and is rolling overboard: you jump, reach, grab—and pull her back in by the scruff of her lifejacket. She gets her hands on sturdy gear-tie-down straps and braces her feet. You grab again for the oars, but the raft is washing broadside onto a rock! Instantly, everyone jumps to the side of the raft nearest the rock—bringing the far side, the upstream side, up, and letting the current gush under rather than into the boat. You plant an oar blade in the current, twirling the raft off the rock, back into the flow. And on you go, plunging on down the rocky slope, plowing bow in through the giant standing waves, riding the wild spume, inundated, holding your breath in the crests, breathing in the troughs, yelling, hooting, gasping. And then the waves gradually become small and finally disappear altogether. The boat slows, you have arrived. The raft floats in a deep, emerald pool. Dripping, breathing deep and fast, up to your knees in water, you see that no one has been lost, that the raft is intact. You give Jill a tender swat on the head, you look around at a place of awesome beauty. As you reach for a bailing bucket your knees begin to shake.

When you launch off on a whitewater voyage you give yourself to the river. You die to the arena of cities and jobs, and are born into a world that is clear, continuous, and flamboyantly colorful—a world of risk and surge, with a flow that wafts you along with colossal motion, easy. The river in its natural, juicy canyon becomes your universe. Its variety, its rhythms form the landscape and tempo of your life, its bends your turns of thought. In the soothing calms you swim, dream, and talk; in the rapids, with heart pounding, you fly, swallow, and maneuver.

With its mystery and magic, rare in the cosmos, pure and relentless, the river penetrates your being. Even in the dark of a moonless night you feel it, the expanse, the presence, something big and moving, flowing, a broad, low murmur like wind in a forest mixed with gurgling and slapping sounds. Always it is there, subtle, spiritual, sustaining, playing a bass to the words, the laughter, the group antics. Real, obvious, yet somehow intangible, the living river carries you along for days on end through the wilderness in an onrushing entry, a headlong passage of mind and body.

Out there on the big flow you see things differently. You understand the beauty of an oar, a thing strong and straight, ten feet of solid ash with a slight suppleness that absorbs shock and strain, a lever that grips the water, zipping the boat along. The raft itself becomes an intimate friend, a home, an embodiment of both security and adventure. In a sense a raft is little more than an illusion, a bag of air, yet it is amazingly sturdy and able to go where hard-hulled boats split and crumble. Able to bounce, rebound, fold, and wallow, it is a pliant, buoyant spirit somehow at one with the river, the colossus. Insubstantial, maybe, but, like a reed in the storm, it thrives, dips, and dives amidst jumbled boulders, treacherous currents, and thousands of tons of wild water. There is truly nothing like the feel of a raft, the big bottom rolling and tossing among towering waves, shifting and sliding on surging hillsides of boiling foam, reveling in the ongoing, onpouring deluge. It is little wonder that rafters spend hours, sometimes whole days fiddling about in their boats, adjusting this strap and tightening that—really doing nothing at all, except savoring the feel of the rambling womb.

The people on a river voyage draw into a tight society. Engulfed in a world of sensation, mood, and skin, they reach out to one another with intensity, talk deeply, and often find rich and supportive rapport. The upwelling events and daily life of a trip create a perpetual explosion of feelings and expression—and draw people out and press them close. The long days bring friendship, free-flowing conversation, water fights, word fights, love affairs—especially love affairs. The entire setting fires the desire for physical and emotional intimacy—the isolation, the sublime natural beauty, the sensual motion of the river, the warm baking sun, the sleepy coolness of the shade, the spark of danger, the sense of voyage. And what an Eden for lovers a wilderness river is—a paradise of swim holes, fireside baths, diving rocks, shared slippery biodegradable soap downs, hot springs, playful dunkings, tense rapid runs. The place is erotic beyond imagining.

Another engaging part of rafting is the backwoods rumble to the river. With gear, companions, and sense of purpose, you roll toward the put in, often far into the back country, encountering mountain folk in their tiny boondock settlements. Contrary to the image conjured up by movies such as *Deliverance,* country people, I have found, are exceptionally warm and welcoming, and enjoy the chance to talk about their lives and the surrounding territory. Interestingly enough, most of these people live in fearful awe of the river near them. Unfamiliar with whitewater technique, they know only that such and such number of people died on the river in years past. They don't realize that, in most cases, these people either attempted the river when the water level was too high or lacked experience or proper equipment. They simply see the river as a killer—and earnestly proffer ominous reports of the river's murderous fury. These warnings invariably terrify the novices in the group—and sometimes even cause them to scribble off last minute letters of farewell to family and friends.

What about this danger element? The truth is that rafting is not nearly as hazardous as is commonly thought. When approached with adequate understanding and equipment, it is far safer, for instance, than driving on a modern highway or walking on a city street. But still, clearly, there is risk—and this risk has its fascination. All of us, men and women, in some deep inner well of the self, have a sense for who we are, what we want to be, how we want to live. And it is this innermost intuition which inspires us to seek novelty, surprise, conflict, and tempts us toward uncertainties, to try, to risk, to grow—always in ways bound up with our feelings of identity and the inner fluctuations of self esteem. Rafting offers an arousing blend of these very things: novelty, adventure, and struggle, risk and growth. Hence its lure, its magnetism.

Go wide-eyed and careful out onto that dazzling flow.

PART I

The Raft and the Crew

CHAPTER ONE

Equipment: The Full Story

The amount of equipment needed for rafting varies with the length of the river voyage. Single-day trips call for a raft, a watertight bag for lunch, maps, bailing buckets, lines, lifejackets, paddles or oars and rowing frame, and, for emergencies, a repair kit, an air pump, a first-aid kit, and a survival kit (see Appendix I for a complete checklist). Extended trips require, in addition to the gear above, waterproof containers, camping equipment, stores of food and clothing, and other items.

While one-day excursions have the advantage of requiring less equipment, it is only in the course of longer voyages that one can begin to respond deeply to the river and to one's companions. A good compromise is to begin with a few one-day trips, and then, after acquiring more experience and equipment, to undertake longer journeys.

Much of the gear mentioned in this chapter is available in local surplus and sporting goods stores, but some things, like rafts designed especially for whitewater, 10-foot oars, and waterproof containers, are harder to locate (see Appendix II for a list of suppliers).

PHOTOGRAPH 1 A 10-man oar raft outfitted for an extended voyage. Numbers correspond to those in photo.

1. Bow
2. Coiled bow line
3. Right spare oar
4. Waterproof black bags secured with special one-knot lashings
5. Ten-foot ash oar
6. Oar blade
7. Oar throat
8. Oar shaft
9. Bailing bucket
10. Watertight wooden kitchen box
11. Thole pin
12. Canvas pouch for odds & ends
13. Oarsman
14. Full-jacket life preservers
15. Taut hand-grip line running to stern
16. Wide-brimmed sun hat with chin strap
17. Stern
18. Tennis shoes to be worn when running rapids
19. 50-caliber, watertight ammo box holding books, maps, cameras, first-aid kit, etc.
20. Short safety line with clip securing ammo box
21. Easy-rower washer
22. Safety lines securing oar
23. Hardwood-block thole-pin mount
24. Elaborate rowing frame
25. Heavy canvas garbage bag, securely lashed to raft, for carrying all unburnable trash out of the wilderness
26. 20-inch buoyancy tube
27. Taut lifeline around raft
28. Left spare oar
29. Elastic cords permitting instant release of spare oar
30. Cold-can sack of heavy cloth to be dipped in the river in calms to cool

Rafting gear is rugged and functional. Each oar, line, and valve has its unique, crucial purpose, and together they form a ship, a bed, a magic carpet for exploring the rivers of the wilderness.

RAFTS: THE TRUE BREED

Inflatable rafts designed for whitewater are a staunch breed. Made of thick, tough material and usually weighing more than 85 pounds, they can withstand the severe punishment dealt out by rocky streambeds and, if punctured, are kept afloat by multiple air chambers. Large buoyancy tubes, combined, in the better rafts, with upturned bows and sterns, keep out big waves and make rough water easy floating. With reasonable care, whitewater rafts will last from year to year, maybe taking a patch here and there and probably needing a bit of extra pumping as time goes by but remaining largely unchanged by wear.

Rafts, like rivers, vary widely in size. But for the optimum blend of stability and maneuverability, the choice sizes range in length from 12 to 16 feet. Not only can rafts this size dodge down the smallest of raftable streams, but at moderate water levels they can also descend even the largest rivers. When paddled or fitted with frame and 10-foot oars, they make ideal expedition rafts, accommodating a small party and its baggage.

The versatility of rafts in the 12- to 16-foot range became clear in the decade following World War II when surplus military assault rafts of the 10-man and 7-man types were tested with great success on all sorts of whitewater. The 10-man raft is now thought by many to be the optimum size. With its 16-foot length and 8-foot beam, it is at once highly maneuverable and extremely stable. Likewise, the 7-man raft is an exceptionally fine all around river boat. Twelve feet long and 6½ feet wide, it is a shade less stable than the 10-man, but in compensation it is more responsive, more frisky. While the 10-man carries from four to six people for river rafting, the 7-man carries three or four. Both of these rugged boats are made of heavy, black, nylon-neoprene fabric.

As the most respected and sought-after medium-sized rafts, the 10-man and 7-man are now practically unobtainable through surplus outlets. However, a number of similar rafts are currently being manufactured commercially. Here is a brief survey of some of the better makes.

The foremost raft maker is Avon, an English company. The Avon Adventurer, with its 13-foot length, 6½-foot beam, 95-pound weight, 17-inch tubes, and upturned bow, is about the same size as a 7-man assault raft (Photograph 2). The Avon Professional, a 15-by-7-foot boat with 18-inch tubes, a 130-pound weight, and upturned bow and stern, is roughly equivalent to a 10-man. And Avon's largest boat, a new model of the 10-man size, is 17 feet long by 8 feet wide with huge 22-inch tubes and magnificently uplifted bow and stern. These are the finest rafts now being made. The very appearance of an Avon exudes staunch dependability, and a close examination of the seams, valves, and so on impresses one with the thoroughness of the Avon craftsmen. The grey, heavy-duty, nylon-Hypalon fabric of Avon rafts is not only extraordinarily tough but also, to a greater extent than neoprene, impervious to sun and resistant to rot. The tubes are tested to 11 psi (pounds per square inch) and designed for an operating pressure of 2¾ psi—giving the rafts a powerful stiffness and a comforting solidity. Careful attention is given to detail: Each raft has bronze, D-ringlike handles bow and stern, nylon side handles, interior hand rails, storage pouches in the bow, and ample D-rings for securing rowing frames. Also, every Avon comes with a sturdy foot pump, a pressure gauge, a rugged carry bag, and, significantly, a warranty.

The most complete line of rafts designed especially for whitewater is made by Rubber Fabricators of West Virginia. Included in this extraordinary flotilla, which ranges from tiny dingies to mammoth pontoons, are a raft of the 10-man style called the Yampa and a raft of 7-man style called the Selway. The Yampa, built to military 10-man specifications, is 15½ feet long by just under 8 feet wide, has 18-inch tubes, weighs 110 pounds, and sports a nicely upturned bow (Photograph 3). The Selway, built to 7-man specifications, is 12 feet by 6½ feet, has 16-inch tubes, weighs 85 pounds, and has an upturned bow and stern. Both these boats of black nylon-neoprene are lighter than their military counterparts, but both have gained the respect of river people throughout the West. In fact, the Yampa is used widely by commercial outfitters. Among the other rafts made by Rubber Fabricators is a superb craft called a Green River Boat (Photograph 4). This nylon-neoprene inflatable owes its prowess not only to its 17-foot length, 8-foot beam, and 18-inch tubes but also to its upturned bow and stern and its extremely

PHOTOGRAPH 2   A 13-foot Avon Adventurer—a lively, rugged boat.

PHOTOGRAPH 3   A Yampa on the Tuolumne. (*Photo by Richard Krieger, courtesy of the American River Touring Association.*)

thick skin—so thick the boat weighs 260 pounds! A favorite on large rivers such as the main Salmon, the upper Colorado, and the Green, the Green River Boat will carry from 5 to 8 people and full expedition equipment.

A unique, self-bailing raft called the Huck Finn has been developed by veteran riverman Bryce Whitmore. The Huck Finn consists of four giant tubes, each 18 or 20 inches in diameter, which are laced together side by side to form an air-mattresslike platform roughly 14 feet long by 6 feet wide. Although it is somewhat more affected by head winds than other rafts, the Huck Finn maneuvers well and handles rather like a 10-man. Because it is unswampable, it eliminates bailing and offers greater safety; unlike other rafts, it cannot be filled with tons of water and rendered sluggish. The tubes are made of extremely thick (class 7) black nylon-neoprene and are almost indestructible. A nice feature of the Huck Finn is that, with removal of the two center tubes, it can be converted into a sporty catamaran-style raft called a Cataraft (Photograph 5). Fast and thrilling, the Cataraft is ideal for small, rocky, steep-gradient rivers. While the Cataraft carries two people or, on mild water, three, the Huck Finn carries six or seven. Bryce, its inventor, operates a river-running outfit in California and Oregon called Wilderness Water Ways. As a reluctant supplier in the raft-selling business, he usually sells just the tubes and hands over plans for the frame, which the buyer must have made separately.

A graceful, rugged boat called the Havasu (Photograph 6) is made by Holcombe Industries of California. With its 17½-foot length, 7½-foot beam, 125-pound weight, and hefty 20-inch tubes, the Havasu is roughly 10-man size. Its pale grey, nylon-vinyl fabric, a recent innovation in the realm of rafting, is exceptionally resistant to abrasion and allows the Havasu to stand up well under the worst conditions of constant scraping over rocks. In design and appearance the Havasu is quite beautiful; its eye-pleasing lines swing smoothly from uplifted bow to uplifted stern. The Havasu also handles well. Unfortunately, some Havasus have had air leaks. The people at Holcombe have been working on this problem, though, and feel that they now have the solution well in hand.

Fabricators in Taiwan and Japan turn out a variety of rafts, some suspect, some adequate. The suspect rafts include a group of cheap, yellow "rubber duckies" which will be discussed later.

PHOTOGRAPH 4   A threesome of Green River Boats running Big Drop in Cataract Canyon. (*Canyonlands Expeditions Photo.*)

PHOTOGRAPH 5   Fast and thrilling, the Cataraft is ideal for small, rocky, steep-gradient rivers. (*Photo courtesy of Bryce Whitmore.*)

PHOTOGRAPH 6   A Havasu on the Stanislaus. (*Photo courtesy of Holcombe Industries.*)

The adequate boats are black or grey in color, range in size from 11 to 17½ feet, and are made of nylon-neoprene or nylon-Hypalon. One line of these rafts, although its boats have mediocre valves, no upturned ends, and relatively thin skins, is satisfactory and stands up well on all but extremely rocky streams. Another line has thick hides, upturned bows and sterns, and good valves. Imported by Campways, these latter boats are remarkably well-made and bear the names Miwok, Shoshoni, and Havasu II.

SMALL RAFTS AND MAD ADVENTURE

Out on the river in a small raft you are on your own. No large, tough tubes offer protection; no broad beam or ample length provides stability. You survive by your wits. Only your skill with oars or paddle keeps your little craft upright and out of danger. When rigged securely with a frame and good-sized oars, small boats are sprightly and nimble, skittering this way and that with the dipping of the oars like flies on the water. Truly they are a delight to row, especially after you've rowed bigger rafts, those barges. Many small rafts are inexpensive and widely available and so may be picked up on the wing. Understand, though, that small rafts require extra care and skill.

The line dividing small- from medium-sized rafts falls between 6-man rafts and 7-man rafts. This is due not so much to a difference in size as to differences in design and materials. With its 12-foot length and 5-foot, 4-inch beam, a 6-man raft is just as long as and only a foot narrower than a 7-man. But the fact is that most rafts of the 6-man size and smaller available today are made in a cheap fashion with thin material and simply are not in the same league with 7-man and larger rafts.

Of the smaller sizes, however, the 6-man is by far the best raft (Photograph 7). It is stable enough for small and moderate rivers at medium and low water levels, yet maneuverable enough for tight, rock-strewn passages. A 6-man may be used for one-day outings or may be loaded with an oar frame and expedition equipment for extended trips for a party of three. Due to variations in materials, 6-mans weigh anywhere from 30 to 60 pounds. Tube diameter is usually 16 inches. The heavier rafts, as always, are far superior, and only the heavier ones should be used on rocky rivers.

PHOTOGRAPH 7   A family in a 6-man on the Copper River in Alaska floats past the sheer face of Mile Glacier, where giant slabs of ice occasionally calve off and crash into the water. (*Photo courtesy of the American River Touring Association.*)

For many years fine, yellow, Air Force 6-mans were sold at very low prices in surplus stores. These were good boats with solid valves, upturned bows, and thin but durable nylon-neoprene hides. In days gone by, I piloted one of these jaunty craft down rivers all over the West, and I would probably still be using it if I had remembered to dry it thoroughly before storing it one winter; as it was, moisture caused the floor to rot. Sad to say, these boats are now rare. Rubber Fabricators, though, makes a comparable 6-man raft called the Rio Grande. Made of green nylon-neoprene and weighing a satisfying 60 pounds, the Rio Grande is currently the finest 6-man available. Like the Air Force 6-man, it is nearly as good as a 7-man.

Unfortunately, most 6-man rafts used today are so much jetsam pasted together out of flimsy, yellow nylon-neoprene and cotton-neoprene. These shoddy craft, which are sold in sporting-goods and surplus stores everywhere, are greatly inferior to 7-mans and to the two 6-mans just discussed. Extremely thin-skinned and lightweight (under 40 pounds), these rafts are commonly called "rubber duckies" and, with gruesome aptness, "kamikaze rafts" because with their first brush against a rock they have been known literally to pop. Although many professional boatmen use these rafts on their personal goof-off trips with no problems, dozens of other less experienced people die in these paltry craft each year. Too often, the poor quality of these rafts corresponds to the owner's poor understanding of what he or she is doing. Therefore, if used at all, these rafts should be well rigged with frame and oversized oars, loaded with one or at most two people, and handled with great alertness and skill.

Another roughly 6-man-size boat is the little Avon Redshank. Twelve feet long and 4 feet, 10 inches across the beam, this tough nylon-Hypalon boat weighs 52 pounds and has a pointed, slightly upturned bow. Like all Avons, it comes with such extras as foot bellows, repair kit, and carry bag. Unfortunately, the Redshank's tiny, 14-inch tubes make it a very wet boat, adequate only for mild rivers.

Rafts smaller than the 6-man size, even though they are extremely maneuverable, are generally unsuitable for river use. They are too small to carry much luggage and their small tubes allow them, like the Redshank, to be swamped easily. There are, however, some small rafts that do fare well on rivers. Four-man boats that have inflated tube diameters of 16 inches or over can navigate many rivers. In fact, in the hands of experienced oarsmen, these rafts can descend, on the low water of late summer, rivers as difficult as the Rogue River in Oregon. A typical adequate 4-man has a 9-foot length and a 4-foot beam.

The other small rafts appropriate for river use are 1-man boats with spray shields or spray covers. Spray shields are short, stiff walls that jut vertically from a raft's bow and stern, while spray covers are poncholike sheets that attach around the top of a raft's outer tube and tie tight around the rafter's waist. When in place, these devices prevent water from entering the raft and allow the tiny craft to pass through moderate rapids that would swamp larger boats.

Of late, newfangled craft such as inflatable kayaks and Sportyaks have ventured out onto the rivers. If these oddball vessels can claim kin, I suppose it is to rafts. In any case, the techniques and other information presented in this book apply or can be readily adapted to these craft as well as to rafts.

Inflatable kayaks, sometimes called "orange torpedoes," are invariably orange in color and pointed at both ends. They range from babysize, about 4 feet long, up to 2-man size, about 12 feet long. Controlled with a double-bladed paddle, they are remarkably stable and are commonly used on rivers as difficult as the main Salmon and the Rogue. Although reasonably sturdy, current makes are not tough enough for extremely rocky rivers. Leslie Jones, the renowned maker of the river scroll maps mentioned near the end of this chapter, has proposed an improved version of the inflatable kayak that could be marketed at a very low price. It would measure 9 feet by 30 inches, be made of thick nylon-neoprene, and have a stiff floor (so the boat wouldn't belly down in the center) of extra thick material. Such a craft would open up thousands of small rivers now regarded as too small for rafts.

Made by Dayton and sold by Inflatable Boats Unlimited and others, Sportyaks are charming little one-man rowboats of rigid plastic. Seven feet long and 3 feet wide, and with spray shields jutting up from bow and stern, these 38-pound boats have run some of the West's most challenging rapids in Grand Canyon, Cataract Canyon, and Dinosaur. They are best suited, though, to milder runs such as the Green River Wilderness. Sportyaks come with good-sized oars and a built-in, watertight duffle compartment.

Avoid round or donut-shaped rafts; they are difficult to maneuver.

A WORD OF CAUTION CONCERNING SMALL RAFTS: Because small rafts are more easily flipped and swamped, they demand greater skill and alertness. If yours is a small craft, master your technique totally on mild rivers before attempting anything difficult. To a little raft, even an easy river is challenging. Know your raft's limit and don't go beyond it. Above all, if your raft has a thin skin, stay off extremely rocky rivers. As in all rafts but even more so in small ones, wear a good lifejacket and carry an adequate repair kit—you will need both. On extended trips most small rafts must be escorted by larger, gear-carrying rafts. Keep your raft extremely light; small boats must dodge and skitter in the foam. For them, survival depends on speed and quickness. Perhaps most important of all, absolutely do not use the undersized oars that come with inexpensive small rafts; instead, use a light but sturdy rowing frame and large oars. Nine-foot boats should have 6- or 7-foot oars, and 11- to 12-foot boats should have 8- or 10-foot oars. When rigged in this way and rowed with skill, small, light boats will dart across the water.

PONTOONS AND THREESOME RAFTS

Inflatable rafts over 20 feet in length are called pontoons (Photograph 8). Although they surpass the needs and probably the

PHOTOGRAPH 8   A pontoon with sponsons upsets in Lava Falls in the Grand Canyon. (*Photo by Twila Stofer, courtesy of the American River Touring Association.*)

means of the average rafter, these mammoth boats are nonetheless noteworthy, not so much because they can carry large numbers of people (who wants to travel with a crowd?), but because they are excellent for large rivers at high water and for giant rivers such as the Colorado of the Grand Canyon.

Although pontoons come in various lengths ranging from 22 to 37 feet, all have tube diameters of about 3 feet and beams of 9 feet. Because these 9-foot beams can be inadequate in the cataclysmic rapids of the Grand Canyon, pontoons used there are often fitted with enormous side tubes called sponsons for added stability. Since the use of motors in the Grand Canyon may be phased out, the largest of these pontoons, which can be maneuvered only with motors, may soon disappear. Smaller pontoons can be controlled either with motors fixed to inboard-motor mounts or with oars, which are, after all, quieter and more appropriate. Even if a motor is used, oars are still essential as a backup mode of control. Pontoons are now unobtainable on the surplus market, but they may be acquired from the distributors of the aforementioned raft manufacturer, Rubber Fabricators. More feasible for the average rafter than pontoons are large rafts created by joining three smaller rafts.

Three rafts of any equal size may be lashed together to form a larger, more stable craft capable of navigating rivers that none of the three rafts would dare approach alone. A formidable raft 12 feet wide and 18 feet long, for instance, may be made by lashing three 6-man boats side by side; this craft can tackle fairly large rivers with confidence. A trio of Green River Boats so joined (Photograph 4) can prevail in almost any kind of whitewater, including Cataract Canyon at high water, which, according to some, contains the world's most treacherous rapids. One celebrated river runner, Georgie White, goes so far as to lash three huge pontoons together to form a floating island for her trips through the Grand Canyon (Photograph 9).

Threesome or triple-rig rafts may be assembled and dismantled on the spot as immediate river conditions require. Where maneuverability is essential, the rafts are run separately, but where stability is the crucial factor, they are joined. In creating and operating a threesome raft, keep these things in mind: The main danger associated with these rafts is that the downstream boat can flip back onto the center boat, badly injuring the people in both boats (this is called "pancaking"). To prevent this, one or more taut lines are run under the rafts from the bow side of

PHOTOGRAPH 9   Georgie White's "G rig" in Lava Falls. It was with this mammoth craft that Georgie pioneered group trips through the Grand Canyon. (*Photo courtesy of Georgie White.*)

the bow raft to the stern side of the middle raft. Threesome rafts are best controlled with sweep oars, that is, oars that extend over the bow and stern. A trio of pontoons, however, should have a motor plus oars as a back up. If the rafts are to be run separately, each must have, of course, a frame and oars of its own. The load should be distributed evenly among the three rafts except for some extra weight in the bow raft to hold it downstream and to help keep it from flipping back onto the center boat.

CARE OF RAFTS

A few precautions will prolong the life of your raft. Do not step on a raft spread out on dry land. Never drag or slide, always lift and carry, your vessel. Before deflating a boat at the end of a trip, stand it up on one side at water's edge and wash it out by splashing bucketsful of water up into it, being especially careful to wash away any small rocks lodged between the buoyancy tubes and the floor join. In order to prevent rot and mildew, a raft should be stored in a cool, dry place; a cement floor is not a dry place. Talcum powder will help ensure dryness during winter storage. The storage place should also be rodent free.

When inflating a raft, add air until the buoyancy tube is just drum tight; this places the air pressure at about 2 psi. Because the bursting pressure of most well-made rafts is between 10 and 13 psi, the pressure may be increased a bit beyond 2 psi without danger. For instance, if the temperature rises by 60° F, the pressure will increase from 2 psi to 4 psi, still leaving an ample safety margin. In a hot climate, however, if a raft is inflated in the cool of the morning and left in the hot sun out of contact with the cool water, it is wise to release a little air so as not to strain the fabric or adhesion.

After a few seasons of scraping against rocks and river bottoms, a raft may need rejuvenation. Heavily abraded areas on the raft's bottom and sides should be patched with nylon-neoprene, nylon-Hypalon, or nylon-vinyl material in the manner described below in "Patching," and mildly worn areas should be painted with a suitable coating. The finest coatings now available are made by Gaco Western in Seattle and are found in paint and rubber-goods stores. These coatings are painted on as liquids and dry to give old rafts new, resilent skins. Because it is important that these coatings dry rapidly, lest the solvent they contain loosen the raft's seams and patches, apply them in the direct sun, preferably where there is a breeze blowing. In time, those parts of the raft that contact the rowing frame will also chafe; they, too, should be protected.

The Repair Kit

A repair kit with tools, patching supplies, and spare parts should be carried in the raft *at all times*. Though seldom used, this kit is one of the most important pieces of gear, for when it is needed, it is absolutely invaluable. A large ammo box makes an excellent kit container. Keep this box secured *very* firmly to the raft.* A list of kit contents should be encased in clear contact paper and taped to the underside of the repair-kit lid.

---

* As with all tie-down lines, keep cords (use at least two, one on each end) *short* so the box won't flop around, banging into legs, and so feet won't become tangled in them in a flip.

REPAIR KIT CONTENTS

2 pints contact cement	For Hypalon and neoprene rafts, A. E. Staley's N151B adhesive or Carboline neoprene adhesive F-1 are recommended.
2 one-ounce eyedropper bottles of catalyst	If needed for adhesive. *Note:* N151B adhesive requires catalyst N151A.
2 pints solvent/thinner	Toluol (same as Toluene) is the recommended solvent for the above adhesives. It is available in paint stores.
2 one-inch, natural-fiber brushes	For mixing and spreading glue. Toluol may dissolve some synthetic fibers. (*Note:* Some rare glues go on best with a putty knife.)
3 sheets emery paper	For buffing
1 buffing tool (optional)	
1 rolling tool (optional)	This is a handle with a little wheel on the end for rolling out air bubbles. Called a stitcher by some. A pair of channel locks will substitute.
1 pair large, sharp scissors	
1 or 2 square yards of thin patching material	Should be same material as raft. Thin material (16 oz./sq. yd.) is best, for it conforms easily to the shape of the raft.
1 rag	
1 small can with lid	For mixing glue
1 felt pen	For marking patch outlines
Several large, heavy-duty, curved, upholstery needles	For stitching ragged edges of rips
Heavy dacron, nylon, or waxed thread	#16 American thread works well.
1 pair channel-lock or vice-grip pliers	For countless odd jobs, including pulling upholstery needles, tightening bolts, and replacing radiator clamps.

1 combination tool that serves as screwdriver, wire cutter, pliers, and adjustable wrench

Epoxy glue	For mending diagonal breaks in oars and paddles
Silicone rubber seal or GACO trowelling compound	For mending and replacing valves

SPARE PARTS

These will vary with the type of raft, frame, etc.

2 thole pins	These get bent in flips.
3 or 4 easy-rower plastic washers 6 inches in diameter	
Numerous radiator clamps	For oar rubbers or clips
Numerous oar rubbers or clips	
Assorted nuts, bolts, caps, etc.	
2 two-inch D-rings	
3 feet of one-inch flat nylon webbing (or 3 feet of ½-inch flat tubular nylon webbing	For replacing D-rings
1 small coil of baling wire	Handy for mending and making things

PATCHING

When applying a patch to a raft of nylon-neoprene or nylon-Hypalon, follow these steps: *

1. Cut one patch 3 or 4 inches wide and 3 or 4 inches longer than the rip. Try to use one continuous patch to cover the entire rip.

---

* These patching techniques and the methods discussed below for attaching D-rings and replacing valves are used by the boatmen of the American River Touring Association and are outlined in ARTA's *River Guide's Manual*.

2. Cut out another patch 6 to 8 inches wide and 6 to 8 inches longer than the rip.

3. Round the corners of the patches (don't leave scraps on the ground). If using heavy material, bevel the edges on these cuts by angling the scissors.

4. Center each patch over the rip and draw its outline on the raft with a felt pen. (The entire patching process goes easier if you stretch the injured area out on a flat, hard surface, such as a broad, flat rock or the top of a wooden gear box.)

5. Thoroughly buff (give a velvety roughness to) both sides of the smaller patch and the side of the larger patch to face the raft. Also carefully buff the area of the raft within the outlines. Remove any loose paint. Clean tape away from seams or avoid patching over seams if possible. Use Toluol during and after the buffing; this acts as a paint remover and cleaning agent and softens the material, allowing the glue to get a better grip. When using Toluol, be careful not to rub too much rubber off.

6. If the rip is on a bend in the tube or is excessively ragged or long, it may be necessary to sew the edges together to avoid wrinkles and ensure matched edges. Use a cross stitch:

DRAWING 1 STITCHING TECHNIQUE

The value of stitching is a matter of disagreement. Many rafters avoid stitching if at all possible, saying both that the strength it adds is negligible compared to the sheer strength of the patch and that it creates a rough surface for patching. But other rafters swear by stitching, and, in fact, one series of tests performed with Scotch Grip adhesive (#2141) indicates that cross-stitching does greatly increase the strength of a patch.*

7. With a rag, thoroughly clean all buffed surfaces. Again, be careful not to rub too much rubber off. Let all surfaces dry *completely.*

8. Following the instructions on the glue container, prepare, in a special can, enough glue for the two patches plus a little

---

* For more on this, consult "First Aid for a Raft," *Oar & Paddle,* July-August, 1974. *Oar & Paddle,* a magazine of interest to all wilderness boaters, may be contacted by writing P.O. Box 621, Idaho Falls, Idaho 83401.

extra. Some glues come ready to use, but many require thinning. When properly mixed with thinner/solvent, most glues are a thin, but not watery, syrup. (*Notes for N151 adhesive:* N151B adhesive, an excellent glue, requires N151A catalyst at a 1:20 ratio, that is, ⅔ eyedropper (16 drops) catalyst per ounce of adhesive. Toluol (same as Toluene) is the only solvent for this glue. Use glue within 20 minutes of mixing in catalyst. Keep activated glue out of the sun. If glue becomes too dry, it can be reactivated with Toluol within 20 minutes of mixing.)

9. Using a brush, put one thin layer of glue inside the smaller outline on the raft, then one thin layer on one side of the smaller patch; repeat once. (When two thin coats are used on both surfaces, the glue dries completely. When one thick coat is used, only the surface of the glue dries and the patch is weak.) Let dry to a tacky but not sticky surface. Try to shade both surfaces so they dry at the same rate. KEEP LIDS ON THE SOLVENT AND GLUE CANS.

10. Now, using the outline as a guide, place the patch, with the glued side down, in *exactly* the desired position. Do this with utmost care because, once the two surfaces make contact, it will be extremely difficult to part or adjust them. With your fingers, press the patch in place from the center to the ends and then from the center to the edges. Then use scissor handles, channel locks, or a rolling tool to insure a solid contact. Begin in the center and work outward to remove bubbles and wrinkles. Press particularly hard along seams if patching over them is unavoidable.

11. Repeat steps 9 and 10 for the larger patch.

12. Paint the edges of the patch with a thin layer of glue.

13. If you feel an inside patch is desirable, use the procedures described in steps 9 and 10. Obviously, an inside patch must be applied before the outside patches.

14. Clean the brush in solvent. Put away all the stuff. Sleep, eat. The big patch job is now complete.

SOME REMARKS ON PATCHING

- Unless you face an emergency, always allow enough time for the glue to cure completely before fully reinflating the chamber. This period varies with the type of glue: Some glues cure immediately, others take 12 hours or longer.
- An undersized patch is not an economy, for it will blister when the tube is inflated.

- If pressure is not maintained, trace the leak by painting the chamber with soap lather and mark the spot where bubbles develop. Then repair as outlined above.
- Pressure-seal cans may allow glue and solvent to dry up. Screw-lid cans are better.
- If water has entered the air chamber, it should be poured or siphoned out before the rip is patched.
- If patching in the rain, rig a rain fly over your work area. If it is both cold and rainy, it may be necessary to heat a dutch-oven lid (or some other heavy metal implement) to dry the patch area and cure the glue. Rest the heated iron, lifting it with channel locks, on golfball-sized rocks directly over the work area.

D-Rings

All things secured directly to a raft are attached by means of D-shaped rings called D-rings. The D-rings used range in size from 1 to 5 inches. The larger the D-ring, the wider the webbing holding it to the raft and, hence, the stronger the ring. Sturdy D-rings may be purchased already mounted on neoprene patches (see Appendix II); these patches are attached to the raft in the manner outlined below in steps 7 and 8. D-rings, nylon webbing, and neoprene or Hypalon material may also be purchased separately and fashioned into D-ring patches as outlined below. This latter course is by far the cheaper. D-rings are available in saddle shops and hardware stores.

ATTACHING D-RINGS

[*Note:* The dimensions given are for 2-inch D-rings, a good size. If you choose a larger size, use wider, longer strips of webbing and a larger patch.]

1. Cut three 1-inch-by-6-inch strips of nylon webbing. (These strips may be cut from 1-inch nylon webbing, or they may be made by cutting three 6-inch strips of ½-inch tubular nylon webbing and slitting them lengthwise.)
2. Cut, buff, and clean an 8-inch-diameter circular patch with a slit in the middle for the D-ring.
3. Cut, buff, and clean a rectangular patch to cover the slit.

4. Mix glue and paint both sides of the nylon strips. When glue is tacky, arrange as below:

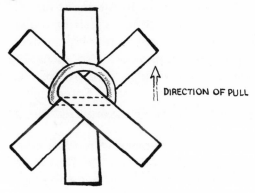

DRAWING 2 D-RING ATTACHMENT

5. Put two thin coats of glue on under side of circular patch and on upper side of nylon-strip assembly. When glue is tacky, press together, then roll.

6. Put two thin coats of glue on upper side of circular patch near slit and on small rectangular patch. When glue is tacky, press together, then roll.

This completes the D-ring patch; now attach this patch to the raft.

7. Place the D-ring patch in the desired position and draw its outline on the raft with a felt pen. Buff and clean the area of the raft within the outline.

8. Put two thin coats of glue on the raft and on the undersurface of the D-ring patch. When the glue is tacky, press to raft and roll.

D-rings should be placed so as to maximize sheer tension and minimize perpendicular tension. At the same time, the pull should be at right angles to the flat side of the D, as shown by the arrows in this drawing:

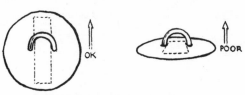

DRAWING 3 D-RING

Valve Replacement

After years of normal wear or in the event of sudden damage, a raft's vital air valves may require repair or replacement.

Peter and Russel one-piece, screw-type valves can often be rehabilitated as follows: Unscrew the six screws. Glue will revive the rubber seal, and the handles of a pair of channel locks can be used to rerivet the valve plug. Spread glue on the valve shoulder and on the hard rubber seat in the raft before replacing screws.

Bridgeport-Schraeder two-piece valves and other similar valves can sometimes be repaired as follows: Remove the plug; use a piece of wire to hold the inside portion of the valve; unscrew the nut; remove the washer. Using Gaco trowelling compound off river, Silicone rubber seal or glue on river (this requires an overnight wait), spread the adhesive around the inner half of the valve as close to the neck as possible. Replace the washer and nut; tighten.

Bridgeport-Schraeder two-piece valves and similar valves can be *replaced* as follows:

1. Cut valve out of boat (4-inch-diameter circle).

2. Cut two 8-inch-diameter circular patches.

3. Cut a valve-sized hole (about 1 inch in diameter) in the center of each patch.

4. Buff and clean a 9-inch-diameter area inside and outside the hole in the raft. Buff and clean one side of each patch.

5. Assemble as below, using Gaco trowelling compound:

6. Put two thin coats of glue on the inside of the raft and on the top side of the lower patch. When the glue is tacky, carefully insert the patch through the hole in the raft, center, press, and roll.

7. Put two thin coats of glue on the under side of the top patch and on the outside of the raft. When the glue is tacky, press and roll.

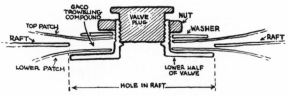

DRAWING 4 VALVE REPLACEMENT

ROWING FRAMES

A rowing frame is a sturdy, usually rectangular contraption that sits astride the raft amidships (Photograph 10). As a baggage rack, this frame, sometimes called an oar frame, holds baggage up off the floor, allowing the raft to slide easily over shallows and reducing wear on the raft's bottom. As a rowing device, it allows the raft to be controlled by a single pair of oars and provides an elevated seat for the oarsman.

PHOTOGRAPH 10   A simple rowing frame. Gear bags are piled onto the rope netting, covered with a tarp, and lashed in place. Notice the tie-down straps running to the D-rings on the inboard sides of the buoyancy tubes. Also notice the hanging straps that prevent the netting from sagging clear to the floor under heavy loads.

A frame offers several advantages. One person with a frame and oars can perform easily what many people with paddles break their backs to accomplish. Because the long oars can maneuver the boat with a speed and certainty that paddles cannot duplicate, passengers in oar boats may also feel safer. On the other hand, since the confrontation is largely between the oarsman and the river, the group is not welded together, as are paddlers, by common effort. But there is an advantage even in this: Because one skilled person controls the raft, other inexperienced people may be taken along, even on difficult runs. Also, I think, a raft's appearance is rendered more snug and riverworthy by a stalwart frame.

Frames range in type from simple, barebones rectangles to elaborate platforms with floors, backrests, and so on (see the various frames in Drawings 5, 6, 7, and 8). Light, simple frames are generally best. They do the job well, are inexpensive, and are easy to carry and store. Moreover, if put together with bolts, a simple frame can be readily disassembled for bush-plane flights to remote put-ins. A light, collapsible frame, in fact, opens up countless otherwise inaccessible runs not only in nearby Maine, Montana, Canada, and Alaska, but also in every far-off, roadless corner of our planet.

Elaborate frames, on the other hand, although they lack many of the advantages of simple frames, do greatly increase a raft's gear-carrying capacity and so are well suited to long voyages. The frame on the right in Photograph 11, for instance, once carried gear and supplies for three people on a 14-day trip down the Middle Fork and main Salmon in Idaho. And the rather extravagant frame on the left in Photograph 11 carried gear and 21 days' food for four people on a voyage through the Grand Canyon. This big frame performed well in the Canyon; its for-

PHOTOGRAPH 11   Elaborate frames not only greatly increase a raft's gear-carrying capacity, they also stiffen and stabilize the boat, rendering it snug, shiplike, and hard to wrap.

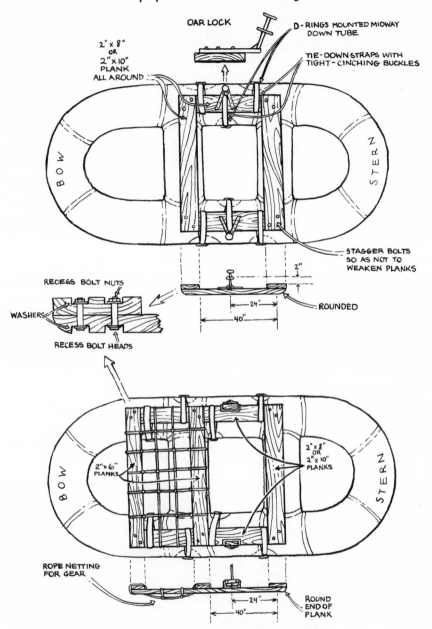

OAR LOCK

D-RINGS MOUNTED MIDWAY DOWN TUBE

2" x 8" OR 2" x 10" PLANK ALL AROUND

TIE-DOWN STRAPS WITH TIGHT-CINCHING BUCKLES

BOW

STERN

STAGGER BOLTS SO AS NOT TO WEAKEN PLANKS

RECESS BOLT NUTS

WASHERS

RECESS BOLT HEADS

2"

24"

40"

ROUNDED

BOW

STERN

2" x 6" PLANKS

2" x 8" OR 2" x 10" PLANKS

ROPE NETTING FOR GEAR

24"

40"

ROUND END OF PLANK

DRAWING 5 TWO SIMPLE WOODEN ROWING FRAMES

DRAWING 6 TWO ROWING FRAMES OF METAL TUBING
Rugged yet exceptionally light, the frames shown here can be made of
1-inch steel or 2-inch aluminum tubing. The sloping seats accommodate
oarsmen of widely varying sizes.

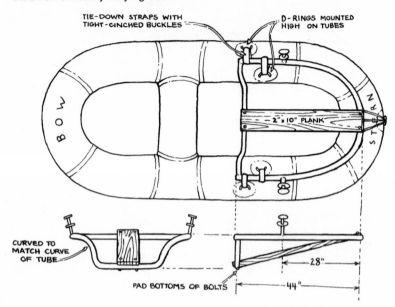

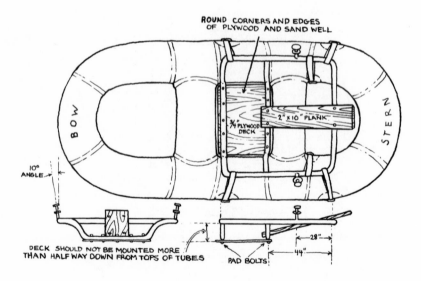

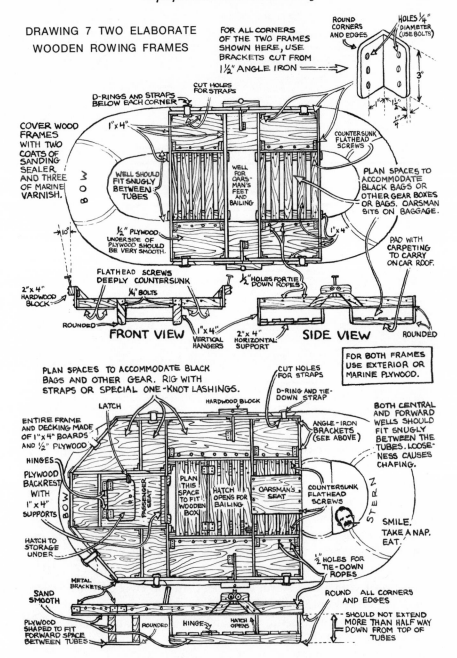

DRAWING 7 TWO ELABORATE WOODEN ROWING FRAMES

FOR ALL CORNERS OF THE TWO FRAMES SHOWN HERE, USE BRACKETS CUT FROM 1½" ANGLE IRON ⟹

ROUND CORNERS AND EDGES

HOLES ¼" DIAMETER (USE BOLTS)

3"

CUT HOLES FOR STRAPS

D-RINGS AND STRAPS BELOW EACH CORNER

COVER WOOD FRAMES WITH TWO COATS OF SANDING SEALER AND THREE OF MARINE VARNISH.

1"x 4"

BOW

WELL SHOULD FIT SNUGLY BETWEEN TUBES

WELL FOR OARS-MAN'S FEET AND BAILING

COUNTERSUNK FLATHEAD SCREWS

PLAN SPACES TO ACCOMMODATE BLACK BAGS OR OTHER GEAR BOXES OR BAGS. OARSMAN SITS ON BAGGAGE.

½" PLYWOOD. UNDERSIDE OF PLYWOOD SHOULD BE VERY SMOOTH.

1"x 4"

PAD WITH CARPETING TO CARRY ON CAR ROOF.

FLATHEAD SCREWS DEEPLY COUNTERSUNK

¼" BOLTS

½" HOLES FOR TIE DOWN ROPES

2"x 4" HARDWOOD BLOCK

ROUNDED

FRONT VIEW

1"x 4" VERTICAL HANGERS

2"x 4" HORIZONTAL SUPPORT

SIDE VIEW

ROUNDED

FOR BOTH FRAMES USE EXTERIOR OR MARINE PLYWOOD.

PLAN SPACES TO ACCOMMODATE BLACK BAGS AND OTHER GEAR. RIG WITH STRAPS OR SPECIAL ONE-KNOT LASHINGS.

CUT HOLES FOR STRAPS

D-RING AND TIE-DOWN STRAP

LATCH

HARDWOOD BLOCK

BOTH CENTRAL AND FORWARD WELLS SHOULD FIT SNUGLY BETWEEN THE TUBES. LOOSE-NESS CAUSES CHAFING.

ENTIRE FRAME AND DECKING MADE OF 1"x 4" BOARDS AND ½" PLYWOOD

ANGLE-IRON BRACKETS (SEE ABOVE)

HINGES

PLYWOOD BACKREST WITH 1"x 4" SUPPORTS

BOW

PASSENGER SEAT

PLAN THIS SPACE TO FIT WOODEN BOX

HATCH OPENS FOR BAILING

OARSMAN'S SEAT

COUNTERSUNK FLATHEAD SCREWS

STERN

SMILE. TAKE A NAP. EAT.

HATCH TO STORAGE UNDER

½" HOLES FOR TIE-DOWN ROPES

METAL BRACKETS

SAND SMOOTH

PLYWOOD SHAPED TO FIT FORWARD SPACE BETWEEN TUBES

ROUNDED

HINGE

HATCH OPENS

ROUND ALL CORNERS AND EDGES

SHOULD NOT EXTEND MORE THAN HALF WAY DOWN FROM TOP OF TUBES

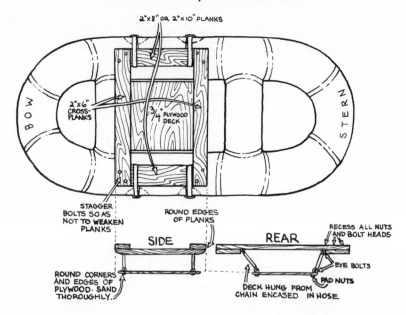

DRAWING 8 A WOODEN FRAME FOR A PADDLE RAFT

ward deck, extending clear to the bow, kept out water and stiffened the boat, allowing it to nose easily through high cresting waves. Both these frames, though cumbersome on land, are elegant on the water, transforming their rafts into solid yet agile little ships.

One solution to the problem of frames and carrying capacity is the poop deck (Drawing 9). This is a flat platform capable of carrying an enormous amount of gear that sits on the stern of a raft; it is normally used in conjunction with a simple, square frame. The poop sits on the stern, the frame rides amidships, and the crew lounges up forward, where the waves come crashing in, where the excitement is. A sturdy, rigid poop deck can be made from a single 4-by-8 sheet of ¾-inch marine plywood: Cut the sheet to fit your raft's stern, then beef up the edges with 2-by-4s on edge. Or a lighter "deck" can be made by suspending a taut, flat rope netting across the stern from the tubes and frame. Like oar frames, poop decks are attached to the raft by means of D-rings. Gear is stacked on the deck, covered with a tarp, and securely lashed down with strong line. Paddle rafts often use bow decks instead of poop decks.

Although it is possible to have frames and poop decks of wood, aluminum, and fiberglass custom made (see Appendix II), there

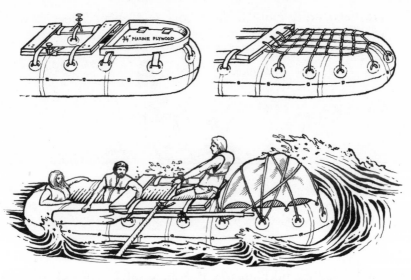

DRAWING 9 THE POOP DECK

is great satisfaction in building your own. A simple wooden frame can be made with ease in the average home workshop. You may choose one of the designs shown in Drawings 5, 6, 7, and 8 or invent a design of your own.

NOTES ON BUILDING FRAMES

- It is important that you buy your raft before constructing the frame, for the frame must be built to fit the width and shape of the particular raft. A frame should span from the top center of one side tube to the top center of the other, as shown in Photograph 10.
- The distance between oarlocks must be coordinated with the length of your oars. Because the oarlock falls slightly less than one-third the way down an oar's length, the distance between oarlocks should be slightly less than two-thirds the length of your oars. For example, with 8-foot oars the oarlocks should be roughly 5 feet 3 inches apart; with 9-foot oars, the oarlocks should be about 5 feet 10 inches apart, and with 10-foot oars, the most common length, they should be about 6 feet 6 inches apart. The distance between the oarlocks and the oarsman's seat should be such that the oar handles are a bit farther forward of the pins at the start of the stroke than they are behind the pins at the end of the stroke. Also, the oarlocks should be slightly higher than the oarsman's seat. Generally, oarlocks

are between 2 and 4 inches above and about 2 feet forward of where the oarsman sits.

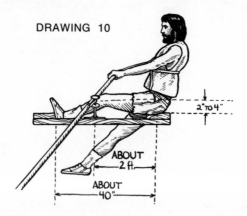

DRAWING 10

- Thole pins should be made of ¾-inch solid steel rod. If at all possible, pins should be removable (and thus replaceable). Therefore, mount pins in rugged sleeves of steel pipe or in extremely deep, very tight holes in hardwood blocks. Then fasten the pins in place not with glue or welds but with ³⁄₁₆-inch, hex-head bolts used as cross pins. Although many thole pins are directly vertical, it is best if pins lean outboard about 10 degrees. Uncapped pins should be plenty long (see Drawings 11 and 12).
- When the frame is mounted on the raft, the oarlocks should be a bit closer to the stern than to the bow.
- The oarsman must have an unobstructed view forward, a place to brace his or her feet, and room to swing each oar a full 180 degrees.
- Wells, floors, and decks that go down inside the raft—these may be hung on rigid vertical supports or suspended on chains —should not go more than halfway down from the top of the tubes. Otherwise, when the raft passes over sharp rocks, the floor may be ground between the frame and rock.
- Frames should not cover or in any way hamper access to air valves. Easy bailing should also be possible.
- All bolts should be countersunk; there should be no sharp or protruding edges; surfaces contacting the raft should be smooth.
- Above all, the frame should be sturdy. An oar frame must be able to withstand severe punishment if it is to survive heavy whitewater.

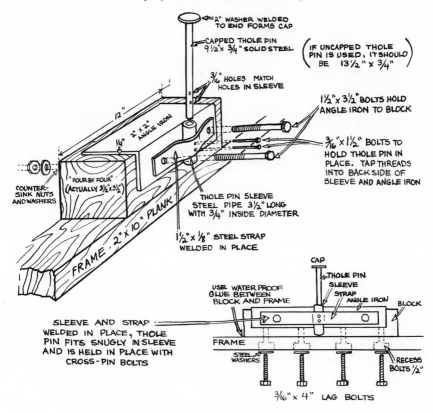

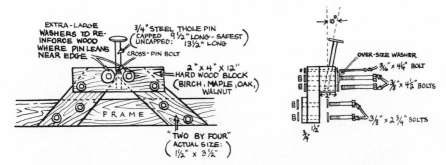

DRAWING 11 STEEL SLEEVE ON ANGLE IRON AND HARDWOOD
BLOCK THOLE PIN MOUNTS

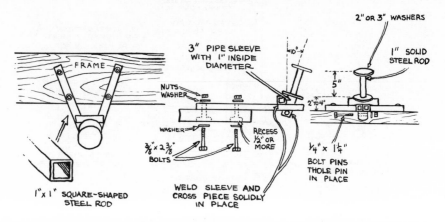

DRAWING 12 OUTJUTTING STEEL SLEEVE THOLE PIN MOUNT

Frames and poop decks are attached to rafts by means of tie-down straps and D-rings. Four outboard D-rings, one below each corner, plus two inboard D-rings suffice (see Photographs 10 and 12). Some rafts have oarlocks already attached to them. A bolt through the earlobe type will help secure a frame, but don't bother securing anything to the swivel type—these pop off under mild strain.

OARS AND PADDLES

Oars

Whitewater oars should be long and strong. Oar length should correspond to boat size.

Boat Type	Boat Length	Oar Length
4-man	9 feet	6 or 7 feet
6-man	12 feet	8 or 10 feet
7-man	12 feet	10 feet
10-man	16 feet	10 feet
shorty pontoon	22 feet	12 or 15 feet
pontoon	27 to 37 feet	12 to 15 feet

Sweep oars range in length from 10 to 15 feet and should also correspond to the raft's size and load. Because few sporting-goods stores stock oars over 7 feet in length, longer oars must usually

PHOTOGRAPH 12 Frames are secured to rafts by means of tight-cinching straps and D-rings.

be acquired from ship chandlers, through special orders with sporting-goods stores, or from the oar suppliers mentioned in Appendix II. The light aluminum oars that sometimes come with inflatable boats should be avoided, for they do not provide effective control.

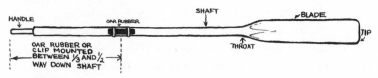

NOTE:

BECAUSE THE SHAFT EXTENDS DOWN ⅔ OF THE OAR, THIS MEANS OAR RUBBER AND CLIPS ARE MOUNTED SLIGHTLY LESS THAN ⅓ THE WAY DOWN THE LENGTH OF THE OAR.

DRAWING 13

When selecting oars, make sure that the grain runs straight along the shaft. If the grain runs even slightly crossways, do not accept the oar. Also, make certain that the wood is thick and strong at the throat, the point where the blade meets the shaft. If the throat is weak, the oar should be either rejected or wrapped with fiberglass in the manner explained in the next section. All rafting oars should be made of hardwood, such as ash or maple.

New, unfinished oars should receive two coats of sanding sealer and three coats of quality spar varnish. When sanding between coats, give particular attention to the handles, making sure that they are quite smooth. The tips of new oars may be fitted with copper guards to protect the blade from rocky river bottoms.

Always carry at least two spare oars aboard your raft, mounted so as to be accessible for immediate use. Oars have a way of breaking at the very moment you need them most.

Oar Repair

If, after breaking or losing several oars, you find yourself in the wilderness with only one oar, do not despair. Long, diagonal breaks can be mended in the field with epoxy glue; let the glue cure in camp overnight. If the oar breaks again, it will probably be in an entirely different place. If necessary, a temporary oar can be made by lashing a few 3-foot sticks to the end of an oar-length pole. For more information on this, turn to Chapter Three.

After you return to civilization, oars with abrupt breaks straight across the throat or shaft should be either replaced or repaired. Although it is probably best to replace them, I usually repair mine because it is cheaper and also because I become attached to my gear, especially old, battered oars. Saw the splintered ends off square, cutting close to the break so as not to shorten the oar any more than necessary, and pin the halves together with a steel pin ½ inch in diameter and 8 inches long. Drill the ½-by-4-inch holes straight into the centers of the squared ends and use plenty of epoxy glue when inserting the pin and sliding the halves together. Then the break should be wrapped with fiberglass.

Working with fiberglass is smelly, messy, and quite satisfying. For fiberglass work you need coarse sandpaper, a cheap 2-inch brush, rubber gloves, a small plastic bucket, fiberglass resin, fiberglass catalyst, one to two dozen fiberglass matting strips 4 inches wide by 2 feet long, newspaper, sawhorses, and acetone to clean your hands and the brush. Prepare the oar by using coarse sandpaper to roughen the entire area around the break, starting about 9 inches above and continuing to a point about 9 inches below the fracture. Next, wipe off the sanding dust and place the oar across two sawhorses or chair backs so that the roughened section rides in mid-air. To protect your floor from the drippings spread some newspapers around. After putting on rubber gloves, mix a cup of fiberglass resin with the proper amount of catalyst, following the directions on the can, and brush this liquid around one end of the roughened area.

At this point, starting at the end of the rough section, begin winding the 4-inch-by-2-foot matting strips around the oar in a spiral fashion so that you maintain a continuous 2-inch overlap. You can experiment with other lengths of matting strips if you wish, but the 2-foot length, I find, is easiest to work with. Brush the fiberglass liquid into the matting strips as they contact the wood, keep the wood just ahead covered with liquid and continue to work confidently in this manner, saturating the matting with liquid as you go, winding tightly, and always being careful to wind in the same direction. For added strength, use double or triple layers of matting immediately around the break, but avoid making the fiberglass too thick, or the oar will be overheavy. The next day, when the resin is hard, sand the fiberglass smooth with an electric disc or belt sander, and if you wish, cover it with special fiberglass paint for a colorful effect.

Repairing Oar and Paddle Tips

Oar and paddle tips sometimes develop splits. These splits can be repaired by cutting out a little rectangle around the split and by gluing a new, hardwood rectangle in the resulting gap with epoxy glue.

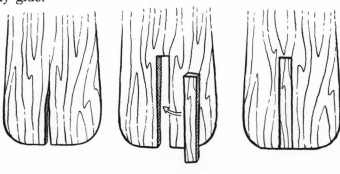

DRAWING 14

Whitewater Oarlocks

Whitewater oarlocks keep the oar blades vertical, freeing the oarsman to concentrate on reading the river and guiding the boat. They also tend to prevent oar breakage, for when an oar jams with near-breaking stress against a rock or against the river bottom, the oar is generally released. In the case of the oar-rubber, thole-pin oarlock (Drawing 15, bottom), a jammed oar will either

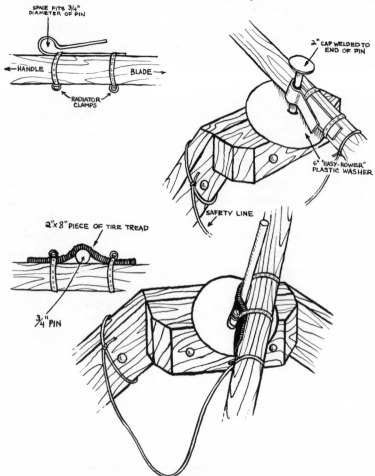

DRAWING 15 WHITEWATER OARLOCKS

The clip type (shown at top) is much safer than the rubber type (shown at bottom), because the former permits the capping of the thole pin. The open end of the clip points toward the blade so the oar will be released should the oar tip jam against a rock or the river bottom. A 6-inch-diameter easy-rower plastic or metal washer under each oar reduces friction. Quarter-inch nylon safety lines prevent the loss of oars in flips. Oars are always placed forward of the thole pins, so the heavy strain of the pull stroke will be borne by the oar, not the clip or rubber.

pop off the pin or the radiator clamps or the rubber itself will break. With the clip-type oarlock (Drawing 15, top), the clip just pops off the pin. I strongly recommended the clip type; it is far safer because it permits the capping of the thole pin. In the tumult of flips, a number of people have been injured by uncapped thole pins. The swivel-ring oarlock (Photograph 12) can also be used, but it does not hold the oar blades vertical.

Paddles

Because they lack the power and ease of oars, paddles demand a robust, strong-winded crew. This very toil, though, is seen by some paddling rafters as a fine thing. Through their united exertions to survive the brutish torrent, these men and women conceive a kind of respect for themselves that is unknown to more leisurely boatmen.

Paddles used by rafters range in length from 4½ to 6 feet, with the in-between sizes of 5 and 5½ feet most common. Paddle length depends on the paddler's size and strength, on the raft's tube diameter, and on whether the paddler is acting as captain or crew member. A small crew member in a raft with small tubes (16 inches or less) will use a 4½-foot paddle. A big crew member on a raft with big tubes (20 inches or more) will use a 6-foot paddle. Crew members somewhere in between in size will use 5- or 5½-foot paddles. Captains, regardless of body and raft size, usually use 5½- or 6-foot paddles, because a large paddle is needed for steering over the stern and for certain key strokes, such as draw strokes, used to turn the raft.

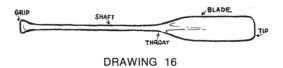

DRAWING 16

The buyer of paddles will have to choose between hardwood, softwood, a laminated combination, and aluminum fiberglass. Paddles of hardwood, such as ash or maple, are tough and will stand up against the battering of submerged rocks and stony river bottoms, but they are also heavy and tiring to use. Softwood paddles, which are usually made of spruce, are not so durable and will have to be replaced much sooner than those of hardwood, but they are considerably lighter and more pleasant to use.

When one has dipped a paddle in water a hundred times, he already knows that the reduction of just a few ounces in its weight makes an enormous difference. Laminated paddles that alternate strips of spruce or pine with strips of mahogany or red cedar combine lightness and toughness. Paddles with aluminum shafts and fiberglass blades are extremely light and rugged. These two latter types, inevitably, are more expensive. When buying wooden paddles, check to see that the grain runs straight along the shaft, that there are no splits or knots, and that the shaft and throat are thick and strong.

A word of caution to paddlers: Do not attempt the more rugged rivers without a veteran crew of well-coordinated and extremely strong paddlers.

IN-RAFT EQUIPMENT

Besides paddles or a rowing frame with oars, there are several other items of rafting equipment that must be carried in the raft and are essential to its performance and safety in whitewater and flat water alike.

Bailers and Bilge Pumps

After each major rapid, a raft that is not self-bailing will have to be emptied of water. If the rapid was fierce and things went poorly, the raft may be as much as half full, but if all went well and the oarsman handled the boat correctly, perhaps only a few gallons entered it. In either case, some sort of bailer must be kept ready at hand.

Large, plastic buckets of the 3-gallon size (Photograph 1) make the best bailers. Smaller scoop bailers can be made without expense by cutting the bottoms out of large plastic jugs with sturdy, comfortable handles, such as gallon-size Clorox jugs. Large bailers of the bucket type are especially necessary on big-water rivers like the Colorado, where tons of water enter the raft each day. Always take several bailers along, because they are easy to lose overboard—and they are essential.

Bilge pumps are probably not worth the expense (which is well over $50). I installed a Henderson single-action pump on one of my rafts only to find that a bucket bailer moves water just as fast and is more relaxing to use. Now I console myself by saying that a bilge pump, in addition to lending a determined, mysterious air to the raft, does remove water, when pumped vigorously, at a considerable rate, and is able, with its flexible hose, to reach any section of the raft and remove every last drop of water from it.

Lines

Rope, with its countless daily and emergency uses, is a basic tool on the river. What follows is a discussion of the various lines carried on a fully equipped raft. While not all these lines are essential, most are. The more rope, the better.

The two principal lines on a raft are the bow and stern lines; these may be of ½-inch manila or ⅜-inch nylon or multifilament polypropylene. Each line should be at least 100 feet long. In addition to these, a spare coil 200 feet in length should always be at hand. Although these lengths may seem extravagant, they are often necessary in securing the raft at night (two ropes should be used for double safety and the nearest tree may be some distance away), in lining the raft through waterfalls and otherwise impassable rapids, in righting the raft after a flip, and in coping with the unforeseen.

For brief stops, most rafts also carry a 20-foot painter line. Attached to the bow of paddle boats and to the stern of oar boats, this handy line is generally the first taken ashore. Grab it, jump ashore, and snug the boat in. When a tie-up point presents itself close by, this little line saves having to drag out a long line.

Rafts on dangerous rivers should carry a heaving line for shore and man-overboard rescue. This is an 80-foot line of ⅜-inch multifilament polypropylene (a rope that floats) with a monkey fist on the end. For a thorough discussion of the heaving line and the rescue of boats and swimmers from shore, consult O. K. Goodwin's article in Chapter Three.

Solo rafts on violent rivers should be rigged with an emergency beaching line. From 200 to 300 feet long and made of ¼-inch multifilament polypropylene, the beaching line is wound on a spool board and mounted low on the outside of the raft so as to be accessible after a flip.

One end of the beaching line is permanently secured to the raft; the other, which contains a small loop, is swum ashore and belayed around a rock or tree to swing the raft in against the bank.

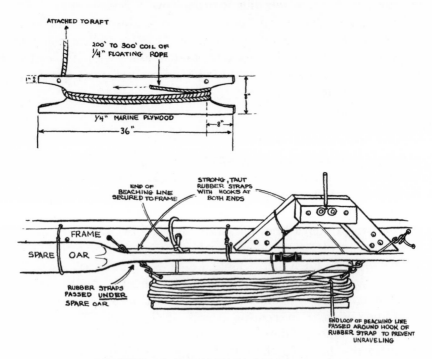

DRAWING 17 EMERGENCY BEACHING LINE

For more on this, see the section of Chapter Three entitled "Flips."

Short lengths of rope are continually needed for random odd jobs in and about the camp and raft. These should be cut from a spare coil of rope set aside for this purpose. Some light nylon line, called parachute cord, is also quite handy.

Of the various types of line available, multifilament polypropylene is by far the best; it is light, strong, easy on the hands, and it floats. Samson Cordage, mentioned in Appendix II, makes a number of excellent multifilament polypropylene lines suitable for whitewater use. If you carry a winch, you should have at least one long, heavy line of manila. Nylon and, to a lesser extent, multifilament polypropylene will stretch enormously under tension and lash dangerously if a break occurs.

On the river, all lines should be kept ready for immediate use and yet be tucked out of the way where they cannot entangle arms or legs. This is achieved by keeping them neatly coiled and either stuffing them into special pouches or wedging them tightly under tie-down straps.

Lifejackets

Because aerated, foaming whitewater provides very little buoyancy, lifejackets are *absolutely essential* in rafting. Life preservers of the full jacket style are by far the best (Photograph 1). With their large flotation chambers front and back, full-jacket preservers not only offer maximum buoyancy, which is good on all rivers and essential on big-water rivers like the Colorado, but also, more than other styles, tend to keep the heads of unconscious people above water. Preservers of the vest or yoke style with collars (these latter look rather like toilet seats) suffice for small, mild rivers. But all belt styles are to be avoided, for they neither offer adequate buoyancy nor keep the heads of the unconscious above water.*

For flotation, life preservers use air chambers, closed-cell foam, or sealed, kapok-filled, plastic bags. Air-filled jackets, such as those made by Flotherchoc, are preferred by some paddle rafters because they allow great freedom of movement. Jackets of closed-cell foam, though least comfortable, are most durable. Kapok-filled preservers, by far the most common, generally offer more buoyancy, provided they are not also used as cushions or backrests. The pressure of sitting or leaning can rupture the kapok-filled bags, causing these jackets to become waterlogged when wet and of little use. Check kapok jackets frequently with a squeeze test; if they are no longer air tight, use them as anchors, not lifejackets! Jackets colored yellow, orange, or red are easiest to spot in the water.

In order to be adequate for hair, that is, immense whitewater, a life preserver must provide at least 33 pounds of buoyancy. Here is a method for checking the buoyancy of a preserver: First, fill a large container, such as a plastic basket, to the very brim with water, and weigh it. Second, stuff the life preserver into the container, forcing it below the surface. Third, after removing the preserver, weigh the basket: The weight of the missing water equals the displacement, or buoyancy, of the jacket.

Nonswimmers should wear their jackets at all times while on the water, but others (unless park regulations specify it) need don theirs only when approaching, running, and lining fast water. Every raft should carry at least one extra lifejacket.

---

* For a definitive discussion of life preservers, consult Carl Trost's thorough article, "Life Jackets?" in *American Whitewater*, vol. 17, no. 1 (Spring, 1972).

Watertight Bags and Boxes

Amid ubiquitous spray and inundating foam, watertight containers are essential if clothing, camping gear, and food are to remain dry. Special bags of neoprene and plastic and boxes of metal and wood are therefore pressed into service.

The most widely used waterproof containers are surplus, neoprene black bags (Photograph 13). These rather heavy, boxlike bags have shoulder straps for carrying and come in a variety of sizes, ranging from a large 22 by 16 by 12 inches to a small 14 by 9 by 7 inches. Thick and rugged, these bags are extremely durable.

When sealing a black bag, carefully match both lips before starting to fold, and pull firmly after each fold. If too much air is trapped inside the bag, unroll one end of the roll enough to create an air passage, and sit on the bag to force the air out. Always fold the ends of the roll up under the top flap and pull all straps tight. When sealed correctly, these bags are almost completely watertight.

Large and small ammo cans, provided they have rubber gaskets, offer cheap, crush-proof, somewhat heavy protection for cameras, repair and first-air kits, and delicate edibles such as bread and eggs. Paint these boxes white or silver to reflect heat. Although the larger sizes, which hold up to 3 cubic feet, have massive handles to use in securing them to the raft, the smaller sizes, such as the 50-caliber ammo cans, have only flimsy wire handles and brackets that cannot be relied upon as tie-down points. So weld sturdy rings to the smaller boxes. Use two spring

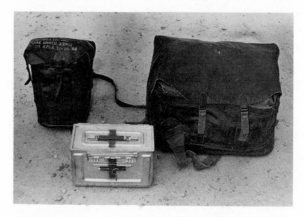

PHOTOGRAPH 13   Waterproof black bags and a 50-caliber ammo can.

clips or carabiners for each box, and tie boxes *short* so no one will be hit by them in a flip.

There are other waterproof containers. Wooden chests with calked seams and tightly sealing, weather-stripped lids are excellent for kitchen supplies, food, and, if you wear them, clothes (Photograph 14). Inexpensive, effective protection may be achieved with water-repellent duffel bags lined with doubled plastic wastebasket or garbage-can liners sealed with heavy rubber bands. Various commercially made plastic and nylon bags are also available. (For a list of sources for waterproof containers, and everything else in this chapter, see Appendix II.) Most "waterproof" laundry bags, however, are best avoided. When in doubt, check watertightness by partially filling the bag with water, sealing it, and rolling it over and over while watching for leaks. Almost all watertight containers will admit a little water if submerged for a long period, so on rivers where flips are likely pack a towel just inside the opening or, better still, line your bags with large, tough plastic bags sealed with rubber bands.

On extended trips, you will need the equivalent of one large black bag (roughly 2½ cubic feet) for each person plus several extras for food and gear.

PHOTOGRAPH 14   A watertight, wooden kitchen box with a grilled fire pan and a stand-up tray for silverware, utensils, spices, etc. Both the grill and the tray legs fold flat, allowing the tray to nestle into the fire pan, which in turn fits snugly into the top of the box (see Drawing 18).

Miscellaneous Equipment

Here are some essential odds and ends. Note these items well.

AIR PUMP: Because even an airtight raft will lose air in the slamming and pounding of heavy rapids, it will probably be necessary, when you are on a rough river, to pump up the raft each morning. And in the event of a puncture, the air pump will be used to reinflate the air chamber after the hole is mended. Avoid standard tire pumps; they do not fit the valves of most rafts and are endless hell to use. Instead, use a special bellows or cannister pump, such as those sold by Elliott River Tours, Inflatable Boats Unlimited, or Avon dealers. These giant pumps are greatly superior because, rather than pumping a small volume of air at high pressure like tire pumps, they pump a large volume of air at the low pressure appropriate for rafts. With canister pumps, prevent rust and make the pumping easier by keeping the chamber well oiled. Human beings, it seems to me, should never undergo the torturing experience of inflating a raft by hand if there is any possible way to avoid it. Country gas stations near rivers will generally let "crazy river rafters" use their air compressors; it is polite to ask permission beforehand. Or you may wish to get a little portable electric pump that will run off your car battery. When using motorized pumps, of course, be careful not to overinflate the raft.

AIR MATTRESSES: On small rafts, short, tough, air mattresses not only transform the bow and stern sections from dank, miserable wells into luxurious couches, they also eliminate the chance of having a knee or tailbone bruised by a rock passing under the boat. These air mattresses, which double as beds at night, will jam smoothly into place when only partially inflated. Understand, though, that air mattresses hamper bailing. On large rafts (10-mans and bigger), where people generally sit up on the tubes, they are rarely used.

PRESERVER CUSHIONS: As a raft careens through a rapid, the people in it shift and jostle around. For this reason it is sometimes good to pad the fore and aft ends of the oar frame with either life-preserver belts or life-preserver cushions such as those used as seat pads in rowboats. These latter cushions also make delightful swimming toys.

SACKS: When canvas sacks are used to hold things unaffected by water such as canned goods, spare bailers, garbage, and so on, there is more space in the watertight bags for the gear that must stay dry. The sacks must be of heavy-duty, tight-weave canvas, or they will rapidly develop holes. Four or more bags will be necessary, depending on the length of your trip and the size of your party. If the sacks do not have a zipper or buckle closure, prepare each with a throat-tie by knotting a 2-foot cord near the mouth, leaving two foot-long strands for tying the sack closed. Set one bag aside for garbage (*all* unburnable garbage *must* be packed out), one for such gear as the shovel, spare rope, and spare bailers, and one for cold cans. This latter sack takes the beverages, like beer, pop, and juice, and should be fitted with both a double throat tie and a sturdy cord woven securely around its middle. By means of this latter cord, the bag may be dangled in the water when the raft is drifting through calms, thus providing cold drinks whenever desired. The other sacks are used for canned goods.

SHOVEL: A shovel is necessary for preparing fireplaces, smoothing down sleeping sites, burying human waste, and smothering fires. Get one of the sturdy little folding shovels sold in surplus stores.

CRASH HELMETS: Crash helmets that have chin straps and that come down low on the sides of the head to protect the temples are necessary on tough, rocky rivers. If you want to know why these helmets are needed, gently put your finger into the outside corner of either eye socket and feel the thinness of your skull at the temple.

WET SUITS: Wet suits or skin-tight long wool underwear are needed for trips through extremely cold water or in early spring. Wet suits of $\frac{1}{8}$- or $\frac{3}{16}$-inch foam neoprene provide adequate protection and, unlike $\frac{1}{4}$-inch suits, do not restrict movement. Although some boaters get by with only a top with beaver tail, a full suit with pants and top provides much greater warmth and comfort. Wet-suit booties, worn inside tennis shoes, keep feet toasty warm.

ICE CHEST: Although extravagantly heavy and bulky, ice chests packed with fresh foods and ice-cold drinks are pure bliss in a hot climate. Chests should have drain plugs, be easily cleanable, and be made of nonabsorbent material. Temperatures inside them, which should be checked now and then with a thermometer, should be below 45° F. Dry ice is best. If regular ice is used, drain the melt three times a day. Because this water is contaminated, foods in the chest should be sealed in plastic bags. Chests should be disinfected with a water-chlorine solution after each trip.

CAMPING AND PERSONAL GEAR

Whether on an overnight or extended wilderness trip, rafters do not spend all their time in rafts; life around the campsite is also an essential part of their experience. In order to have enough of the things you will need and to avoid burdening yourself with things you will not need for camping, carefully plan what gear you will take with you.

The Kitchen Box

Put all your cooking and eating things into a single wooden box or black bag and call it the kitchen box. A wooden chest, like that shown in Photograph 14, with nesting tray and fire pan makes for smooth and easy camping, but a big black bag will also suffice. A sturdy cardboard box inside this black bag will make the contents more accessible and will let you pack large flat items, like the grill, newspapers, and paper plates, in the slots between the boxes. Not only kitchen things but also noncanned food and small camping gear, like flashlights and toilet paper, may be kept in this one handy box. The kitchen box should contain:

1. Aluminum foil
2. Biodegradable dish soap
3. Can openers
4. Collapsible bucket
5. Cord
6. Dutch oven (optional)
7. Egg containers (optional)
8. Fire pan with grill or asbestos blanket and grill with wire legs
9. Flashlights with spare batteries and bulbs
10. Fry pan (also serves as pot lid)
11. Gloves for oarsman
12. Big knife
13. Lunch sack
14. Wooden matches
15. Napkins
16. Newspapers or lighter fluid
17. Paper plates
18. Paper towels
19. Paring knives (2)
20. Plastic bags with fasteners

21. Plastic or canvas basin (optional)
22. Pot-gripper pliers
23. Pot-holder gloves of asbestos
24. Pot scrubber with handle
25. Pots (nesting set of 3, 4, or more)
26. Salt, pepper, and other spices (see Chapter Five for details on spices, foods, etc.)
27. Sierra Club cups (2 per person)
28. Silverware
29. Spatula
30. Long spoons (2 or 3)
31. Stove(s) and fuel
32. Sugar in container with tight lid
33. Tea towel (optional)
34. Toilet paper
35. Water containers of canvas or plastic. These should be collapsible and have a 2- to 4-gallon capacity. Also, an insulated jug is good for carrying mixed drinks on the river. (All are optional.)
36. Water purification supplies, with eye-dropper—Clorox, Purex, iodine, or halazone (see Chapter Five)

Newspapers make a fine fire starter, so take plenty. A set of four nesting aluminum or stainless steel pots with lids suffices nicely for a party of four. Often such a pot set comes with a light frying pan that, if used with skill, is quite serviceable. Big wooden matches are the best. A couple of asbestos glove-type pot holders plus a pair of pot-gripper pliers facilitate the lifting of hot pots. The advantage of having several is that you can find at least one when you need it. A long (18-inch) spoon-and-fork set helps with campfire cookery and serving. Sierra Club cups serve as bowls, cups, and plates, so have at least two per person. Take plenty of knives, forks, and spoons; in the wilderness only big tablespoon-size spoons make any sense. A large plastic bowl makes a good wash basin for you and your dishes. A collapsible canvas bucket provides a convenient fireside water supply and also many a smooth, truly unforgettable shower. A collapsible water container with a 2- to 4-gallon capacity can be convenient on rivers where the water is not potable. A handled metal pot scrubber is essential. A big knife is good to have. One roll of toilet paper usually lasts four people a week or more. Have extra batteries and bulbs for your flashlights. Salt and pepper shakers should be packed with their lids closed. Pack sugar in a container with a tight lid. Put honey, jam, syrup, and such like into handy, refillable squeeze tubes. One way to preserve eggs is to place them in special protective cases available in mountaineering shops. Paper towels, napkins, paper plates, and aluminum foil are all good to have. A pillow slip cover packed with bags

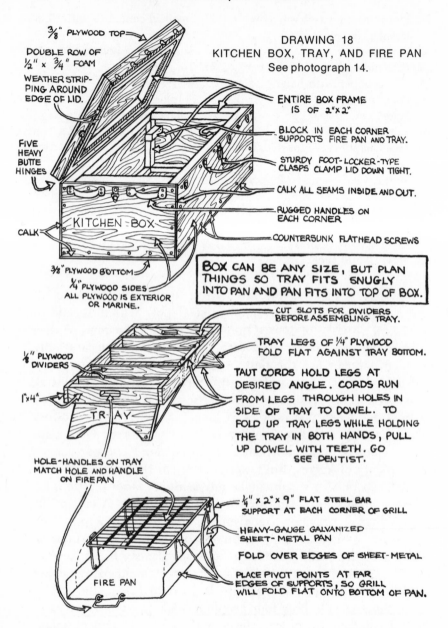

DRAWING 18
KITCHEN BOX, TRAY, AND FIRE PAN
See photograph 14.

3/8" PLYWOOD TOP

DOUBLE ROW OF
1/2" x 3/4" FOAM

WEATHER STRIP-
PING AROUND
EDGE OF LID.

FIVE
HEAVY
BUTTE
HINGES

KITCHEN BOX

CALK

3/8" PLYWOOD BOTTOM

1/4" PLYWOOD SIDES
ALL PLYWOOD IS EXTERIOR
OR MARINE.

ENTIRE BOX FRAME
IS OF 2"x2"

BLOCK IN EACH CORNER
SUPPORTS FIRE PAN AND TRAY.

STURDY FOOT-LOCKER-TYPE
CLASPS CLAMP LID DOWN TIGHT.

CALK ALL SEAMS INSIDE AND OUT.

RUGGED HANDLES ON
EACH CORNER

COUNTERSUNK FLATHEAD SCREWS

BOX CAN BE ANY SIZE, BUT PLAN
THINGS SO TRAY FITS SNUGLY
INTO PAN AND PAN FITS INTO TOP OF BOX.

CUT SLOTS FOR DIVIDERS
BEFORE ASSEMBLING TRAY.

1/8" PLYWOOD
DIVIDERS

1"x4"

TRAY

TRAY LEGS OF 1/4" PLYWOOD
FOLD FLAT AGAINST TRAY BOTTOM.

TAUT CORDS HOLD LEGS AT
DESIRED ANGLE. CORDS RUN
FROM LEGS THROUGH HOLES IN
SIDE OF TRAY TO DOWEL. TO
FOLD UP TRAY LEGS WHILE HOLDING
THE TRAY IN BOTH HANDS, PULL
UP DOWEL WITH TEETH. GO
SEE DENTIST.

HOLE-HANDLES ON TRAY
MATCH HOLE AND HANDLE
ON FIRE PAN

1/4" x 2" x 9" FLAT STEEL BAR
SUPPORT AT EACH CORNER OF GRILL

HEAVY-GAUGE GALVANIZED
SHEET-METAL PAN

FOLD OVER EDGES OF SHEET-METAL

FIRE PAN

PLACE PIVOT POINTS AT FAR
EDGES OF SUPPORTS, SO GRILL
WILL FOLD FLAT ONTO BOTTOM OF PAN.

of raisins, nuts, cheese, salami, bread, and chocolate makes an
irresistible lunch sack; keep this sack out in a special watertight bag so that it will be handy for your lunch stops. And carry
a pair of light cotton or leather gloves in the kitchen box in case
the oarsman or a paddler develops blisters.

On dam-controlled rivers, where no annual floods cleanse the riverbanks, it is important to keep the shores entirely clean and pure. Since the ash and charcoal of campfires can mar a beach badly, build fires in fire pans or on fireproof blankets and then pack out the ash and charcoal or, on large rivers like the Colorado, dump them into the fast midstream current. Although almost any large metal pan can be used, the better fire pans are custom made of heavy-gauge, galvanized sheet metal and are designed to stow neatly somewhere on the raft, such as around the bottom of a black bag or, as in Photograph 14, inside a wooden box. Fire blankets, available in sporting-goods stores, are easier to transport and are more widely used; these work well with a grill with wire legs.

A compact propane or white-gas stove with a large fuel capacity is useful on any river and is essential on popular rivers with assigned campsites, where firewood is often scarce.

Camping Equipment

SLEEPING BAGS: Form-fitting bags of duck or goose down surpass all others in both warmth and compactness. Sewn-through seams are to be avoided as they cause extreme and unnecessary heat loss. If you intend to descend eventually the magnificent rivers of the North, get a bag that will keep you warm down to 10° F. Zippered bags may be kept partially open on warm nights.

AIR MATTRESSES: A person can tolerate immense hardship during the day so long as he or she can escape completely into womblike sleep at night. Deepen and soften your sleep with an air mattress. Foam pads are generally rather bulky and less comfortable, but you don't have to blow them up.

PONCHOS: A nylon or plastic poncho serves as a raincoat, a ground cloth under sleeping bags, and as a makeshift shelter. Have one per person.

TENTS: Tents are advisable in some climates, especially the rainy Pacific Northwest. Tents should fold into compact bundles and should, if they are to provide thorough rain protection, have fly roofs and waterproof floors.

Clothes and Personal Things

For a one-day trip all that is essential in the way of clothing is a pair of nonslip tennis shoes, a set of clothes that can get wet, and a set of dry clothes to leave in the car for the ride home. Depending on the weather and on your inclinations, you may also want to take some of the things mentioned below. (In cold weather it is essential that you also have a change of dry clothes in a waterproof bag.)

For extended trips each person should have the following personal gear:

STANDARD

Waterproof dirty-clothes sack

Wide-brimmed sun hat with chin strap. Straw and tennis hats both good. Keep hat wet to remain cool in hot weather.

Insect repellent

Lip ointment

Pants (2 or 3). Avoid corduroy and wool; they take too long to dry.

Shirts (2 or 3) not sweat shirts; they take too long to dry.

Nonslip tennis or deck shoes (2 pairs). Canvas wading shoes are all right, but uncomfortable. Do not wear thongs on the river; they can be dangerous.

Biodegradable hand soap

Socks (several pairs)

Sunglasses with secure head strap

Sun cream

Sweater—a warm one

Swimsuit

Toothbrush

Toothpaste

Comb or brush

Towel

Underwear

Windbreaker—together, windbreaker and sweater serve as a coat.

Grand piano

OPTIONAL

Botanical, zoological, or geological equipment

Bandana—serves as scarf, towel, pot holder, and tourniquet if need be.

Books

Camera with plenty of film—a waterproof gas-mask bag or a 50-caliber ammo box will protect cameras and film from wetness. Check for leakage before your trip. Paint boxes aluminum or white to reflect heat. Line with foam padding to avoid damaging camera and lenses.

Change of fresh clothes to keep in car for drive home

Chess set

Wool or down coat (should not be bulky)

Fishing gear (Light fly or spinning gear which disassembles into compact protective case is generally best.)

Warm hat

Hiking boots

Kleenex

Knife (Folding type in sheath is best.)

Musical instrument in sturdy case

Pillowcase (Stuff with clothes to form pillow at night.)

Plastic bags with fasteners. These keep your things in some kind of sandfree condition. Have one for underwear and sox, one for sweater, etc.

Playing cards

Sanitary napkins or tampons

Scarf

Shaving gear

Extra optical glasses, if worn

Extra sunglasses

Songbook

Writing materials

Add to this list as you wish, but keep in mind the size of the bag or box that will hold your things. Try to keep your kit under 25 pounds.

Books

On a recent voyage down the Rogue in Oregon, some of our finest times were spent reading aloud to one another a novel of wilderness adventure. Drifting lazily through the calms, at times avidly absorbed in the tale and at times detached and amused, we were not only entertained, we were awakened to a new sense of romance and adventure, and we saw more clearly the unlimited possibilities of nature, life, and thought.

In selecting books appropriate for reading aloud, I suggest that you lean away from dense, convoluted works and favor those whose style is open and clear. Novels and stories concerning wilderness adventure are especially apropos. Here are some suggestions: *Captain Blood* by Rafael Sabatini offers gripping adventure and exalted romance; *Treasure Island* by Robert Louis Stevenson is another tale of adventure on the high seas; *Deliverance* by James Dickey concerns an intense and bloody river trip in canoes; Homer's *Odyssey* is *the* tale of seafaring adventure; *Man on a Raft* by Kenneth Cooke is a true account of men drifting for weeks on the open sea; Mark Twain's *The Adventures of Huckleberry Finn* deserves its position as the most famous river tale; *Robinson Crusoe* by Daniel DeFoe concerns a lone man's experiences on a wilderness island; *Wind in the Willows* by

Kenneth Grahame is a lyrical, philosophical story of a mole and a water rat; *Walden* by Henry David Thoreau presents a sensitive, mystical response to nature; *Siddhartha* by Hermann Hesse tells of enlightenment found beside a river; Ernest Hemingway's *The Sun Also Rises* involves a deep and absorbing pilgrimage to nature; and C. S. Lewis's *Perelandra* is a work of science fiction which, in its vivid portrayal of a foreign planet, sharpens one's perception of earth.

For a short trip try these briefer works: *The Fox* by D. H. Lawrence throbs with a mysterious, arresting sense for nature; *The Open Boat* by Stephen Crane depicts four men who, as they confront a cruel sea, explore brotherhood and fear; *Big Two-Hearted River* by Hemingway is an intense view of a man in the out-of-doors; *To Build a Fire* by Jack London is a tale of hypothermia in the Far North; and Joseph Conrad's *The Heart of Darkness* and *An Outpost of Progress* probe man's inner nature as it manifests itself in uncivilized settings.

Books dealing with specific rivers are mentioned in the sections on those rivers in Part II. These factual books, whether read before or during a trip, add greatly to one's experience of it.

The Ditty Bag

For the sake of comfort when on the river by day, have a ditty bag or box handy with sun cream, chapstick, tissues, sunglasses, and toilet paper. A small waterproof rubber pouch or ammo box works well for this. This is a good place, too, for maps and books.

EMERGENCY AND SURVIVAL GEAR

Go prepared for hard times, and you will enjoy the good times more. A hand winch or hefty block and tackle can be useful in freeing a raft that is wrapped around a midstream rock (see Chapter Three). Carry a complete medical kit (see Chapter Four). On wilderness rivers, have a compass, a folding sheath knife on your belt, lots of dextrose (high-energy tablets), and extra food. All rafts should have emergency signalling equipment; aerial flares and signal mirrors of the United States Air Force type are standard. Daring expeditions to the edge of nowhere should probably have ground-to-air transceivers on frequency 122.8. In isolated parts of the world or under unusual, dangerous circumstances, such as are encountered in winter rafting, each person should have a waterproof survival kit sewn into his or her lifejacket; this kit should contain matches, signal mirror, flares, dextrose, a knife, and a compass. Wilderness travelers would do well to read Bradford Angier's *How To Stay Alive in the Woods,* a comprehensive manual of survival.

MAPS

Detailed maps of the river make a voyage safer and more interesting, allowing one both to foresee rapids and waterfalls and to identify tributaries, mountains, and other salient features of the landscape. In addition, they aid in keeping track of one's position, knowledge of which allows one to coordinate his progress down the river with his schedule, if he has one, and with the state of his supplies. Accurate knowlege of one's position is especially necessary in the event of an emergency, such as a serious injury, in which case it is important to know the shortest route back to civilization.

Ideal maps for river runners are made by riverman Leslie Allen Jones. The continuous strip, or scroll, maps lovingly produced by Les Jones not only show every bend, island, rapid, and fall in the river, they also include names, difficulty ratings, brief descriptions, and running and scouting advice for the more difficult rapids and falls. They show campsites, the contour of the canyon, and other features close by the river. Their clear, cross-sectional views of the river's gradient enable the rafter to note at a glance the river's drop at any given point. Occasional historical notes add a fascinating dimension by indicating the locations of past events on the river, such as where so-and-so drowned in 1869. And the more recent maps include extremely useful water-flow information. Each scroll map comes with a special plastic bag that serves as a transparent, watertight mapcase, allowing one to keep the next 5 or 10 miles of river continuously in view without exposing the map to wetness.

These thorough, professional maps are available for a large number of Western rivers, including: Green River Lake to Daniels ($2.50); Green River—Red Canyon, Canyon of Lodore, Whirlpool Canyon, Split Mountain Canyon, Desolation Canyon, and Gray Canyon ($3.00); Colorado River—Gore Canyon to Grand Junction ($2.80), Westwater Canyon ($1.80), Cataract Canyon

($1.10), Grand Canyon ($3.20); Yampa River ($1.80); Dolores
River ($2.75); Black Canyon of the Gunnison River ($2.50); San
Juan River ($1.80); Hell's Canyon of the Snake River ($2.50);
Middle Fork of the Salmon River ($2.00); Salmon River ($2.30);
Clearwater River of Idaho and Selway River ($3.00); Rogue
River ($2.00); MacKenzie River of Oregon ($1.80); Columbia
River in British Columbia ($2.50); British Columbia's Fraser
River—Tete Jaune Cache to Yale ($3.00); North and South Fork
of the Flathead River of Montana ($3.00); and the Grijalva River
of Mexico ($1.50). These maps may be ordered from Leslie A.
Jones, Star Route Box 13A, Heber City, Utah 84032. It should
be noted, of course, that no map is so flawless that it eliminates
the need for on-site inspection and good judgment. Although
they do name side canyons and tributaries, scroll maps concentrate largely upon the river, making additional maps necessary if broader coverage is desired.

Detailed views of both the river and the surrounding countryside may be found in the topographic quadrangle maps of the
7½-minute and 15-minute series published by the United States
Geological Survey. Especially useful if one is forced to leave the
river or has the desire to take side trips and a great help in
finding put-ins, these colorful maps show all rivers, streams, variations in terrain, trails, roads, airstrips, man-made structures, and
some waterfalls and rapids. Obtain the 7½-minute quadrangles
whenever they are available, because their detailed scale of 2⅝
inches to the mile offers a much better view of river and country
than the 1-inch-per-mile scale of the 15-minute quadrangles. Although many of these maps have been either recently drawn up
or recently revised, some are over twenty years out of date; thus,
the roads shown have sometimes been improved or abandoned,
and some of the rivers shown have long since been turned into
lakes.

For information on which quadrangle maps cover particular
rivers, obtain indexes to the topographic maps of the states in
which the rivers are located. For a list of the quadrangles covering each of the rivers discussed in Part II, see Part II. State indexes and quadrangle maps covering areas west of the Mississippi
River may be ordered through the mail by writing to the United
States Geological Survey, Distribution Section, Denver, Colorado
80225. For state indexes and maps east of the Mississippi write
to the United States Geological Survey, Distribution Section,
1200 South Eads St., Arlington, Virginia 22202. Always order

by map name, state, and series. The current price is 75¢ per map. Each order should be accompanied by exact payment in cash or by money order or check made payable to the Geological Survey. State indexes and a folder describing topographic maps are furnished free on request. Private dealers sell quadrangle maps at their own prices. Names and addresses of such dealers are listed in each state index.

Canadian topographic quadrangle maps, on a scale of 1¼ inches to the mile, are available at the price of 50¢ per map. Regional indexes, which will tell you which maps cover which rivers, and the maps themselves may be ordered from the Canada Map Office, Department of Energy, Mines, and Resources, 615 Booth Street, Ottawa, Ontario, K1A 0E9, Canada. The telephone number is (613) 994-9663.

Accurate, inexpensive maps of certain rivers are also available from the Forest Service of the Department of Agriculture, from the states themselves, and from other sources. For information on maps such as these covering a particular river, see Part II.

In addition to occasional river maps, the Forest Service furnishes maps of national forests. If your river runs through or borders one of the many national forests, get a free map of the forest from the Forest Service regional office nearest the river. Addresses of the Forest Service regional offices are Federal Bldg., Missoula, Mont. 59801; Federal Center, Bldg. 85, Denver, Colo. 80225; 517 Gold Ave., S.W., Albuquerque, N. Mex. 87101; Forest Service Bldg., Ogden, Utah 84401; 630 Sansome St., San Francisco, Calif. 94111; P.O. Box 3623, Portland, Oreg. 97408; 6816 Market St., Upper Darby, Pa. 19082; 50 Seventh St., N.E., Atlanta, Ga. 30323; 710 N. 6th St., Milwaukee, Wis. 53203; Fifth Street Office Bldg., P.O. Box 1631, Juneau, Alaska 99801.

Because maps sometimes get washed overboard, it is wise to carry an extra set. On this extra set always mark all possible escape routes; if you are ever unable to proceed by river, this could save days—and lives. In order to make quadrangle maps or other flat or folding maps waterproof and durable, spray them on both sides with clear acrylic or varnish. But don't use shellac; it turns white when wet.

RIGGING AND PACKING THE RAFT

After inflation, rafts are normally rigged on the beach and then lifted into the water for loading. With an oar raft, cinch the frame (and poop deck, if you have one) tight with straps to D-rings. Mount spare oars so that they are readily accessible; although some rafters mount spares in a vertical position, letting them stick up into the air, most hang them just below the outboard edges of the frame with stretch cord. Place working oars forward of thole pins, and make sure the pins are tight. Secure all oars with strong, light, nylon lines; use 3- or 4-foot lines, and tie one end to the oar shaft just below the clip or rubber and the other to the frame. If necessary, pad the frame where people might bruise themselves against it.

Rig paddle rafts with webbing, or rope across thwarts in such a way that paddlers can wedge their knees under them without risking entanglement (Photograph 15). Some paddle rafters lash their gear to the floor, while others put their gear on a frame or on a bow deck of wood or netting.

For all boats, rig grip ropes or handles for each crew member; these often run around the top or the inside of the buoyancy tube.

PHOTOGRAPH 15   A paddle raft in the sediment-laden waters of the Grand Canyon. Notice the webbing thwarts passing over the paddlers' inboard knees. (*Bob Krips Photo.*)

As well as long bow and stern lines, rig a short 20-foot painter line for brief tie-ups; put this line on the stern of oar boats and on the bow of paddle boats. Solo rafts on tough rivers should have beaching lines.

Pack gear so that the load is as low and sleek as possible. There should be no protruding edges, and the load should not interfere with rowing or paddling. Balance the boat from side to side, but, to help keep the bow downstream, position people and gear so that more weight is *forward*.

When the gear is lashed down correctly, nothing need ever be lost, not even in a flip. But tying everything in well day after day requires a quick and easy system. Give some thought to this. The simplest, fastest method is to put everything into a neat, tight pile, cover it with a tarp, and lash it down securely. Another method is to use a well-planned system in which each piece of gear has its designated spot and its own special fastenings. With this latter method, boxes are double-clipped on short lines and bags are secured either with fitted straps or with special one-knot lashings.

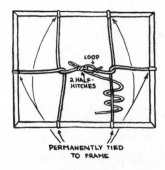 

DRAWING 19 SPECIAL ONE-KNOT LASHING
Once the four ropes are attached to the frame, this lashing can be fastened or released simply by tying or untying the two half hitches at the top.

Regardless of the method you choose, all loose pieces of gear, like lifejackets, camera cases, and the ditty bag, should be clipped to the raft. Use spring clips and carabiners but not compression clips. Compression clips of the sliding-pin type often won't hold thin handles or lines in the frenzied underwater wrenching that occurs after a flip.

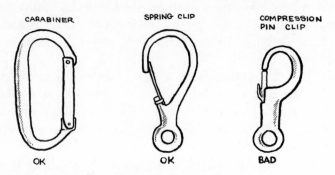

CARABINER   SPRING CLIP   COMPRESSION
                                    PIN CLIP

OK   OK   BAD

DRAWING 20 CLIPS

TWO PHILOSOPHIES OF RIVER GEAR

The waggish characters who run rivers in rafts are of two philosophies concerning river gear. One school, hypnotized by the constant sway of spray and foam, takes nothing that is not essential. For them, the light surge and agile play of the raft among the rocks and big waves is the vital thing, and so they streamline their boat, keeping it trim and light for the dance. The other group, eyes glowing with visions of big trout, hearty meals, the conquest of *War and Peace*, stupendous photographs, and air-cushioned sleep, pack their rafts with all the paraphernalia of their hobbies. From badminton to gold panning, from painting watercolors to painting on cosmetics, from lounging in folding chairs to cooking elaborate feasts with the aid of ice chests, dutch ovens, and iron griddles, the members of this group voyage into the wilds equipped to enjoy themselves in the ways they love best. The beauty of rafting is that it can accommodate both groups—and all those in between.

CHAPTER TWO

Guiding the Raft Through Whitewater

A mystique surrounds rafting. People unfamiliar with rivers imagine rapids as terrifying infernoes and river rafters as supermen or fools. The truth is less dramatic: River rafting is relatively easy, and anyone in good physical condition can learn to guide a raft through rapids.

Rafting skills do, however, take time to develop. The ability to spot hazards and read the river depends not only on an intellectual knowledge of river characteristics but also on a great deal of practice studying and running actual rapids. In the same way, skill in maneuvering a boat requires an understanding of rowing or paddling techniques and much practice. The key elements are knowledge and experience. First, read this book, studying most carefully this chapter and the next—they are the core of the book. Then, go out on the river and see how things move in unison there. Join your knowledge to experience by beginning on mild rivers and gradually work your way up the scale of difficulty. Take this book along and refer to it often.

PHOTOGRAPH 16   A paddle raft climbs over a towering haystack in the Grand Canyon. (*Bob Krips Photo.*)

OAR TECHNIQUE

It has only been in recent times that men have understood how to row whitewater. Before Nathan Galloway appeared, they ran rivers in the same way they rowed still water. Looking backward and rowing blind, they rowed long-keeled, unmaneuverable boats pell-mell downstream, increasing their closing speed with obstacles and scanting maneuvering time. It is small wonder that early river explorers like those of the Powell expedition, the first men known to have run the Grand Canyon, met with frequent disaster and were terrified by whitewater. But in 1896 Nathan Galloway changed all this. With the rare ability to do the obvious that we call genius, Galloway turned around to look where he was going and rowed *against* the current to slow his closing speed with obstacles and to gain time to avoid them. Combined with his use of a flat-bottomed boat called a dory that was easy to turn and maneuver, this simple innovation transformed river running from a nightmare undergone unwillingly for purposes of exploration into a thrilling sport to be enjoyed for its own sake. The inflatable raft, with its flat bottom and light weight, follows in the wake of Galloway's wooden dory; it is at once stable and maneuverable, and it is at home in whitewater when rowed in the Galloway fashion.

PHOTOGRAPH 17   An oar boat rowed in Galloway position, that is, with the oarsman facing the bow, which is pointed downstream.

The Ferry

As the rush of water propels a raft through a rapid, the boatman scoots the raft from side to side to avoid obstacles. This sideways motion is achieved with the ferry, the most basic of rafting techniques (Drawing 21). You are at the oars of your boat in Galloway position, that is, facing the bow, which is pointed down-

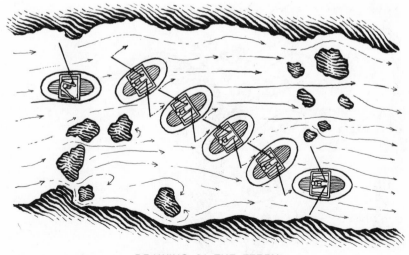

DRAWING 21 THE FERRY
To ferry, angle your stern toward the side you want to approach, and back-row.

stream. *To ferry right, swing the bow about 45 degrees left—to ferry left, swing right—and backrow.* (To backrow, lean forward extending your arms, dip the oars to the throat, and pull back with arms, back, and legs in one smooth effort.) This action both slows the boat's downstream progress and moves it sideways in the current. If you are more concerned with moving to the side than with slowing downstream speed, you may increase the angle until the boat is at right angles to the current. By the same token, you may decrease this angle if you want more to slow your speed than to move sideways. In general, however, 45 degrees is the optimum angle. Bear in mind that I am talking about the boat's angle to the current, not the banks. On bends, where the current turns later than the banks, a boat may at times even be perpendicular to the banks while maintaining a 45-degree angle to the current (Drawing 22).

DRAWING 22 FERRYING AROUND A BEND

In ferrying, the important thing is the boat's angle to the current, not the banks. On bends, where the outswinging current turns later than the banks, a boat may at times be perpendicular to the bank while maintaining a 45-degree angle to the current.

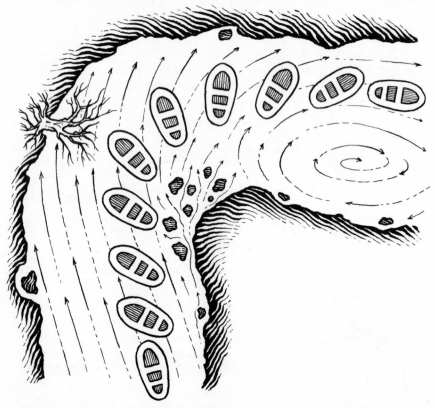

In slow current it is possible to ferry straight across the river like an actual ferry, but in fast water the most a rafter can do is angle across. Use the ferry whenever you want to avoid obstacles or approach the bank in fast water.

The Portegee

The portegee (Drawing 23) is a style of rowing used by Portuguese fishermen. To do it, just point your bow in the direction you want to go and push on the oars. (To push on the oars, lean back pulling back the oar handles, dip the blades, and push forward by simultaneously leaning forward and straightening the arms.) Because only the arms and stomach come into play, this is not a strong stroke. Use it only in moderate water when you have plenty of maneuvering time.

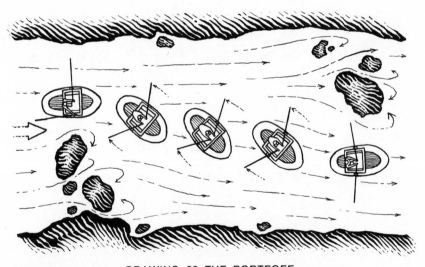

DRAWING 23 THE PORTEGEE
To portegee, point your bow in the direction you want to go, and push on the oars.

The portegee is especially handy in the calm, shoaling water just above rapids. It allows you at once to look at the rapid, ease forward toward the brink, jockey into correct entry position—and all the while you are also ready to shift into the more cautious and powerful ferry position whenever necessary.

The Double-Oar Turn

Mastery of the double-oar turn requires practice. To swing the bow right, simultaneously pull on the right oar and push on the left (Drawing 24). To turn the bow left, reverse this; that is, push on the right oar and pull on the left. Initially this may seem a bit like trying to pat your head with one hand while rubbing your stomach with the other, but in time it will become second nature. Practice the double-oar turn relentlessly; make it instinctive.

DRAWING 24 THE DOUBLE-OAR TURN
To swing the bow left, simultaneously pull on the left oar and push on the right. To rotate the bow right, reverse this, that is, push on the left oar while pulling on the right.

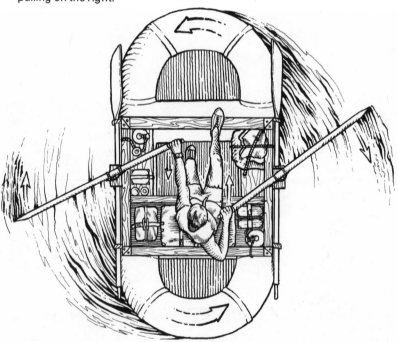

As you run heavy water, the waves will constantly attempt to twist your boat around sideways; only the instant and forceful use of a double-oar-turn stroke will keep the bow into the waves and prevent the raft from flipping. But this stroke is not only used to prevent broaching in waves, it is also the basic stroke used to turn the raft. Whether it be to enter or leave a ferry or portegee position, or just to turn the raft around, this is the stroke to use.

The double-oar turn is quick and easy and spins the raft on a dime. The single-oar turn, which consists of pulling the right oar to turn right or the left oar to turn left, is slow in comparison and causes an unnecessary backwards motion of the raft. The single-oar turn is used only for minor adjustments of raft angle or when backward motion is desired.

The Pivot and Back Pivot

The pivot consists simply of turning the raft from a ferry position to a bow-downstream position (Drawing 25, left). It is used to narrow the passing space of the raft in order to slide closely past rocks and is executed with a double-oar turn.

DRAWING 25

THE PIVOT	THE BACK PIVOT
The pivot is used to narrow the raft's passing space in order to slide closely past obstructions. Note the use of the double-oar turn and the folding in of the oars.	The back pivot is used to pass rocks closely when recovering from an extreme ferry angle. Because it leaves the raft running backward, the back pivot is used only as a last resort.

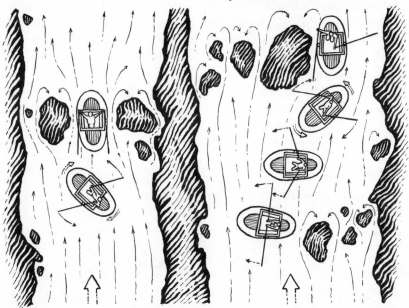

Similarly, the back pivot is used when passing rocks closely (Drawing 25, right). But because it leaves the boat running backwards, the back pivot is used only in tight situations where an extreme ferry angle must be maintained as long as possible. At the last second, with no space for a standard pivot, the boat is swung around, often with frantic pulling on the oar *farthest* from the rock because the near oar has insufficient room to operate. Then, running backward, the oarsman must keep the *stern* into the waves until he gets a chance to spin the boat around into the bow-downstream position.

Handling the Oars

Oars can easily jam and snap. Never use them to fend off rocks or brush, even to avoid a collision. Never let them dangle in the water regardless of whether the water is swift or calm. And when ferrying in shallows, the great enemy of oars, keep a keen eye peeled and use quick, shallow strokes to avoid jamming the downstream oar. It is better to hit a few rocks with the raft than to break an oar.

A few tips on handling oars: Because the greatest power is applied in the ferry, not the portegee, take the strain off the oar rubbers by placing the oars *forward* of the thole pins. To avoid breaking oars when rowing, apply power smoothly and steadily, rather than suddenly. Don't flail; take solid, deep strokes, dipping the oars to the throat. To move swiftly through calms, turn your boat around and backrow in rowboat fashion; but here, as always, be alert for rocks and snags.

There is more than one way to stroke with the oars when ferrying, portegeeing, and rowing in calms. You can pull on both oars at once, in the standard manner, or you can pull on each oar alternately. With the alternating technique, as one oar is powering through the water, the other is being returned through the air. Just as one oar leaves the water, the other enters it. When done with a bit of polish, the alternating stroke can be very graceful and relaxing.

PADDLE TECHNIQUE

Paddles unite a raft's crew into a pack of uncomfortable, fatuously happy slaves. Everyone in a paddle raft must pull like a wild demon to guide the raft through rapids. Sitting astride the buoyancy tubes cowboy fashion, paddlers meet the river head on, taking the waves in their teeth and often getting washed overboard. In paddle rafts the people are drawn close by their shared exertion, which forms a tight bond of trust and good feeling between them. It is paddlers who experience the most

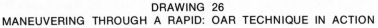

DRAWING 26
MANEUVERING THROUGH A RAPID: OAR TECHNIQUE IN ACTION

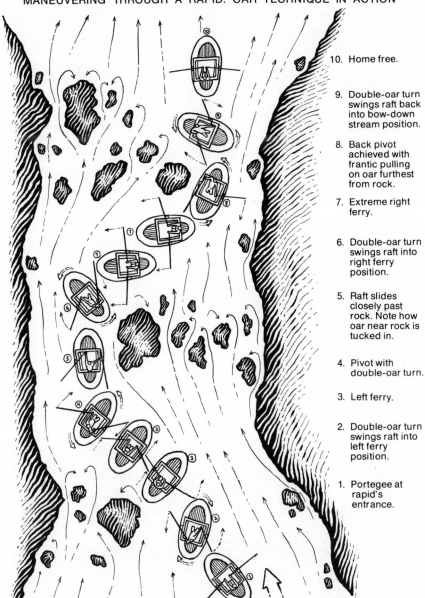

10. Home free.

9. Double-oar turn swings raft back into bow-down stream position.

8. Back pivot achieved with frantic pulling on oar furthest from rock.

7. Extreme right ferry.

6. Double-oar turn swings raft into right ferry position.

5. Raft slides closely past rock. Note how oar near rock is tucked in.

4. Pivot with double-oar turn.

3. Left ferry.

2. Double-oar turn swings raft into left ferry position.

1. Portegee at rapid's entrance.

intense adventure; there they are, with nothing but inefficient paddles between them and disaster.

In large rafts paddlers can sit either cowboy style, gripping the buoyancy tube betwen their knees, or atop the tube with both feet inboard, twisting slightly to paddle. In small rafts paddlers also have the option of sitting down inside the boat and reaching over the bouyancy tube to paddle. Sitting atop the tube with both feet inboard offers greater comfort, but the cowboy straddle offers more excitement. Cowboys keep the outboard foot out of the drink by tucking it back and up, and they keep themselves out of the drink by locking their inboard leg under a rope thwart (but in such a way that it cannot get tangled) or by grasping a rope handgrip similar to that used by rodeo riders. Never strap or tie yourself in lest you be held underwater in a flip. Of course, paddlers riding cowboy style must be alert to pull in their outboard legs when the raft scrapes or collides with rocks.

Paddle crews divide their strength evenly on both sides of the raft, with the odd man, if there is one, steering over the stern and assisting on one side or the other as necessary.

The Strokes

Develop strong yet comfortable forward, back, and draw (sideways) strokes by moving naturally and easily. In mild water,

PHOTOGRAPH 18   Ecstatic slaves. (*Photo courtesy of the American River Touring Association.*)

don't overreach and don't go in for excessive twisting of the torso. But when extra speed is needed, lean deeply into the strokes, bringing the stomach, torso, and entire body into play. For all strokes, place the inboard hand across the top of the paddle grip and the outboard hand well down the shaft.

To do the *forward stroke*, first thrust the blade forward with the outboard arm. Next, momentarily keeping the outboard arm stiff, push the grip forward to bite the blade deep into the water. Then smoothly continue the stroke by pushing on the grip while pulling on the shaft, keeping the blade at right angles to and close to the raft. A full follow-through provides little forward power, so stop the stroke just after the blade comes past the hip. Slide the blade from the water by swinging the grip down toward the inboard hip, and feather the paddle on the return by keeping the blade's surface parallel to the surface of the water. Feathering cuts wind and wave resistance.

The *backstroke* is a forward stroke reversed. Plunge the blade into the water just behind the hip; apply power by simultaneously pushing forward on the shaft and pulling back on the grip; end the stroke where the forward stroke begins.

The *draw stroke* is a sideways grab, and its opposite, the *pry stroke*, is a sideways push. To do the draw stroke, reach out from the raft, dip in the blade and pull straight in with the blade parallel to the raft. Do the pry stroke by reversing this. With small rafts, say 9 feet long and under, these complementary strokes come in handy for small sideways maneuvers, and when used by a key stern man in any boat, they are good for turning the raft.

A fifth stroke, aptly called the *calm-water crawl*, provides much-needed variety when alternated with the standard forward stroke during hellish paddles through long calms. Sit cowboy fashion facing the stern; hold a long paddle diagonally in front of you with the shaft held by the outboard hand against the outboard hip and the grip held by the inboard hand before the inboard shoulder. Extend the inboard arm to swing the blade behind you, dip the blade to the throat, and pull back on the grip to pry strongly, using the hip as a fulcrum. With assisting motion from shoulder, hip, and hand, the crawl is powerful yet easy.

DRAWING 27 PADDLE STROKES
Notice the various sitting positions. All of these strokes can be done in any sitting position.

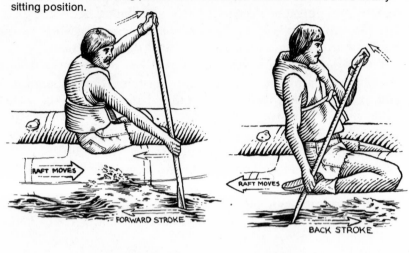

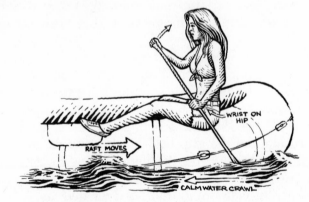

The Captain and the Commands

Because rapids demand fast, decisive action, a paddle raft needs a captain to unite and quicken the crew. A raft captain does not have lofty status or power; he is simply a member of the crew who is, for the moment, controlling the raft through commands. The happiest, closest crew is one where the role of captain is shared equally, with everyone getting a chance to captain the raft through major rapids. Beginners should be advanced in accordance with their ability; they should begin by captaining the raft through easy riffles and then, with an experienced person ready to step in if necessary, they may take over for rapids of gradually increasing difficulty.

Since communication between captain and crew is crucial, each crew must agree on a set of short, clear commands. Possible commands:

Forward	Crew paddles forward.
Backpaddle	Crew does backstroke.
Turn right	Right side backpaddles.
	Left side paddles forward.
Turn left	Left side backpaddles.
	Right side paddles forward.
Draw right	Right side uses draw stroke.
	Left side uses pry stroke.
Draw left	Left side uses draw stroke.
	Right side uses pry stroke.
Stop	Paddlers relax.

Commands must be carried out immediately. Green crews should practice until they can snap through any series of commands without hesitation, without any crew member having to think, "Turn right . . . let's see . . . I'm on the left side, so I should, ah, paddle forward."

Because the captain influences the response of his crew both with his tone of voice and with the commands, he controls not only the raft's direction but also its speed. A captain's control of speed and his ability to anticipate how the water ahead will affect the raft allows him to avoid under- and overcompensation when maneuvering among obstacles. Good captains think well ahead and move the boat with, rather than against, the river. They issue commands sparingly and precisely, working their crews as little as possible and maneuvering the boat in a tight fashion. When used in harmony with the river's currents, a few strong strokes can scoot the boat fast and far. With a good captain, paddling can even be easy.

In situations where instant action is not necessary, the captain may say, "Paddle at will." When time and the rapid's booming din allow, the captain should preface commands with a brief statement of plan, such as, "We're going to ferry to the left of that big rock. OK . . . (gives command)." If a command is not understood, it should be repeated with gusto.

Paddle Maneuvers

The ferry (explained in detail above in "Oar Technique") is the basic maneuvering technique for paddle as well as oar rafts. Used to navigate bends and to sidestep obstacles in swift current, the ferry involves paddling upstream at an angle to move the raft sideways in the current. Paddle rafts can ferry with the bow angled either upstream or downstream. The bow-upstream ferry is stronger because it employs the more powerful forward stroke; it is executed by placing the boat at a 45-degree angle to the current with the bow angled upstream and toward the side you want to approach (Drawing 28). The bow-downstream ferry, on the other hand, though weaker because it uses the less powerful backstroke, does offer certain advantages: it allows paddlers to look ahead without craning their necks and makes it easy to put the bow into waves. It is done by backstroking with the *stern* angled upstream at about a 45-degree angle toward the side you want to approach. Practice both ferries at every opportunity; they are the foundation of paddle rafting technique.

In calm and moderate water where there is ample maneuvering time, the straight forward paddle is used. Just point the bow in the direction you want to go and paddle forward. The pivot and back pivot are simply turns, and are called out as such (see "Oar Technique—The Pivot and Back Pivot").

Sprawling and indifferent, a river waits to test all comers; only careful and intelligent practice can prepare a paddle crew for this confrontation. When first on the water, crews should review all strokes and commands. They should also run through practice patterns that encompass all the commands and ferries. Here's a sample pattern: Beginning with the bow pointed downstream, (1) turn 135 degrees right (clockwise), (2) paddle forward to ferry right (that is, toward the right as you look downstream), (3) turn 90 degrees left (counterclockwise), (4) backpaddle to ferry left, (5) turn 180 degrees right, (6) paddle forward to ferry left, (7) turn 90 degrees right, (8) backpaddle to ferry right,

DRAWING 28 THE PADDLE FERRY
A bow-upstream ferry. With the bow angled upstream toward the side it
wants to approach, the crew does the forward stroke; this moves the boat
sideways across the current. Because it employs the more powerful forward stroke, the bow-upstream ferry is faster than the bow-downstream
ferry, which employs the weaker backstroke.

(9) turn 45 degrees right to face downstream, (10) draw right,
and then, (11) draw left. Don't try to remember this pattern.
Just remember the various commands and ferries and work them
into your own spontaneous patterns.

SWEEP-OAR TECHNIQUE

Sweep-oar technique is straightforward. The boat is kept in line
with the current with the bow pointed downstream, and the
long sweep oars extending over bow and stern are used to move
the boat directly sideways in the current. No ferrying is possible,
and the boat can be slowed only by ducking into eddies or by
deliberately hitting and rubbing against rocks. Nor is it possible
to row swiftly downstream through calms; as a result, most sweep
rigs are either heavily laden commercial rafts, which sit low in

DRAWING 29

the water and move along with the mild current of calms even against headwinds, or threesome rafts, which split up to row in the usual way through calms. Because sweep-rig boats tend to be big and sluggish, their boatmen must perpetually think well ahead and take action early when avoiding obstacles.

Considerable skill and muscle are needed to handle big-bladed, 12- to 15-foot sweep oars. Use big, rhythmic strokes and put your whole body into them. Learn to save strokes when possible by *planting* the big blades into currents and eddies that will push or pull the boat where you want to go. For instance, to enter an eddy (a place where the current turns upstream just downstream from an obstruction) slide closely past the obstruction, plant the bow oar in the eddy to swing in the bow, and then, just as the stern clears the obstruction, pull strongly on the stern oar to bring the boat entirely into the eddy. To leave the eddy, plant an oar in the downstream current and let it pull you back into the mainstream. When planting an oar in this manner, brace your feet well; a large sweep oar caught in a current can easily knock you overboard. Take care never to dip the bow oar in a place where it could jam and break against a rock or the riverbottom.

Sweep-oar rigs handle well in heavy rapids. Just keep the bow into the waves and pull to one side or the other as necessary.

Because the stronger stroke is a pull stroke, many boatmen switch sides for maneuvers which would otherwise call for a lot of pushing. Some sweep rigs are handled by one man in the center of the boat, while others require a man at each oar.

The one-man sweep-oar rig imparts a grand feeling to the oarsman. Stand in the center of the raft, lean heavily into the strokes, feel the raft buck beneath your feet, learn to move with the big oars. Do it once and you will know why no true Idaho riverman will row anything else.

RAPIDS

Rapids vary greatly in size and shape. Some are short, abrupt drops while others are half-mile-long chutes. In some the river broadens to filter through labyrinthine boulder fields; in others it pinches down to rush between narrow cliffs. The channels of some rapids are straight; the channels of others twist to send the

PHOTOGRAPH 19 Warm Springs Rapid on the Yampa River. This rapid has claimed the lives of at least three professional boatmen, largely because the broad holes (reversals) at its foot are extremely hard to avoid. Numbers correspond to those in photograph.

1. Pool above rapid
2. Tongue
3. Holes (reversals)
4. Nasty rocks just the surface
5. Eddy

main current crashing into the canyon walls. Some have moderate slope and can be surveyed from upstream; others fall so steeply that they appear from upstream as a mere horizon line across the river. The variations are endless, but the causes of rapids are few.

The fast, turbulent water of rapids is caused by four things: *Gradient* or slope of the riverbed; other things being equal, the steeper the slope, the faster the water. *Roughness* in the form of rocks, boulders, ledges, and gravel formations; the rougher the floor of the river, the greater the turbulence. *Constriction* of the river channel through narrowing and shallowing; the smaller the bottleneck, the faster the water. And last, water *flow/volume;* this one is very important. Some rapids become more difficult as the flow increases; others become easier. In general, higher flow increases difficulty. Spring run-offs, in fact, turn many mild rivers into unrunnable raceways of boiling foam. Usually, two, three, or all of these factors combine to make a rapid, but any one of the four is capable of creating a rapid alone. Mule Creek Canyon Rapid on the Rogue River, for example, is caused mainly by con-

PHOTOGRAPH 20   Blossom Bar on the Rogue River—a boulder garden. The raft in the upper center is running the only navigable passage through the maze of boulders. (*Photo by Karl Kernberger, courtesy of the American River Touring Association.*)

striction; sheer granite cliffs squeeze the river into a thin ribbon of speeding water made wild by heavy waves rebounding off the banks.

Contrary to what is commonly imagined, the water in most rapids flows at no more than 10 mph. At all its thousands of gauging stations throughout the United States, the United States Geological Survey has recorded in the last forty years only a handful of instances in which a river's speed exceeded 13 mph. In comparison to modern highway speeds this may seem slow, but when you move in an open raft through a sea of lashing waves at this speed, you will think it very fast indeed. A river flows fastest near the surface in its center, for here there is least friction with banks and riverbed and with the slower-moving water near them. Because the surface tension of the water slows the flow somewhat, the fastest speed is attained just below the surface.

A rapid's difficulty hinges mainly on how hard its obstacles are to avoid. Roughly speaking, the faster the current and the greater the number of obstacles, the tougher the rapid. But a large number of things play a part in determining a rapid's difficulty, including sharpness of bends, length, width, depth, turbulence, waves, rescue potential, and water temperature. A comprehensive chart explaining the Western and International scales for rating rapid and river difficulty will be found in Part II. We turn now to the components of a rapid.

The Tongue

At the beginning of most rapids a smooth *tongue* of fast water, in the shape of a V pointing downstream, marks the path of the main current (Drawing 30). As the water entering the rapid speeds up, obstructions above and below the surface send wakes fanning out downstream. When two wakes meet they form a tongue. Each V-shaped tongue prominently points out a channel between obstacles and marks what is often (but not always) an optimum point of entry. When there is more than one tongue, the largest that terminates in a regular succession of standing waves is the main channel.

Standing Waves

Unlike ocean waves, which move while the water in them remains

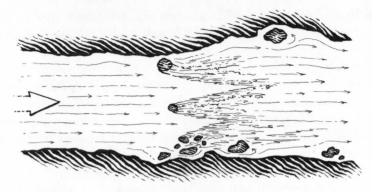

DRAWING 30 THE TONGUE
The largest V usually marks the main channel and optimum point
of entry.

relatively still, the big waves of a river stand in a fixed position
while the water rushes through them. Shaped like big steep-sided
mounds or haystacks (in fact, they are called haystacks), standing waves are generally found in orderly rows in long chutes or
at the foot of rapids. Caused by fast-moving water dissipating
its energy as it slams into slow-moving water, haystacks commonly mount to heights of 8 and 10 feet, and, on gargantuan
rivers such as the Fraser in British Columbia, occasionally mount
to altitudes of 20 feet and more. The first, or upstream, haystack
in any given row is the largest, and each suceeding wave is
slightly smaller than the one before. Thus each row gradually
peters out into little low waves that diminish into calm.

Straight rows of evenly spaced haystacks usually mark the
deepest water and fastest current and so are more likely to be
rock-free than the surrounding water. If a row has standing
waves with extremely steep sides and breaking tops, it should
be avoided by keeping to the alley of lesser turbulence off to
either side. But when the crests are rounded, rafters may run
these rows right down the middle, revelling in the roller-coaster
ride which, in big-water rivers like the Colorado in the Grand

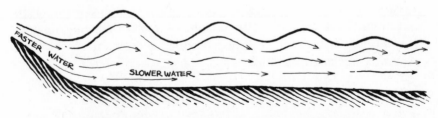

DRAWING 31 A ROW OF STANDING WAVES

Canyon, can last for hundreds of yards. Interestingly, the very large waves can be the safest because their peaks are far apart and the boat has ample time to rise to them.

RUNNING STANDING WAVES: As the boat climbs the crests and slides into the troughs, keep the bow pointing into the waves. If you must ferry, do so with the bow pointing downstream as much as possible. As the boat slams into each trough, some boat-men backrow to reduce spray and allow the bow to rise to the next crest without nosing under and taking on a lot of water. As you crest, read the river ahead, checking your general position and focusing keenly on the third or fourth haystack immediately downstream. Remember that uniform waves are usually safe, while breaks in the pattern spell danger. Mounds of water with no haystacks showing below often conceal rocks, and flat pancakelike patches of water indicate holes just upstream.

Reversals

A reversal is a place where the river's flow swings upward and revolves back on itself, forming a treacherous mouth. As one of the most dangerous of river obstacles, reversals are a focus of attention and have many names—holes, souse holes, hydraulics, stoppers, stopper waves, keepers, white eddies, curlers, side-curlers, roller waves, and backrollers. Some of these terms are used loosely to refer to any sort of reversal, while others have more precise shades of meaning and denote certain types of re-versals. Each of these terms is discussed in the glossary at the back of this book. Despite all these names, however, there are basically only three types of reversal (Drawing 32).

The most common type of reversal is the surface backflow below, that is, immediately downstream of, rocks just under the surface. After the swift water spills over the rock, it plunges to the river bottom where it remains for a short distance as it flows on downstream. In plunging to the river bed and remaining there, the water leaves a gap on the surface below the rock which must be filled in by water moving back upstream. An upstream re-versal of current results, consisting of white, aerated foam which offers meager buoyancy.

Small reversals of this type can hold a raft momentarily and cause it to take on water, while large reversals of this sort can swamp or flip a raft or stop it dead. These holes often kill

DRAWING 32 THREE TYPES OF REVERSALS

Reversal caused by a rock just below the surface.

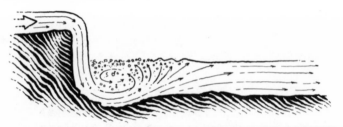

Reversal below a vertical fall.

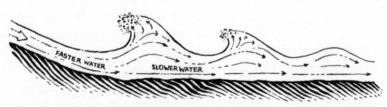

Cresting standing waves.

swimmers. They should be avoided whenever possible and, when unavoidable, should be hit bow-on with considerable forward momentum to drive the raft through. Plunge oar and paddle blades deep to grab the forward-moving water near the bottom, or, if possible, swing blades wide to catch the downstream flow at the sides of the hole.

The most perilous reversals are those found below vertical falls. Similar to but usually stronger than the rock-caused roller wave, this reversal, sometimes called a hydraulic, is caused by a current plunging down a vertical drop and remaining on the

PHOTOGRAPH 21   A reversal (hole). The downstream current is pouring into the hole from the left, while the foaming surface backflow is moving right, or upstream. Notice the distinct line formed where the opposing currents meet.

river bottom, leaving a gap on the surface that must be filled by water moving upstream. Although this flat, bubbly backflow often looks benign, it casually flips rafts and drowns swimmers. Regardless of the height of the fall above it, *never attempt to run a vertical-drop reversal.* If you do not flip in the mid-air plunge, you will flip in the foam below.

The only sudden drops that can be run are those that angle out at a 45-degree angle or more and have a strong run-out below, not of aerated foam but of solid water. If a low, sheer fall spans the entire river, walk below it and look for a point in the fall's lip, such as a deep nick, where the flow shoots out and has a strong run-out of fairly solid water. This point is dangerous but may be runnable.

A third type of reversal is the back-curling standing wave. Generally found only in very tough, steep rapids where a broad current is severely pinched, high, steep, curling standing waves can easily swamp and flip a raft. They should definitely be avoided but, if unavoidable, should be hit dead-on with strong forward speed. These cresting waves often come in pairs. The first one sets you up by spinning the raft sideways, and the second wave finishes the demolition by overturning the boat. Defend against this by taking strong corrective strokes with paddles or oars the second the raft starts to go sideways.

There is some difference of opinion as to whether these curling waves can be considered proper reversals, or holes. Some river people call them curlers and distinguish them from the two types of reversal already described, while others group them all together. Certain river runners, including myself, draw a line between mildly curling and heavily curling waves, but this distinction tends to be arbitrary and hinge largely on individual feeling. The reader will have to resolve this one for him- or herself. Let the juices in the pit of your stomach be your guide.

Reversals can trap and roll a swimmer. Due to their very buoyancy, logs are sometimes held and spun for days where the opposing currents meet. Obviously, you should avoid swimming in reversals at all costs. But if, because of some mishap, you find yourself in the water and see that you are going into a reversal, take in a lungfull of air and relax; you will most likely be sucked under and flushed out downstream, where your lifejacket will bring you to the surface. If trapped, swim sideways out the end of the wave or swim *down* in order to escape into the downstream current. If this does not work, *take off your lifejacket and again swim down* to reach the downstream current that will eventually bring you to the surface. Bear in mind that taking off your lifejacket is risky and is done only as a last resort.

Eddies

An eddy is a place where the river current either stops or flows upstream. Eddies are found just downstream from obstructions in the river or from outjutting sections of bank. The current, in shooting past these obstructions, causes a low-pressure area just below them that must be filled in by water moving upstream. The more powerful the current, the stronger the eddy. The zone of turbulence between an eddy and the downstream current, usually marked by swirling water and bubbles, is called an eddy line, or fence. If an eddy is strong, its fence can be so turbulent that it becomes a navigation problem; eddy fences have flipped rafts in the Grand Canyon.

Eddies are most numerous in swift water and are useful to the whitewater boater because they provide handy stopping

DRAWING 33
ENTERING AN EDDY WITH A SUDDEN, STRONG FERRY

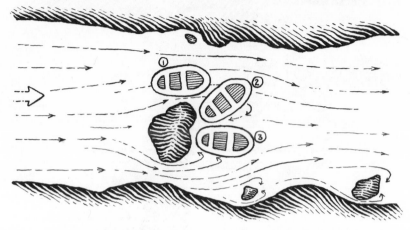

This technique works best with light rafts.
1. The raft slides closely past the eddy-causing obstruction.
2. The raft tucks under the rock with a sudden, powerful ferry.
3. The raft floats easy in the eddy.

places in the midst of rapids. If you need some time to bail or a quiet interlude while running a real smoker, pull into an eddy. Eddies can be entered in two ways: You can slip closely past the obstruction and pull into the eddy with a sudden, strong ferry (this method works best with light rafts). Or, with careful advance timing, you can accelerate diagonally downstream for a short distance so as to power into the eddy (paddle boats do this bow first, while oar boats row backwards in what is called a reverse ferry and drive into the eddy stern first) (Drawings 33 and 34). Bear in mind that a mild eddy can be entered anywhere along its length, but a powerful eddy with a turbulent fence is best entered at its head or tail, that is, at its extreme upstream or downstream end. In general, leave the eddy by way of its weak lower end. Learn to use eddy currents when moving toward shore or into the mainstream.

Bends

The faster current and deeper channel swing to the outside of river bends (Drawing 35). Carried by centrifugal force, the faster surface current rushes toward and piles up along the outside bank. *Swift-water bends should be approached along the inside bank.* This gives you the option of swinging to the outside

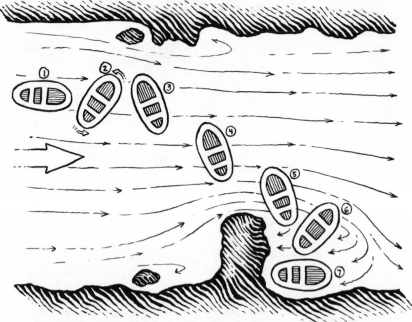

DRAWING 34 ENTERING AN EDDY WITH A REVERSE FERRY
Sometimes the only way for a heavy raft to enter a small or violent eddy is
with a reverse ferry. The steps detailed here are for an oar raft; a paddle
raft uses basically the same technique except that it approaches the eddy
bow first and finishes up in a bow-upstream position.
1. Raft approaches wide.
2. Raft turns around to angle its stern downstream.
3. With careful timing, the oarsman begins to pull powerfully on the oars.
   The boat's angle to the current can be be close to 90 degrees, but is
   best at about 45 degrees.
4. While aiming for the eddy, the oarsman continues to pull on the oars
   and gain momentum.
5. With the oarsman still pulling on the oars, the raft breaks through the
   eddy fence.
6. The eddy turn: With the stern in the upstream eddy current and the bow
   still in the downstream current, the raft is spun into a normal ferry angle.
   The oarsman continues all the while pulling on the oars to bring the
   boat entirely into the eddy.
7. The raft rides easy in the eddy.
Note: The reverse ferry and eddy turn are not only used to enter eddies,
they can also be used to dodge through tight places. The reverse ferry (or
sometimes an extreme ferry) scoots the raft sideways, the eddy turn snaps
the bow into a bow-downstream position, and the raft, rather than entering
the eddy, rides the eddy fence past a major obstruction or hole.

of the curve or of staying on the inside. Rafts approaching along
the outside bank often have no options because they are sucked
inexorably to the outside by powerful outswinging current.

Fallen trees are a common navigational hazard on the outside of bends. The outswinging current undercuts the outside bank causing trees to fall in across the swift water. Unlike rocks, which bend the current around them, fallen trees strain the current through their dead branches like a sieve. Boats and boaters colliding with these trees and other types of strainers, such as flooded brush and bridge pilings, can be disastrously pinned by immense pressure. Approach all bends cautiously, always on the inside, and always ready to stop quickly should the need arise. Scout all blind, swift-water bends.

Shallows

Found where rivers widen, shallows force the rafter to pick his way gingerly, often among exposed rocks, searching for some kind of channel. When seeking an elusive channel, bear these facts in mind: The biggest waves generally indicate the best

DRAWING 35   BENDS

A raft on the inside of a bend can either swing to the outside or keep to the inside, but a raft on the outside is usually drawn inexorably to the outside.

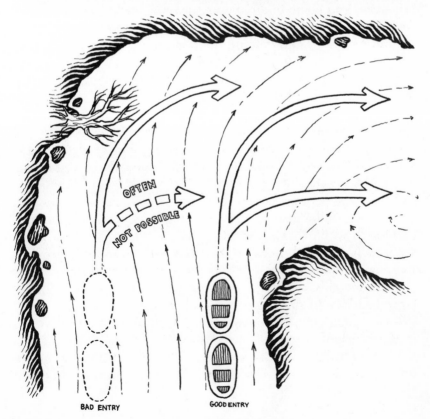

BAD ENTRY   GOOD ENTRY

depth and fastest current. If one bank is high while the other is low, the channel will most likely lie near the high bank. On curves, the channel is on the outside of the bend. Once found, channels have a way of petering out; when this happens, move to another. Sometimes a sideways motion of water will indicate the direction in which a new channel can be found. Places to avoid are areas of small choppy waves, called sandpaper, which generally signal severe shallows, and patches of foam that indicate a rock just below the surface immediately upstream. During the low-water levels of late summer and fall, even the most talented rafters occasionally have to do the unthinkable, that is, get out and push.

SCOUTING

Scout all rapids that cannot be seen clearly from upstream. Since boulders, sharp bends, and steepness all make a rapid more difficult and hide it from the viewer upstream, hidden rapids are often the most difficult and are the very rapids one *must* scout. Whenever you come to an obscure or tough-looking rapid, beach your boat well upstream and walk down to study it.

With an eye to determining the best course for your raft, note the rocks, waves, holes, the tongue or tongues, and the direction of the current in each section of the rapid. Judging the direction of a current can be tricky. One way to see if a flow is pulling to one side or another is to toss in a chunk of driftwood and watch which way it goes.

Give particular attention to all heaped mounds of water. Rocks just at surface level can create humped mounds of water that look like haystacks. As a result, the big waves over a submerged rock patch sometimes bear a dangerous resemblance to standing waves. The difference is that standing waves are regular and patterned, while the waves concealing a submerged rock patch are usually jumbled. Because the foam and spray surging over a rock can be quite thick, it is sometimes necessary to stare fixedly at these mounds, watching for a glimpse, a faint, dark outline, a jagged surface to show itself between surges of water. Be intent! Without intentness, it is possible to look at white death and think it easy, innocuous foam.

Walk right down to the foot of rapids. Water heaps up on the upstream side of rocks, obscuring both rocks and holes from the viewer upstream. But water is dished out from the downstream side of these same rocks, making rocks and holes plainly visible from downstream (Photograph 22). Do not be seduced into cutting short your scouting trek by an appearance of easy water. Green boatmen are continually hurrying into easy-looking rapids only to be undone by hidden holes and other hazards. One rapid on the Salmon River in Idaho called Big Mallard has a treacherous hole completely invisible from upstream because it is camouflaged by another hole nearby. As one walks down along the bank, Big Mallard looks easy until one reaches its very foot. Rapids that are wide or especially difficult should be scouted from both sides if possible.

After a rapid has been thoroughly scouted, a crucial decision must be made: Are you going to run or line it? If a rapid has an unavoidable vertical drop or fallen tree, or is for some other reason just too difficult, line it. If it looks extremely tough but you still think you can run it, consider asking passengers and poor swimmers to walk around and also consider placing line throwers at key rescue points.

ROCK HOPPING: Scouting is a long and tedious business if you step around and over and between the myriad rocks covering

PHOTOGRAPH 22 Water piles up on the upstream side of rocks, and is dished out from the downstream side.

most rapid banks. Learn to hop along swiftly in nonslip tennis shoes, taking long strides and *stepping only on the tops of rocks.* To do this you cannot be gazing off at the rapid, but must keep your head down and pay close attention to your footing. Think always a step ahead, focusing not on where your foot is now landing, but on where your next step will be. Falter and you crash in a heap.

PLANNING A COURSE

When planning a run through a rapid, choose the simplest, most direct route that avoids the obstacles and goes with the current. The more closely you can follow the current, the easier your run will be. So take into account the direction of the current in each part of the rapid. Above all, choose your point of entry with care. If entered correctly, many rapids require little or no maneuvering, and in others the amount of maneuvering can be greatly reduced (Drawing 36).

DRAWING 36   PLANNING A COURSE

The sophisticated raft enters on the far left to minimize maneuvering. The uncouth raft enters on the right and must ferry.

Remember that the speeding current reduces maneuvering time. Although a 50-yard stretch in slow or moderate water provides ample time for intricate maneuvering, even to the point of spinning in circles, a similar stretch of fast water flashes by in about 9 seconds, cutting time very short.

Minimize maneuvering in heavy water. Unless it is absolutely necessary, don't plan to ferry in waves that may swamp or flip your boat if taken at an angle. In extremely heavy water like that of Lava Falls in the Grand Canyon, about all anyone can do is keep the bow into the waves.

In deciding on a particular course, consider the risks involved should you make a mistake. There is a route down the left side of Lava Falls which, though far calmer than other routes through the rapid, is seldom run because there is a point near its head where the missing of a single stroke would send you into the biggest hole in the rapid. Rather than chancing a disappearance into this vast hole, most rafters run a tumultuous path of slightly smaller holes on the right. It is better to hit many relatively small holes than to risk hitting a single large one.

Oftentimes, the best or only course through a tough rapid involves first tucking under one obstacle and then scooting sideways to pass just above another. In especially tight maneuvers of this sort, the key to a successful passage is often *momentum.* Rather than dropping straight down and trying to pick up speed sideways in the short space between the obstacles, the wise rafter enters far over and, with careful timing, begins a powerful ferry early, so that by the time he tucks under the first obstacle the raft is already up to speed to zip sideways fast across the tight space (Drawing 37).

Once you and your companions have settled on a course, retrace it mentally many times over from tongue to foot. Note the entry. Memorize key rocks along the route to use as points of orientation during your run. Visualize the course as it will appear from the moving raft. Then retrace the rapid still again, planning an *alternate course.* Decide where and how you can initiate the alternate plan, should the first plan prove unworkable.

RUNNING THE WILDWATER

Prepare for each run as though preparing for a flip. Strap and tighten lifejackets. Put on tennis shoes. Pack away stray items such as books and sun cream. Seal all gear bags. Check gear tie-down straps. And make sure no loose lines are lying around to entangle feet.

In the calm above the rapid move into position for correct entry. As you drift down toward the brink, check, standing if

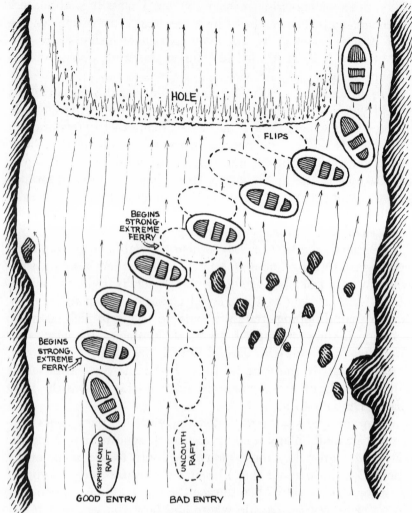

DRAWING 37   MOMENTUM AND POINT OF ENTRY

The sophisticated raft enters far over, with careful timing begins strong, extreme ferry early, and gains speed beforehand to cross the tight space between rock and hole. The uncouth raft drops straight past the rock, cannot pick up speed fast enough to miss the hole, and flips.

necessary, to see that you are lined up to enter at precisely the desired point. Make whatever adjustments are necessary by portegeeing or ferrying. This is a tense moment.

As you slip over the lip swing your bow downstream. You drop into the rapid; everything speeds up. Look downstream along the grain of the current to see where it's taking you. Scan the general pattern of the rapid. Quickly evaluate your plans. If they

PHOTOGRAPH 23 Running Rainie Falls on the Rogue River. (*Photo by Robert Sawyer, courtesy of the American River Touring Association.*)

seem good, follow them. If not, improvise something better. Look and think well ahead. As you ferry to avoid immediate hazards, consider where you're going to wind up. Keep the bow into big waves. If you feel good, yell to let the world know.

Relax when the river keeps you in the channel and takes you where you want to go. Relax when the hazards are moderate and the holes small. In moderate water, react only when necessary and don't move too far when avoiding rocks and holes. A miss is a miss; if it saves effort to pass a rock closely, pass it closely. In light water the seasoned oarsman takes one stroke for the beginner's ten.

But when the river pulls you toward danger, stroke like a devil. When holes are large and when the current slams against a cliff, know that the risks are high. Be afraid. Keep the adrenalin flowing. Crowd in those strokes! Move that boat! Skirt those big holes by a wide margin.

Keep your attention on the rapid throughout the run. A common mistake is to run the first tough drop fine and then, with a feeling of enormous relief at having made it through the worst, to relax so completely that you fail to cope with the lesser but still dangerous obstacles that follow.

In violent rapids, sometimes all plans collapse and things rush at you so fast that you have no time to come up with a new strategy. When this happens, hang in. Take each obstacle as it comes. Spin off the rocks. Fight to miss the holes. Put the bow into everything you can't avoid. And trust the toughness and stability of your raft. This is, after all, what rafting is all about. When you make it through all right, the feeling is euphoria. But if something goes wrong, you have an emergency (see Chapter Three, fast).

A Special Technique for Big Water

Because it is almost impossible to flip a raft that is full of water, one way to run heavy rapids is to deliberately swamp your boat. But a raft full of water is both sluggish and vulnerable to rocks—rocks near the surface will tear the bottom off a flooded raft—so this technique can only be used in deep-water rapids like Lava Falls where no maneuvering is required and where gigantic waves and holes are the only obstacles. Fill the raft either with buckets or by taking the first waves (waves that won't flip you) sideways. As you submarine through the foam, hold on and breathe when you can.

SAFETY

Because river touring is an inherently dangerous activity, it must be approached with a solid understanding of and keen respect for established rules of safety. Observing safety guidelines does not eliminate risk; it merely reduces the risk to an acceptable level. Life and health are precious. Be careful.

The following safety code is based in large part on the safety code of the American Whitewater Affiliation.

A SAFETY CODE FOR WHITEWATER RAFTING

Personal Preparedness and Responsibility

Thoroughly Research Rivers You Plan to Run; get detailed maps and guides; learn the river's volume, gradient, season, weather, difficulty classification, current water level, and special hazards. Be aware of possible sudden changes in flow conditions due to rain, snow melt, or dam-release fluctuations, and know how these changes can affect the difficulty of the run.

Be a Competent Swimmer with ability to handle yourself under water.

Wear a Lifejacket when approaching, running, or lining rapids.

Wear Crash Helmets on Rocky, Hazardous Rivers.

Be Aware of and Avoid River Hazards. Following are the most frequent killers:

HIGH WATER. The danger, the power, and the difficulty of rescue increase tremendously as the flow increases. A safe river at a low level is often a killer at higher levels.

COLD. Cold quickly robs one's strength, along with one's will and ability to save oneself. Dress to protect yourself from cold water and weather extremes. When the sum of water-plus-air temperature is less than 100°F, a rubber wetsuit is essential for safety if there is any possibility of an upset. Next best is wool clothing under a windproof outer garment such as a splash-proof nylon shirt; in this case one should also carry a complete change of clothing in a waterproof bag. If, after prolonged exposure, a person experiences uncontrollable shaking and has difficulty talking and moving, he must be warmed immediately by whatever means available—fire, dry clothes, sleeping bag, warm liquids, bare-body sandwich, etc. (see Chapter Four).

STRAINERS. Brush, fallen trees, bridge pilings, or anything else that allows the river current to sweep through but would pin a boat and boaters against the obstacle. The water pressure on anything trapped in this way is immense, and there may be little or no whitewater to warn of danger.

REVERSALS AND WEIRS. The water drops over an obstacle, then curls back on itself in a stationary wave. The surface water is going *upstream,* and this action will hold any floating object trapped between the drop and the wave. Once trapped, a swimmer's only hopes are to dive below the surface to where current is flowing downstream or to try to swim out the end of the wave. (See the section on reversals in this chapter.)

Be Suitably Equipped. Wear shoes that will protect your feet during a bad swim or a walk for help, yet will not interfere with swimming. Tennis shoes are recommended. Carry a knife, and furnish yourself with skin protection, raingear, etc., as the situation requires. If you need eyeglasses, tie them on and carry a spare pair. Do not wear bulky clothing that is easily waterlogged.

Have a Frank Knowledge of Your Boating Ability, and do not attempt waters you are not ready to handle. Oarsmen and paddle crews should work their way up the scale of difficulty *gradually.*

Know First Aid Including Artificial Respiration and carry a first-aid kit with fresh and adequate supplies (see Chapter Four).

Be Practiced in Emergency Procedures; know how to handle swampings, flips, and collisions with rocks, and be able to swim through rapids and line unrunnable falls and rapids (see Chapter Three).

Float Plan. If your trip is into a wilderness area or for an extended period, your plans should be filed with appropriate authorities or left with someone who will contact them after a certain time. Establishment of checkpoints along the way at which civilization could be contacted if necessary should be considered. Knowing the location of possible help could speed rescue in any case.

Raft and Equipment Preparedness

Use Only Well-Made Rafts with Multiple Air Chambers.

Test-Inflate Rafts Before Each Trip; check both used and new boats for air leaks by running water smoothly over the buoyancy tubes while watching for bubbles, and check for water leaks by swishing a few gallons around inside the raft while the raft is up on saw horses. New rafts are subject to manufacturing errors, material flaws, and shipping damage, and stored rafts fall prey to rot and rodents.

Test New and Unfamiliar Pieces of Equipment, such as rafts, frames, oars, paddles, pumps, and lifejackets, on easy water before relying on them for difficult runs.

Have Strong, Adequately Sized Paddles or Oars, and carry a complete set of spares accessible for immediate use.

Have at Least One Extra Lifejacket per Raft.

Lines: Have 50- to 100-foot bow and stern lines, plus at least 200 feet of line for rescue and lining work. All lines should be strong—3000-lb. test or more. Keep lines coiled for immediate use and tucked securely out of the way to avoid entanglement with arms, legs, or feet.

Solo Rafts Should Carry an Emergency Beaching Line for use in case of a flip. (See Chapter One, the section on lines.)

A Taut Grab Line or Sturdy Handles Should Be Placed Around the Outside of a Raft's Buoyancy Tube; these allow you to hold on after an upset.

Carry an Air Pump and a Complete Patch and Repair Kit. These are your life! Keep them firmly tied to the raft. (See Chapter One.)

On extended trips, carry food, camping gear, and survival equipment in *Waterproof Bags Securely Lashed and Clipped to Raft.* Ammo cases for cameras, etc., should be tied *short,* so no one gets hit by them. Bailing buckets are a hazard when tied with a cord; snap them to the frame with a carabiner.

On the River

Have Two or More Rafts in Your Party, and be familiar with group modes of operation such as signaling and rescue support (see the next section). The only exception to this rule is the seasoned whitewater rafter, who, after many years on the river, has mastered every aspect of the sport including self-rescue techniques.

Approach Hazards with Caution. Be Able to Stop Before Being Sucked In. Keep an eye peeled for eddies, pools, and unobstructed shore suitable for stopping your raft should the need arise. Bowmen in paddle boats and sternmen in oar boats must be ready to jump ashore with painter lines.

Thoroughly Scout All Rapids That Cannot Be Seen Clearly from Upstream. (See section on scouting in this chapter.)

Line or Portage Rapids That Are Beyond Your Ability or Too Difficult for Your Raft.

On Especially Long, Difficult Rapids Consider Placing Line Throwers at Key Rescue Points. (See Chapter Three.)

Keep Raft Well Bailed; a fully or partially swamped boat is sluggish and vulnerable to puncture. *Exception:* In enormous rapids were the main concern is not maneuverability but stability, do not bail.

Do Not Overload the Boat; a raft's whitewater capacity is roughly half its nominal designation; for example, a 6-man can take three people (see Chapter One).

Rig the Raft with Care: Secure the frame firmly to the raft; lash and double clip all gear; tie light safety lines to oars; fix strong handgrips for all crew members.

Use Knots That Are Strong Yet Easily Untied. (See Appendix III.)

Avoid Entanglement: Be certain there is absolutely nothing to cause entanglement when you are coming free from an upset raft. Lines are the biggest danger; keep them neatly coiled and out of the way (yet ready for immediate use) either by stuffing them into special pockets on the raft or by wedging them tightly under gear tie-down straps. Never wedge legs under frame. Above all, never tie yourself to the raft or to anything else.

Avoid Twilight and Night Rafting; poor visibility increases rapid difficulty many fold; make camp early.

Be Certain All Crew Members Are Familiar with This Safety Code. It is especially important that newcomers learn (1) to swim through rocky rapids with feet downstream, (2) to jump to the downstream side of the raft if the raft broaches on a rock, and (3) to keep lines neatly coiled and tucked out of the way so as to avoid entanglement.

GROUP MODUS OPERANDI

Because the safest mode of river travel is in groups of two rafts or more, group voyaging has become a refined art. At the heart of this art is a spirit of cooperation, a sense of mutual dependence, and a willingness constantly to look after one another. A group of rafts is a tight team, with each boat ever alert to the other's needs, ever ready to offer quick support.

A party of rafts threads its way single file down river in deliberate, precise fashion. The raft with the most experienced crew or boatman goes ahead as lead boat while another competent crew brings up the rear as sweep boat; the lead boat is never passed and the sweep never passes any other boat. To keep the string compact and united, each boat continuously keeps the one behind it in sight, waiting if necessary. Thus, if one boat stops, all stop. Each raft looks after the raft behind it, passing on signals, indicating obstacles, and seeing it through bad spots. To suggest a better course through a rapid or channel, a fully extended arm is used to point right or left as necessary. Like all signals, this signal is repeated until communicated.

In dangerous rapids where flips might occur, the rafts stand by to provide one another with rescue support. As each boat finishes the rapid, it assumes a strategic position for potential rescue of the following raft, which in turn positions itself to assist the raft behind it. And so the line of rafts moves haltingly through the threatening water.

If a rapid is extremely long and perilous, several rafts may be stationed at strategic places along its length. Although this kind of support cannot be provided for the lead boat, some rescue support, when necessary, can be offered by posting men with throwing ropes at key points along the bank. In the event of a flip, rescue boats first save the people in the water and then go after the upset raft if this can be done safely.

Although generally close together, the boats should greatly increase the distance between them in fast water. Bunching up in rapids not only restricts maneuverability, but also invites one of the most horrible of river accidents, the raft sandwich. Following boats should drop back enough so that, if the preceding boat gets hung up in a hole, they can stop before entering the rapid. To signal for increased spacing, someone in the lead boat, using a fully extended arm, waves backward and holds his hand up in halt fashion.

PHOTOGRAPH 23A Women are taking to the white-water in ever increasing numbers, both as professional guides and as private adventurers. (*Mike Fahey*)

NOTES FOR BEGINNERS

Begin on mild rivers, and gradually work your way up the scale of difficulty, never taking on more than you are ready to handle. In this way you can perfect your rafting technique in relative safety. Remember, most of the people who die on rivers annually are foolhardy beginners who launch themselves headlong into difficult water without knowing what they are doing. Be wary of spring floods. If possible take your first trip either with an experienced friend or with one of the many fine whitewater schools offering guidance on rivers all across the United States (see Appendix VII). Learn all you can about whitewater, boat handling, and emergency techniques; begin by studying Chapters Two and Three of this book. Strive to be skillful in maneuvering your boat, for in skill there is safety. Above all, especially while you are a novice, exercise all safety precautions. Particularly, use rugged rafts with multiple air chambers, voyage in groups of two boats or more, wear good lifejackets, carry a patch kit and a spare *set* of oars or paddles, and on rocky rivers wear crash helmets. These precautions will allow you to survive your mistakes.

OARSMEN: When you first hit the river, play around a while to get a "feel" for the oars and for how the boat moves on the river. First practice the double-oar turn and the ferry: Ferry back and forth across the river, and when turning the boat, always use *both* oars. Use the portegee for a while. In both the portegee and the ferry, learn not only the standard stroke but also the alternating stroke, in which only one oar is in the water at a time. Try a few pivots and back pivots.

PADDLE CREWS: When paddle crews launch onto the water for the first time, they should review all strokes and commands. To quicken their reflexes they should run through practice patterns that encompass all commands and ferries, including bow-upstream and bow-downstream ferries. To give everyone a feeling for what the captain must do, let each crew member play captain for a while.

EDDIES: Both paddlers and oarsmen should learn to spot and use these handy stopping places. Practice eddy hopping, that is, entering and leaving eddies at every opportunity. There are two ways to enter an eddy: You may slide closely past the eddy-causing obstruction and then tuck the raft under the obstruction with a powerful ferry, or, with careful timing, you may power diagonally downstream for a short distance so as to sweep into the eddy. To leave an eddy, row out its weak lower end. When the current is powerful and the eddy strong, the turbulent eddy fence may restrict entry to the head and tail. Learn to use eddy currents when moving toward shore or into the mainstream.

RAPIDS: To run a rapid, first identify the obstacles. Second, plan both a primary course and an alternate course. Decide how and at what times the alternate course can be initiated if the original course proves unworkable. Run the rapid. Afterwards, talk about the run with an eye to improving your technique.

SAND DIAGRAMS: The sand diagram is a useful aid to the beginning rafter. After scouting a rapid, the novice makes a diagram of it in the sand on the river beach, using pebbles and twigs to represent obstacles. An experienced rafter then draws anywhere from three to six lines across the diagram at an angle perpendicular to the current. The novice then shows how he feels the rapid should be run, using short twigs to indicate the angle and position of the raft at each of the cross lines. The proposed course is then discussed, and differences of opinion are resolved before the run.

SWIMMING RAPIDS: Early in his river life every rafter should swim through a rapid in a lifejacket. Choose a rapid with a channel that is wide, deep, and unobstructed, and have a manned raft positioned below the rapid ready to pick up anyone who has difficulty swimming ashore. This swim accustoms the swimmer to the coldness and power of the river and helps him remain calm in a flip (see Chapter Three, "Man Overboard—Swimming Rapids").

PRACTICE EXERCISES: One interesting way to develop ferrying and pivoting ability is to row around a single large rock as slowly and as closely as possible. Obviously, the current around the rock should be moderate. Another exercise is to row through a mild rapid of scattered rocks as slowly as possible. Enter every eddy, and ferry from side to side across the rapid as often as possible. This exercise tests skill in boat control and in reading currents and eddies.

ON HARMONY—AND FEAR

Learn to work *with* the river. Study its moods, its motions. Use its power to push you where you want to go. It is only in harmony with the colossus that we men survive, and it is for the sake of experiencing this harmony that we go to the river.

Remain alert. Remain *afraid*. Even as you run more and more rivers and gain confidence and skill, do not lull yourself into thinking that danger is gone. To run dangerous rapids is to be near the edge; to pretend otherwise is to invite disaster. When you know that the stakes are high, adrenalin flows strong, reflexes quicken, and you damn well get in those extra strokes of oar or paddle that can spell the difference between thrill and catastrophe.

Say you are ferrying hard right to avoid a gigantic hole. If relaxed you pull right until it looks as if the boat will make it, and you straighten out expecting to slide to the right of the hole— and maybe you do, maybe you don't. Maybe the river pulls left more than is apparent. Maybe the boat dives into the hole, spilling you, your companions, your gear, everything, into the foam. But if you have some healthy fear in you, you pull a little harder on the oars, you crowd in a few more strokes, you make *sure* the boat will clear the hole.

This is not to say you should cringe around with a haunted look or constantly over-row your boat; relax physically as much as possible. But somewhere inside yourself maintain a primitive pocket of fear, a frank, clear perception that what you are doing is dangerous.

CHAPTER THREE

Emergencies

Now and then emergencies that demand fast, effective action occur on the river. When handled correctly, these events are rarely disastrous and, in fact, hardly seem serious at all. Even the much dreaded flip causes only minor inconvenience when handled properly. Study this brief chapter and learn to respond to trouble quickly and efficiently. Of course, no book can cover all possible mishaps, so be resourceful when in danger and learn to use your own wits. To grapple with emergencies skillfully and spontaneously is to feel completely free and alive.

COLLIDING WITH A ROCK

Collisions with rocks that break the surface are commonplace and rarely result in serious mishap when handled in the correct manner. If you see that you cannot avoid a rock, either spin your raft powerfully just before contact or hit the rock bow-on. Spinning, called cartwheeling, will generally rotate the raft off and around the rock. Hitting the rock bow-on will stop the raft momentarily but will allow you to spin off either way with a few

PHOTOGRAPH 24   Trouble in Big Drop Rapid in Cataract Canyon. (*Photo by Bob Elliott, courtesy of the American River Touring Association.*)

turn strokes. *Important: When hitting a rock bow-on, just before the impact the people in the stern should move quickly toward the center of the raft.* This action raises the stern and lets the rushing current slide under the raft. If the stern is low, water will quickly pile against it and suck it under, swamping and even flipping the boat.

If the raft winds up broadside against the rock, *the entire crew should immediately jump to the side of the raft nearest the rock* (Drawing 38). This will always be the raft's downstream side. The command for this action is "JUMP TO!"—jump to the downstream side of the raft. Unless the crew responds instantly, the river will swiftly heap up against and suck down the raft's upstream tube, flooding the raft and wrapping it flat around the rock under great pressure. An alert crew anticipates collisions and hops to the downstream side of the raft *before contact*. When this is done, no water is shipped. In fact, if the current is not too fast, the rock not too sharp, and the raft adequately inflated, the collision may lead to a pleasant interlude of rest. The tranquility of the rock contrasts nicely with the violent motion of the rapid, and the rounded nature of midstream rocks causes them to be superb backrests. Of course, you should never deliberately broach on a

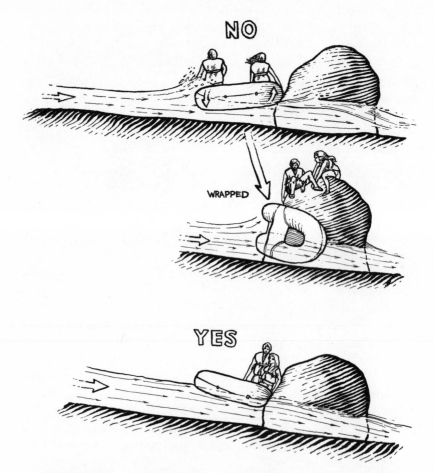

DRAWING 38   HANDLING A BROADSIDE COLLISION WITH A ROCK

Just before a raft broadsides on a rock, the crew should jump to the side of the raft nearest the rock. This lifts the upstream tube and allows the current to slide easily under the raft. If the crew is not quick to hop toward the rock, swift water will speedily swamp the raft and wrap it flat around the rock's upstream face.

rock, but when you do, after hopping to the raft's downstream side and seeing that everything is all right, relax a moment, look around, chat with your mates.

An unswamped raft broached on a rock (a raft in this predicament is said to be *hung up*) can usually be freed with little difficulty (Drawing 39). Push on the rock with the feet to swing or slide the boat in the direction favored by the current. Help swing the boat with the free oar by stroking or by planting the blade where it catches the current. Shift the crew, which always stays on the side nearest the rock, to the end toward which you want the raft to swing. When used with determined effort, these methods rarely fail. But if the raft just won't budge, free it by using the enormous power of the current. Tie several waterproof bags into a bunch and use them sea-anchor fashion to swing the boat off the rock. Because a large gear bag can catch a half-ton of pressure in swift current, use extremely strong line doubled or tripled for additional strength, lash the bags very securely, and attach an extra safety line to avoid losing the bundle. This safety line should, if possible, be long enough to extend beyond the foot of the rapid. When the bundle is ready, securely attach its main line, which need only be a few feet long, to the end of the raft which you want to swing downstream. Then, after making certain that the safety line is secured and will unravel without tangling, heave in the bundle. As the raft twirls off the rock, get set

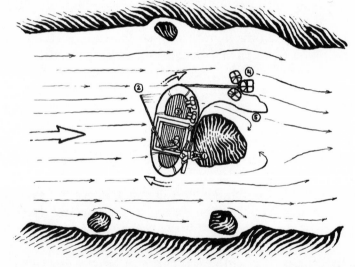

DRAWING 39 FREEING AN UNSWAMPED RAFT BROACHED ON A ROCK

A raft broadsided but not swamped or wrapped can be freed with a combination of techniques:

1. Agile crew member pushes on rock with feet. Often this push alone will swing the raft free.
2. Oar is held in current to help swing boat off rock.
3. Crew stays on side nearest rock and at end which will swing downstream. For an extra assist, these people bounce up and down and stand on the floor of the raft.
4. Securely tied waterproof bags are used sea-anchor fashion. Extra long safety line prevents loss of bags.

to haul in the bundle and man paddles or oars. *A bold alternative:* Some rafters dispense with the bundle and jump into the swift current themselves while holding tightly (but *not tied*) to a loop in the bow or stern line. If these techniques fail, use a winch to free the boat.

FREEING A WRAPPED RAFT

A raft wrapped around a rock in swift water may be pinned by many tons of force. Use a hand winch or block and tackle, anchored to a rock or tree on shore, to pull it free (Drawing 40). Unless the raft is symmetrically balanced on the rock, it will move more easily one way than the other; choose the easier path. Attach the hauling line to at least two points in such a way that the pull is equally distributed. One of these points should be on the far end of the raft: Secure the line to an extremely sturdy D-ring —the pull should be at right angles to the flat side of the D—or cut a small hole in the floor to pass the line around the tube. The second tie-off point should be either a frame or a cross tube. Use line that doesn't stretch, such as manila or dacron. Elastic material like nylon will stretch rather than move the boat and, if it breaks, will lash dangerously through the air. More than one winch or block-and-tackle take-up length is usually required, so beforehand tie a number of butterfly loops (see Appendix III on Knots) in the hauling line. After each winching, the line should be snubbed around a tree or rock while the winch cable is switched to the next loop. As the winch is cranked in, try to heave the far end of the raft up out of the water. (It may, in fact, be easier to free the raft if you tip it fully over.) Have a bow or stern line in hand to bring the freed boat to shore. In extreme cases, consider deflating the far end of the raft and making a large U-shaped cut in the floor of the far end to reduce the current's grip on the boat. If you have no winch or block and tackle, it may still be possible to free the raft with sheer muscle; tie butterfly grab loops—one for each member of your party—into a long line and heave away like Egyptian slaves.

MAN OVERBOARD—SWIMMING IN RAPIDS

If you find yourself being swept overboard, shout to alert your

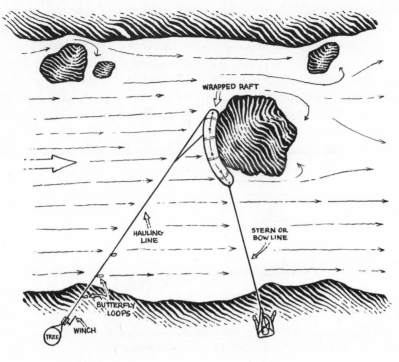

WRAPPED RAFT

HAULING
LINE

STERN OR
BOW LINE

BUTTERFLY
LOOPS

TREE   WINCH

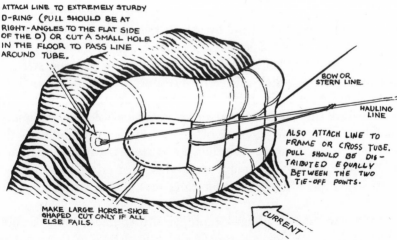

ATTACH LINE TO EXTREMELY STURDY
D-RING (PULL SHOULD BE AT
RIGHT-ANGLES TO THE FLAT SIDE
OF THE D) OR CUT A SMALL HOLE
IN THE FLOOR TO PASS LINE
AROUND TUBE.

BOW OR
STERN LINE

HAULING
LINE

ALSO ATTACH LINE TO
FRAME OR CROSS TUBE.
PULL SHOULD BE DIS-
TRIBUTED EQUALLY
BETWEEN THE TWO
TIE-OFF POINTS.

MAKE LARGE HORSE-SHOE
SHAPED CUT ONLY IF ALL
ELSE FAILS.

CURRENT

DRAWING 40   FREEING A WRAPPED RAFT

An arrangement of winch and lines for pulling a wrapped raft off a midstream rock. Butterfly loops are tied in the line beforehand to allow for the
resetting of the winch cable. During each repositioning of the cable, the
end of the hauling line is snubbed around the tree. A person holding the
bow or stern line pulls the freed raft to shore.

companions. In violent rapids, where flying spume inundates the
raft, your exit may not be noticed, and unless you are missed,
you will not be rescued. Once in the water, be calm but not
complacent. *When swimming rocky rapids face downstream keeping your feet out in front of you to ward off rocks, and use the
backstroke* (Drawing 41). *But when swimming huge, heavy
rapids with no rocks to speak of, swim on your stomach flat and
fast.* Move toward shore only if this seems best, otherwise approach a raft, which may toss you a heaving line and which will
maneuver to pick you up if it can. In heavy waves, breathe in

DRAWING 41   SWIMMING IN A RAPID

In rocky rapids, swim facing downstream with your feet out in front of you
to ward off rocks. Your toes should just break the surface.

the troughs, and hold your breath in the foaming crests. If you
have to avoid an obstacle, begin evasion early, swimming at right
angles to the current. Above all else, do not let yourself get
crushed between rock and raft. Prevent this lethal crunch by
staying away from the raft's downstream side. If you are holding
onto a raft that must maneuver to avoid trouble, let go immediately and rejoin it later. A boatman's first responsibility is the
safety of his raft; as a result, he should wave away any swimmer
who hampers the raft's maneuverability at a critical moment. A
vertical paddle signals to other rafts that a man has gone overboard.

Minimize man-overboard problems by telling people beforehand to hold fast in wild rapids and by cautioning them not to
jump in after others washed overboard—two people in the water
magnifies the problem many times. *Exception:* If someone has no
lifejacket or for some other reason needs immediate help, then
do jump in. If a swimmer is unconscious when rescued and has
stopped breathing, administer artificial respiration immediately;
every second is crucial (see Chapter Four).

Though swimming in rapids is dangerous, fast-water swimmers

can take some comfort in the eddy cushion. An eddy cushion is a layer of slack or billowing water on the upstream side of rocks that reduces risk of injury by easing a swimmer's impact. The size of an eddy cushion is determined by the shape of the rock's upstream face. If the face is rounded or pointed, the eddy pad will be minimal, but if the face is broad and flat, the rock will have an ample water pillow.

Cold water can cause serious problems and should be approached with caution. It quickly saps strength and dims the mind. Ten minutes in cold water leaves a swimmer so weak that he can barely hold onto a rescue line. Yet when this happens to you, you may not realize how weak you are. You float along in the water feeling calm, noticing only that your arms seem heavy, while actually you are becoming a helpless sack. Only after you are pulled into the boat or crawl on hands and knees onto shore, do you realize how weak you are; your muscles go into spasms of uncontrolled shivering. Yet even then you may not comprehend the danger of your condition. Enormously relieved to be out of the icy water, you think the worst is over. But even after you dry out, the cold of your own blood and flesh penetrates deeper into your body. You desperately need warmth from sources other than your own body: Lie on a hot boulder in the sun, sandwich yourself between two bare bodies in a sleeping bag, cuddle up to a big fire, or fill yourself with hot food and drink (see discussion of hypothermia in the next chapter). *But get yourself and others out of cold water as fast as possible.* Bear in mind that water temperature below 50° F doubles the danger rating of deep rivers and makes long woollies or wet suits essential.

FLIPS

Just before a flip there is a fleeting moment in which to respond to the situation. If the raft is diving into a big hole, the main danger is being thrown violently forward into something hard like the rowing frame or a wooden gear box: Instantly drop low and flatten yourself against the aft side of baggage or a cross tube. But if the raft is being upset by a rock, fallen tree, or other obstacle, jump clear so that you are neither crushed against the obstruction nor clobbered by the falling raft. If the raft is pinned flat against an obstruction, stay with the raft if you can do so safely and climb up on the rock or tree.

Swimming in rock-strewn water, backstroke with feet down-stream to ward off rocks; in huge rivers with few rocks, swim flat and fast. If there is a dangerous rapid immediately down-stream, head straight for shore. Otherwise, head for the raft; a crew that stays with its boat doesn't get spread out along a mile of bank. Avoid getting crushed between the raft and a rock by staying away from the downstream side of the boat, and rescue any gear floating loose by heaving it onto the overturned bottom of the raft. If the water is cold, crawl up on the raft yourself. Try to keep track of your companions; if someone is missing, check beneath the raft to see if he or she is caught.

An assisting boat should never attempt rescue in the pande-monium of heavy water but only in the calm between rapids. The rescue boat should approach from upstream in position to ferry, pick up the bow or stern line of the disabled boat, and ferry toward shore. The painter is held or snubbed, not tied. In a powerful current, the upside-down boat may drag both boats toward trouble, in which case it is released and rescued later.

Solo rafts must be rescued by their own crews. Empty boats on small rivers can sometimes be swum ashore, but most boats must be beached with a special line made of floating rope (see Chapter One, "Lines"). Carried by all solo rafts, this emergency beach-ing line is wound on a spool board to prevent tangling and is mounted low on the outside of the raft so as to be accessible after a flip. One end is permanently secured to the raft, and the other contains a small loop. In a calm, after a flip, while someone on the overturned raft gradually feeds line off the spool, a strong swimmer with the loop gripped in his teeth—*never tie a line to anyone*—swims the line ashore and belays it around a rock or tree to swing the raft in against the bank. Paddlers, who should hold onto their paddles during a flip, may be able to climb atop their overturned raft and paddle it ashore. If the raft cannot be turned upright by hand, right it with ropes and river power in the man-ner shown in Drawing 42.

Once a flipped raft is brought to shore, check damage and losses; if the gear was lashed and clipped with care, everything should be intact. Replace bent thole pins and prepare to continue downriver. People strung out along shore should rejoin the group at the raft as soon as they can, lest their companions think them injured and begin a search.

DRAWING 42   RIGHTING A FLIPPED RAFT

A typical arrangement of righting ropes and anchoring line for righting a heavily laden raft. As the crew tilts the raft, the current gains a powerful grip on the raft's upstream edge and brings the raft upright. Because the crew winds up in the water, this operation should be performed in mild, not fast, current. The line anchoring the raft to the rock upstream and the shorter righting ropes, which have figure-eight grip knots at regular intervals, are tied to the downstream side of the frame.

Floating low under tons of water, a swamped raft is difficult to maneuver and is easily damaged by rocks below the surface. Bail at the first opportunity in either an eddy or a long calm. Fortunately, no matter how much water gets into a raft the air-filled buoyancy tubes always ride just above the surface, allowing use of oars or paddles. Don't try to stop in swift water, for the raft is heavy and low and clenched powerfully in the current. If there are no calms or eddies, the best way to stop is to swim a long, sturdy line ashore and quickly snub it around a stout tree or large rock.

LINING UNRUNNABLE RAPIDS

To line unrunnable falls and rapids, float your raft through un-

manned while controlling it from shore with lines. When lining
complex rapids with shoreline calms and eddies, work the raft
through slowly, maintaining tight control with bow and stern
lines. But to line straight-shot, eddyless rapids, such as steep,
narrow chutes, walk a strong, very long line with one end secured to the raft down below the rapid's midpoint, and then
send the raft clear through to the foot, where it is stopped by the
long line (Drawing 43). Be certain this line will not hang up
anywhere along the bank as the boat sweeps through. Also, have

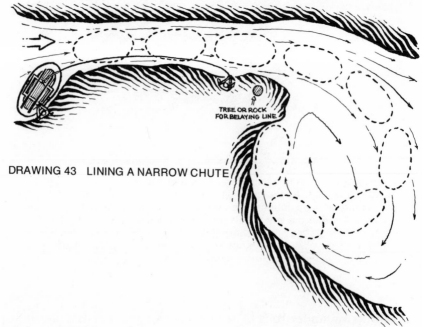

TREE OR ROCK
FOR BELAYING LINE

DRAWING 43   LINING A NARROW CHUTE

plenty of line, for should the line come up short with the boat
still in the rapid, the boat will either be swamped or get away
downstream. (If the raft does float off downstream and there is
no other raft below the rapid to give chase, either swim to catch
it or hope that it gets caught, as it usually will, in an eddy not
too far away.) Before lining falls or rapids, carefully lash and
double-clip all gear. Then, if the unmanned raft flips, just pull it
ashore and right it—without loss. Some horrendous stretches of
water should be portaged, not lined.

THE HEAVING LINE RESCUE

By O. K. Goodwin

[When running perilous rapids, it is sometimes wise to post line throwers at strategic rescue points along the banks. The following article by O. K. Goodwin, Safety Chairman of the American Whitewater Affiliation, is the definitive work on the subject of the heaving line rescue. It is reprinted with a few modifications and with the author's blessings from *American Whitewater,* the Journal of the American Whitewater Affiliation.] *

A successful whitewater heaving line starts with the selection of the line to be used. A good choice is Samson #12 Supreme MFP (see Appendix II). It is good for the following reasons:

1. It has excellent strength and elastic characteristics.
2. The braided construction can be coiled neatly and quickly; it does not kink or hockle.
3. It floats.
4. It is easy on the hands of the rescuer and the rescuee; it does not have loose or coarse fibers and has less tendency to produce a friction burn when sliding through your hands.
5. It does not retain soil and is easily cleaned.
6. It is not affected by temperature.
7. The size (#12, about ⅜") is large enough that it can be gripped and small enough that a 70-foot coil, even when wet, can be extended the full 70 feet. Anything smaller would be difficult to hold; a larger size would be heavier and would limit the distance that could be covered.

Since the monkey-fist knot [Drawing 44] requires about 10 feet of this line, a completed 70-foot heaving line, with monkey fist, requires about 80 feet of line.

To date, we have seen this particular line available in grey only. Since our usage is in rapids or whitewater, where the visibility of the line in the water is reduced, it would be

---

* With its articles on rivers, innovations in boating technique, river conservation, safety, and so on, the bimonthly journal *American Whitewater* is a must for all whitewater boaters. Subscriptions can be arranged by writing American Whitewater Affiliation, Circulation Manager, Box 1584, San Bruno, Cal. 94066.

DRAWING 44   THE MONKEY-FIST KNOT

more effective if the line had a bright color (red, yellow or blue) to make it easier for the swimmer to see.

Tying the monkey-fist knot is easier than it looks [Drawing 45]. Basically, it is an arrangement of three coils of the line tightened so that they are interlocked. The first and

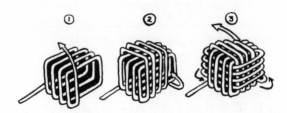

DRAWING 45   STEPS IN TYING THE MONKEY-FIST KNOT

second coils are just that: coils. The third must be worked through the first two, weaving in and out to turn them all into a unit. While forming the knot, the coils are left somewhat loose. The strands are pulled up "snug" only after adding the "load" to the center. Then the free end is secured by knotting, whipping, and/or taping to help prevent it becoming the cause of entanglement.

The load may be any of numerous materials. Its purpose is to add weight (and in this case, flotation) to the monkey-fist. A closed-cell, resilient plastic foam, such as the Dow

Chemical Co. Ethafoam, works well. It is formed into a ball about the size of a baseball and inserted into the center of the loose coils.

In tightening the monkey-fist, it is best to pull each strand "away" from the short, free end. If you left enough length to tie the free end securely, this length would not be altered in the tightening process. A small spike, prick-awl, or screwdriver will prove invaluable in pulling the strands snug.

It is possible to tie a monkey-fist in several ways; the method shown is simple and reliable. The intentional interlock of strands between coils will help provide a smooth knot that will not deform or unravel and it will wear more evenly.

One objection that is given to the use of a knot on the end of a heaving line is that in the whitewater situation they may hang-up in the rocks or bushes and make retrieval of the line difficult. The smoothness of the monkey-fist and the added flotation material, however, reduce this possibility, and, if the site where the line is to be used is carefully selected, this problem may be avoided. Sometimes a slight clearing of tree branches or "chinking" of rock crevices is all that is necessary.

If a line does get hung up in the rocks or bush, try this: Slack off slightly on the line, let the force of the water work on the floating ball, "whip" the line slightly from side to side or "roll" a loop of line from your handhold toward the hang-up. With a little practice the monkey-fist can be made to do tricks that may free it. If all else fails, then go after the hang-up. *This is the only time that a line should be tied to shore.* It can be used to steady you in the current while you reach the snag and free it.

The Coil

Coiling a heaving line so that it will throw well requires one simple trick. As you reach out for a new length of line to form a loop, grasp it with thumb and fingers so that it can be rolled between them [Drawing 46]. By applying this roll you will find that the loop you add to your coil can be formed without any twist or tendency to twist. The flat coil that results will feed from your hands more freely and be less likely to snarl.

With the line lying in the water, practice making your coil

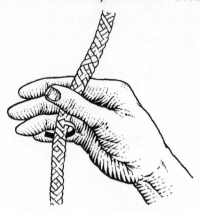

DRAWING 46   THE FINGER ROLL

rapidly, forming the loops as you haul the line in. This quick recovery will help you to be prepared to render assistance and may, on occasion, allow you a second throw after you have flubbed the first one.

A neatly made coil is easy to "split" into two coils [Drawing 47]. The throwing hand should hold ⅓ to ½ the total.

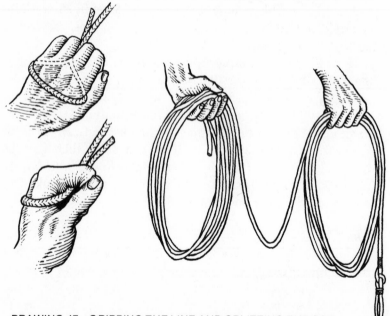

DRAWING 47   GRIPPING THE LINE AND SPLITTING THE COIL

The unknotted handhold shown on the left allows you to hold the line securely without it holding you; when the fingers are straightened, the line snaps free. Also, notice the position of the monkey fist.

The monkey-fist should be hanging just slightly below the bottom of the loops to avoid causing an entanglement as you throw.

The Throw

Throwing a heaving line for distance and accuracy is a skill which requires practice [Drawing 48]. One coil is thrown as the rope from the other hand is allowed to feed out freely. The throw is made with an underhand motion and the throwing arm is kept straight. The whole action should be done smoothly to give the line a chance to flow. When properly done, the loops of the coil will straighten in the air and the line will fall to the water with its length fully extended.

When this is further complicated by adding a moving target, then you must learn to "lead" it, aiming not directly at your target but at the spot where the target will be when the line falls to the water.

To reach a swimmer most effectively, the thrower should deliver the line to a point in front of him and within his

DRAWING 48   MAKING A RESCUE

reach. If his swimming technique is proper, he will be facing downstream and the line should fall on his downstream side. If it lands behind him (upstream side), he probably will not see it. If time allows, the swimmer's chances for making contact will be improved by alerting him that help is imminent.

After the throw—Brace Yourself! Either have plenty of assistance or be prepared to quickly belay (not tie) the line around a rock or tree. If the swimmer rescues the raft or if two or more swimmers grab the line, the pull will be enormous.

The Safety Station

Picking the right spot for a safety station where a heaving line is to be used is important to the effectiveness of the safety effort. There are two approaches to this choice. The site should be located either just downstream of a point where upsets are likely to occur or upstream of any hazardous water, the swimming of which might be undesirable. Several stations may be required to provide good safety coverage for a long and hazardous rapid.

The site should provide clear unobstructed space in which to make a throw, yet should have a handy rock or tree for belaying the line. It should be located as close as possible to the path a swimmer might follow as he flushes by. It should have space to "swing" a swimmer into safer water without additional hazard and *without crossing the main current*. The site should not be any higher above the water than is necessary for a good throw.

Since the line is less visible in turbulent whitewater than in calmer water, the swimmer is more subject to entanglement there. As the degree of turbulence increases, so also should the care with which the site for the safety station is selected.

A Word to the Rafter

If you should ever need the help of a safety line, you should know several things:

1. The location of the safety station(s).

2. If the line lands just beyond your reach, don't expect the current to bring it any closer. Swim quickly to it or it will escape you.

3. The line and water will exert a very strong pull on your arms. Be prepared. This pull can be eased somewhat by body surfing.

4. Take a deep breath and hold it; the current may cause a wave to cover your head.

5. Avoid entanglement.

6. Avoid rope burn. Hold the line at the monkey-fist. Do not let the rope slide through your hands after you feel the initial shock. Grip it tightly. But *do not* wrap it around your hand or wrist!

7. If you have the strength and opportunity, you may be able to save your raft too. Hold the raft's perimeter line and the heaving line together, if possible. Holding the raft with one hand and the line with the other will tend to pull you in two.

8. Once you reach shallow water, use the line to steady you as you walk to shore.

9. One last, crucial point: The line thrower should always wear a life jacket. In most rescue situations the possibility is very real that a rope man will be pulled into the water or that he will go in intentionally in an emergency.

When on the river, never tie a line to your body in any way; instead, tie a loop and hold it. A person at the end of a fixed line in strong current will be sucked below the surface, regardless of buoyancy.

Not long ago on the Middle Fork of the Salmon, a man tried to swim a line ashore from a raft hung up on a midstream rock. After unwisely tying the line around his waist, he dove into the swift current. Instantly, he was swept to the end of the line, sucked under, and bent double with the line digging into his belly. He was unable to free himself, and his companions back in the raft either lacked the presence of mind or were unable to cut or untie the line. When the man's body was finally brought ashore, his companions saw that the waist had been squeezed by rope and current down to the size of a 50¢ piece.

The correct way to run a line ashore in this situation is to attach a weight to the line's end and throw it in the manner described above. People usually get ashore by swimming through the heavy water to the calm below the rapid, where they gain the shore with ease and walk back up the bank.

MAKING A TEMPORARY OAR OR PADDLE

Shallow rivers can break oars at an alarming rate. But if you carry epoxy glue, diagonal breaks can be mended in the field (see Chapter One). In the event that you find yourself with only one serviceable oar, you can make a temporary oar by lashing several 3-foot sticks to the thick end of an oar-length pole (Drawing 49). If no such pole is available, have two people paddle on the oarless side of the raft with the blades of your broken oars or with 6-foot poles having several two-foot sticks lashed to their ends. Wrap or tape broken oars to prevent splinters.

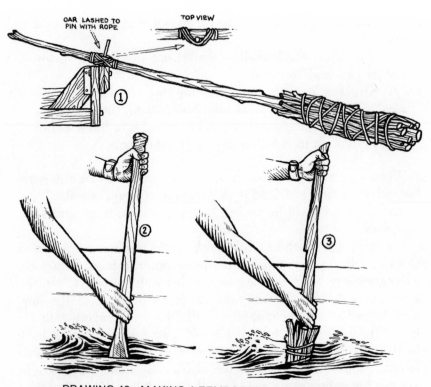

DRAWING 49   MAKING A TEMPORARY OAR OR PADDLE

1. A crude but effective temporary oar can be made by lashing a number of three-foot sticks to the thick end of an oar-length pole.
2. A broken oar used as a paddle. Wrap or tape the break to prevent splinters.
3. A makeshift paddle: a 5- or 6-foot pole with sticks lashed to the end. Two of these do the work of one good oar.

RAFT DAMAGED BEYOND REPAIR

Well-made rafts are rarely damaged beyond repair. But if a raft does incur irreparable damage, the other rafts in the group should be able to accommodate the entire party. If the fates truly conspire against you and mutilate more than one raft, consider continuing downriver in the damaged rafts. Even when lacking a tube chamber or a floor, most rafts can still be rowed or paddled through calms and lined or portaged around rapids. If your rafts disintegrate or disappear altogether, either hitch a ride out of the wilderness with another group of rafters or hike out relying on U.S.G.S. quadrangle topo maps to show the shortest route back to home and bed.

SERIOUS INJURY

If a member of your party suffers serious injury needing immediate medical attention, administer first aid and take the fastest route back to civilization. The quickest path to help is often down the river. A raft that sets off at first strong light and is rowed hard all day can generally cover some 50 miles before nightfall. On most rivers, where there is a remote lodge or ranch with radio and air strip at least every 15 or 20 miles, this means that a raft is never more than a few hours from help and rarely more than two days from its take-out. Another possibility is to signal aircraft for assistance. Also, you can request aid from passing commercial rafting outfits, which often have doctors among their passengers and which, in the Grand Canyon, sometimes carry radio transceivers. The fact that help is often available in the wilderness does not, of course, lessen the need for thorough planning and training. Each party must prepare, as much as possible, to take care of its own needs if it is to truly savor the pioneer spirit of a wilderness voyage.

DISTRESS SIGNALING*

3 DRAWING 50A Three flares, shots, or fires signal distress.

Note: FIRE Lay three fires in a straight, evenly spaced row where they can be seen from the air. Light when aircraft are heard or seen. Use smoke by day, bright flame by night. Add green leaves, moss or a little water to send up clouds of white smoke.

DRAWING 50B HOW TO USE A SIGNALING MIRROR

Hold mirror a few inches from face and sight at airplane through hole. Spot of light through hole will fall on face, hand or shirt. Adjust angle of mirror until reflection of light spot in rear of mirror disappears through hole while you are still sighting on airplane through the hole.

DRAWING 50C S O S signals distress.

● ● ●　━━　━━　━━　● ● ●

dididit　　dahdahdah　　dididit

short short short　long long long　short short short

MORSE CODE

A ·—	J ·———	S ···	2 ··———
B —···	K —·—	T —	3 ···——
C —·—·	L ·—··	U ··—	4 ····—
D —··	M ——	V ···—	5 ·····
E ·	N —·	W ·——	6 —····
F ··—·	O ———	X —··—	7 ——···
G ——·	P ·——·	Y —·——	8 ———··
H ····	Q ——·—	Z ——··	9 ————·
I ··	R ·—·	1 ·————	O —————

*This information has been drawn from the Army Air Force Survival Manual, the Naval Air Force Signaling Guide, and the Boy Scout Handbook.

When sending messages other than SOS in Morse code,
use these procedure signs:

Attention (I have a message for you; make ready to receive.)	. _ . _	AA
Go ahead (I am ready to receive.)	_ . _	K
Wait (I will be ready to receive you or to finish in a moment.)	. _ ...	AS
Cannot receive you	. _ _	W
Break (Signals beginning of text of message.)	_ ... _	BT
End of word	space	
End of sentence	. _ . _ . _	AAA
Error (Have made mistake and will repeat.)	....	EEEEEEEE
Word received (Made by receiver after each word to indicate word received.)	_	T
Repeat	.. _ _ ..	IMI
End of Message	. _ . _ .	AR
Message received	. _ .	R

DRAWING 50D WIGWAG FLAG SIGNALS

Make a wigwag flag by attaching a 2-foot square of red or white to the end of a 6-foot staff. Signals start with the flag held straight up. Hold the bottom of the staff belt-high in the palm of the hand; grasp the staff a foot above the bottom with the other hand. Use Morse code. Make a dit by swinging the flag 90 degrees right and back to vertical. Make a dah by swinging the flag 90 degrees left and back to vertical. The interval between words is made by dipping the flag forward and back.

Swing the flag smoothly, easily without jerking. Keep it as flat as possible toward whoever is receiving the message. To avoid twisting the flag around the staff, swing it in a slight loop. Thus in sending "A" you make a slim figure 8 with the tip of the staff. When a wind is blowing, face slightly into or away from it to keep the flag flying fairly flat.

DRAWING 50E
GROUND-TO-AIR EMERGENCY CODE USED TO AMPLIFY DISTRESS SIGNALS

Lay out these symbols with orange life jackets, pieces of wood, stones, or anyother available material. Maximize color contrast between symbol and background. Make symbols 8 feet in height or larger.

Require doctor. Serious injuries.	**I**	Require map and compass.	▢	Probably safe to land here.	△
Require medical supplies.	**II**	Require signal lamp with battery and radio.	**i**	NO	**N**
Unable to proceed.	**X**	Indicate direction to proceed.	**K**	YES	**Y**
Require food and water.	**F**	Am proceeding in this direction.	↑	Not understood.	**JL**
Require firearms and ammunition.	⋎	All well.	**LL**		

AIRCRAFT ACKNOWLEDGEMENTS:

Aircraft will indicate that signals have been seen and understood
1. Rocking from side to side, or
2. Flashing green light

Aircraft will indicate signals *not* under-by:
1. Making a complete righthand circuit, or
2. Flashing red light

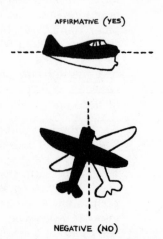

AFFIRMATIVE (YES)

NEGATIVE (NO)

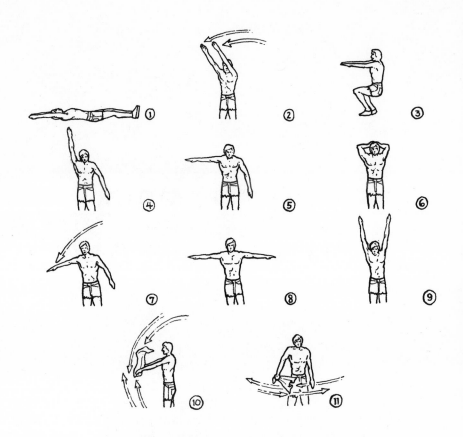

DRAWING 50F   BODY SIGNALS

1. Need medical assistance—urgent. (Lie prone.)
2. Do not attempt to land here.
3. Land here. (Point in direction of landing.)
4. All O.K. Do not wait.
5. Can proceed shortly. Wait if practicable.
6. Our receiver is operating.
7. Use drop message.
8. Need mechanical help or parts—long delay.
9. Pick us up.
10. Affirmative (Yes)
11. Negative (No)

CHAPTER FOUR

First Aid for River People

Out on the river, it is vital that each group have a complete medical kit and that at least two people in the group be thoroughly acquainted with first-aid techniques, especially artificial respiration, closed-heart massage, and the treatment of hypothermia and snakebite. This chapter covers these crucial areas plus a few common, minor river ailments. Since it is by no means a complete first-aid guide, however, it is essential that the reader and all rafters study and carry a detailed first-aid guide such as the Red Cross' comprehensive *Advanced First Aid & Emergency Care*.

Those who plan extended trips through exceptionally isolated country like the Canadian or Alaskan wilderness would do well to carry a medical manual that goes beyond mere first aid. First aid, after all, is intended primarily to ease the suffering of the patient until the doctor arrives. Thus, in areas where it will be impossible to reach a doctor within a few days, it is of utmost importance to have a thorough medical manual and a medicine kit even more complete than that outlined below. One such manual, which contains an outline of an all-embracing medicine kit, is *Being Your Own Wilderness Doctor* by Dr. E. Russel Kodet and Bradford Angier.

Trip leaders should be aware of and should be familiar with the special first-aid techniques for those members of the party who are diabetic, epileptic, or asthmatic, who take daily prescription drugs, or who are allergic to bee or scorpion stings.

RIVER MEDICAL KIT

An expanded version of the first-aid kit carried on Sierra Club outings, this kit has been designed with the assistance of William Thompson, M. D., a veteran riverman, and is based in part on Dr. John Blosser's fine article "Wilderness Medicine," which appeared in the July, 1972, issue of *Emergency Medicine.* Show this list to your doctor, for you will need prescriptions for many of the drugs mentioned in it, and follow his advice concerning substitutions, for improved medicines are continually being developed. At the pharmacy, ask the druggist to write the expiration date on the label of each bottle; this will enable you to keep the supply fresh. *Caution:* Some people are allergic, that is, oversensitive, to many of these drugs. So ask about allergy *before* administering any of them, and even then be alert for ill effects.

DRUGS

aspirin (5-gr. tablets)	To relieve mild pain or headache, to reduce fever, to ease shock
aspirin and codeine (½-gr. tablets)	1 or 2 tablets every 4 hours hours as needed for severe pain
morphine (¼-gr. tablets)	1 tablet for extreme pain; can be repeated in 3 or 4 hours
Lomotil (tablets)	For diarrhea: adult dose, 1 or 2 tablets every hour until diarrhea stops, but not more than 4 tablets per day
Donnatol (tablets)	For abdominal cramps, 1 or 2 tablets every 8 hours
Compazine (5- or 10-mg. tablets or 25-mg. suppositories)	For nausea or vomiting, 1 tablet every 4 hours. If vomiting is severe, tablets will not stay down, so drug is administered in suppository form.

Seconal (100-mg. capsules) — 1 capsule to induce sleep or ease hysteria; can be repeated in 4 hours

Surfadil cream — For sunburn, hives, insect bites, poison oak & ivy

Pyribenzamine (Lontabs) — Long-acting antihistamine: 1 tablet effective for 12 hours against reactions to poison oak & ivy, bites, stings, and other allergy problems

Prednisone (cortisone tablets) — For severe poison oak & ivy, other allergic reaction, or traumatic shock

Betadine solution — Antiseptic

Antibiotic ointment (Myciguent, Neosporin, Polysporin, etc.) — For combating infection of wounds and burns; not an antiseptic

Antibiotic tablets (Erythromycin, Cleocin) — For infection: 1 tablet every 4 hours 4 times daily for a minimum of 3 days. Do not skip a dose. Ask about allergy before using. Keep person out of sunlight or rash may develop.

Oil of cloves — For toothache, apply directly to sore area with Q-tips.

Collyrium — Eyewash for neutralizing irritation

Zinc oxide ointment — To soothe and protect sunburned skin

Salt/dextrose tablets — For prevention and treatment of dehydration and heat exhaustion

Milk of magnesia (tablets) — Antacid or cathartic

Vitamins B complex and C in high potency, stress doses — The stress of severe accident or illness depletes certain vital substances, such as endocrines, which are essential for recovery. Maintain adequate nutrition—emphasizing vitamin B complex, vitamin C, and protein.

Earache drops

Burn spray

Snakebite and insectbite kits with antivenin and complete instructions	Antivenin is especially necessary if children or allergy-prone people are along. Keep antivenin under 90° F.

WOUND CARE

Band-aids (large assortment)	For small wounds and burns
Butterfly strips	For closing cuts
Sterile gauze squares (2 by 2 in. and 3 by 3 in.)	For small wounds; to control bleeding
Sterile gauze squares (4 by 4 in.)	Combination dressing and bandage for large wounds
Telfa sterile pads	For burns
Q-tips	For applying medication
Adhesive tape (3 in. wide, 5 yd. roll)	To hold dressings in place, to close small cuts, to hold splints in place, to protect blisters, etc.
Gauze roller bandages (1 in., 2-in., and 3-in. rolls)	To bandage wounds, to hold compresses in place, to stop bleeding, etc.
Elastic bandages	Use half-strength to wrap sprained ankle, knee, wrist, etc. Use one or more, fully stretched, to control severe bleeding. (Unlike a dangerous tourniquet, this permits circulation and can be used anywhere, not just on extremities.) Use for strapping chest tight to exclude air in puncture wounds. Also, use to bandage fractures and dislocations.

MISCELLANEOUS

Needles and safety pins	For securing bandages, removing splinters, etc.

High-quality scissors	For cutting bandages, cutting away clothing from around wounds, etc.
Precision tweezers	For removing thorns and splinters. Sterilize to handle dressings.
Thermometer	Normal temperature is 98.6; fluctuations of 1 degree are generally not regarded as significant.
Inflatable arm and leg splints	For immobilizing fractures of arm or leg. One may also splint a toe to a toe, a finger to a finger, a leg to a leg, and tape an arm to the torso; but always put padding in between to absorb sweat and to avoid grinding bones together.
Artificial respiration airways	Adult size and, if necessary, child size
Matches	For sterilizing and emergency fire building
Moleskin foam	For foot blisters
Several tubes of sun cream	A reserve supply
Chap sticks	A reserve supply
Insect repellent	A reserve supply
Halazone tablets	A reserve supply for water purification
Bar of soap	For washing hands before applying first aid and for cleansing wounds
Advanced First Aid & Emergency Care	This thorough first-aid manual is available from local chapters of the American National Red Cross.
List of medical kit contents	

COLD WATER: DROWNING AND HYPOTHERMIA *

The early spring (and late fall) boater is confronted with the most serious hazard a river has to offer—COLD WATER. Sudden immersion in cold water may produce serious consequences. Immediate death may result from drowning or cardiac arrest. Exposure to cold water for anywhere from a few minutes to an hour or more leads to hypothermia, a lowering of the core body temperature (measured by rectal, not oral, thermometers). Unconsciousness and consequently a risk of drowning occur whenever the core body temperature is reduced appreciably. A further lowering of body temperature inevitably leads to death.

Sudden immersion in water colder than 50° F causes immediate and intense difficulty in breathing. Gasping and inability to control breathing may cause the dunker to panic within a few minutes following a cold-water tipover. Whenever the head of a gasping dunker is covered by a wave (even if only for a few seconds), he is likely to inhale water and possibly drown. Gasping and rapid breathing can produce hyperventilation within 10 seconds, and this can lead to unconsciousness. Consequently the likelihood of drowning increases because even the best lifejacket cannot be expected to hold the head of an unconscious dunker above the water in turbulence.

In addition to the breathing difficulties associated with cold-water immersion, the dunker's body rapidly loses heat at a rate MUCH FASTER THAN THE DUNKER REALIZES. Depending on skin thickness and the amount and kind of protective clothing worn, the dunker's core body temperature drops from a normal value of 98.6°F to about 96°F within 2 to 10 minutes. At these low core body temperatures, useful work becomes difficult and often impossible. Consequently the dunker is unable to swim or in any other way assist in his own rescue. A drop in core temperature to 88°F leads to unconsciousness, and a further drop to about 77°F usually results in immediate death.

To understand hypothermia, consider how the body gains,

---

* This section is reprinted from *Whitewater: Quietwater* by Dr. Robert Palzer and Jody Palzer. Minor changes have been made in cooperation with the authors.

conserves, and loses body heat. The human body is heated in two ways, externally and internally. Heat is produced internally by the oxidation of food (metabolism) which occurs at one rate in a resting individual and at a higher rate during exercise. Shivering is an involuntary form of muscular exercise that produces heat at the expense of body food stores. The body can also receive external heat from the surroundings (sun, fire, another body, etc.). Body heat is conserved by the insulative layer of subcutaneous fat and by constriction of the blood vessels to the extremities. Body heat is lost by exhalation of warm air, by sweating, and by radiation, convection, and conduction from exposed body surfaces. To the boater, convection and conduction are the most significant means of heat loss.

Rapids boaters are generally subjected to continual wetting even in the absence of tipovers. Wet clothing drains heat from a boater's body at an alarming rate because water conducts heat away from the body at a rate 20 times faster than air. Complete immersion is an even more serious hazard to the boater. Within seconds after immersion, clothing loses its insulative properties; these are due primarily to trapped air which prevents heat loss by reducing convection. Unless a garment is waterproof, wet clothing cannot prevent the rapid circulation of cold water past the skin (convection). Within minutes, the skin temperature of the dunker who is not wearing waterproof clothing will drop to within a few degrees of the water temperature. The dunker's body automatically responds by cutting off blood circulation to the skin in an attempt to conserve heat. Reduced blood circulation prevents the transport of energy stores required by the muscles to perform voluntary work. Thus voluntary movement of the extremities becomes increasingly difficult, sapping body strength and incapacitating the dunker.

Muscular activity on the part of the dunker creates a dilemma. Muscular activity is needed for the dunker to rescue himself, but it also increases the rate of heat loss since blood forced to the extremities is cooled rapidly by the cold water. In short, the dunker should ALWAYS GET OUT OF COLD WATER AS QUICKLY AND WITH AS LITTLE EXERTION AS POSSIBLE. If feasible, he should lie on his back in a feet-first position and let the current carry him downstream as he works his way to shore. He should forget about saving his boat and rescuing other equipment. Unconsciousness can occur within 5 minutes after immersion in cold water. Scientific experiments and personal experience have shown that even good swimmers cannot swim a distance of 200 yards when the water temperature is less than 40° to 45°F. Differences in skin thickness, basal metabolic rate, and other physiological parameters produce variability in the *timing* of an individual's responses to immersion in cold water. Therefore, the following table should be considered only as a rough guide. We can't tell you how long YOU will last in cold water. Physical fitness is not an indicator. The physically fit person may be the first to go because body fat provides protection against cold.

Water Temperature	Useful Work	Unconscious
32.5°	less than 5 min.	less than 15 min.
40°	7.5 min.	30 min.
50°	15 min.	60 min.
60°	30 min.	2 hrs.
70°	45 min.	3 hrs.

Source: A. F. Davidson, "Survival—the Will to Live," *American Whitewater*, vol. 12, no. 1 (Summer 1966) [adapted].

Protection against the serious consequences of cold-water immersion may be obtained either by acquiring a substantial layer of body fat or by wearing protective clothing. The above table lists estimates for a person clothed appropriately for the air temperature. Wearing waterproof outer layers extends these times somewhat, but wearing a neoprene wet suit extends them considerably. Woolen underwear worn under a wet suit (and lifejacket) provides the best protection against cold water that we know of.

Paddlers who have been wearing wet clothing for several hours may experience a mild case of hypothermia. This causes a reduction in the times listed in the above table. Consequently, be on the alert for signs of hypothermia in yourself and your companions. Symptoms include a lack of coordination, thickness of speech, irrationality, blueness of skin, dilation of pupils, and decrease in heart and respiratory rate. These symptoms are similar to those of a drunken person, and the judgment of a hypothermic boater is generally equally irrational.

Treatment: At least two people in every boating party should be versed in mouth-to-mouth resuscitation and external cardiac (closed-heart) massage, so that if one of the first-aiders becomes a victim, there will be another available to provide assistance. Whenever a boater has been in cold water for more than 10 minutes, hypothermia is almost certain. Under these conditions artificial respiration should be given only if breathing has stopped completely, and then it should be applied "at no more than half the normal rate." * Otherwise the would-be rescuer may cause the victim to become hyperventilated since during hypothermia metabolism is slower and less oxygen is consumed.

If the victim has experienced only mild hypothermia, replacement of wet clothing with dry apparel usually suffices. However, in instances of extreme hypothermia, external heat must be applied because the victim is incapable of warming himself up regardless of the amount of dry clothing supplied. Be fast. The victim should be quickly stripped; two rescuers should do likewise and envelop the patient skin-to-skin. Then all three should be wrapped in a sleeping bag. This prompt and massive delivery of warmth to the victim's body is the only way to protect against the phenomenon known as "after cooling," which occurs when the constricted outer blood vessels relax in the first relief from the icy water and allow supercooled blood to flow back to the heart, sometimes causing it to fail. Meanwhile, other rescuers should build a fire to provide warmth and hot nonalcoholic drink; but because this takes time, it is only a supplementary measure. You may also give the victim small portions of high-energy, easily digested food such as honey.

It should be apparent from the above that the spring boater runs the most risks. A spring boating trip is not the time to practice new maneuvers learned from books over the winter months. It is not the time to introduce your friends to boating. It is not the time to make a spur-of-the-moment trip

---

* W. R. Keatinge, *Survival in Cold Water: The Physiology and Treatment of Immersion Hypothermia and of Drowning,* Oxford: Blackwell Scientific Publications, 1969, p. 73.

alone because the rivers are high and you can't round up suitable companions to shoot the rapids.

Expert boaters prefer spring boating and are well prepared to protect themselves against its hazards. Know your limitations and equip yourself properly. If you have any doubts about your ability to safeguard yourself, wait for warmer weather.

ARTIFICIAL RESPIRATION

The mouth-to-mouth or mouth-to-nose method of artificial respiration is superior to the old manual methods, for it allows the rescuer to inflate the victim's lungs immediately, even while the victim floats in the water. Also, because he is closer to the victim, the rescuer can more accurately judge the volume, pressure, and timing of efforts needed to fill the victim's lungs.

If a swimmer is unconscious and not breathing, begin artificial respiration *immediately.* A rescuer in a boat can lean down and deliver the first few puffs while the victim is still in the water (Drawing 51); a swimming rescuer can render mouth-to-mouth resuscitation while floating beside the victim. Of course, it is important to get the victim out of the water, dried off, and warmed up without undue delay, but the more immediate those first ten lungsful of air, the greater the chance of revival. *Be fast!*

DRAWING 51

The more immediate the first ten puffs of air, the better the chance of revival. Be fast!

MOUTH-TO-MOUTH METHOD *

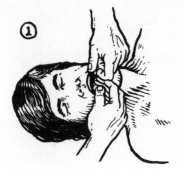

1. If foreign matter is visible in the mouth, wipe it out quickly with your fingers, wrapped in a cloth, if possible.

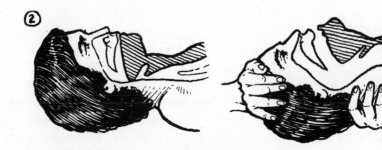

2. Tilt the victim's head backward so that his chin is pointing upward. This is accomplished by placing one hand under the victim's neck and lifting, while the other hand is placed on his forehead and presses. This procedure should provide an open airway by moving the tongue away from the back of the throat.

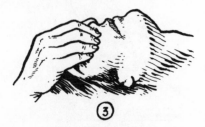

3. Maintain the backward head-tilt position and, to prevent leakage of air, pinch the victim's nostrils with the fingers of the hand that is pressing on the forehead.

---

* Reprinted with permission of the American National Red Cross.

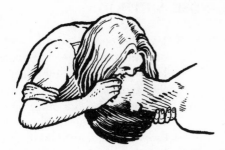

Open your mouth wide; take a deep breath; and seal your mouth tightly around the victim's mouth with a wide-open circle and blow into his mouth. If the airway is clear, only moderate resistance to the blowing effort is felt.

4. Watch the victim's chest, and when you see it rise, stop inflation, raise your mouth, turn your head to the side, and listen for exhalation. Watch the chest to see that it falls.

When his exhalation is finished, repeat the blowing cycle. Volume is important. You should start at a high rate and then provide at least one breath every 5 seconds (or 12 per minute). (If victim is suffering from hypothermia, deliver these lungfuls of air at half the normal rate. See previous section.)

When mouth-to-mouth and/or mouth-to-nose resuscitation is administered to small children or infants, the backward head tilt should not be as extensive as that for adults or large children.

The mouth and nose of the infant or small child should be sealed by your mouth. Blow into the mouth and/or nose every 3 seconds (or 20 breaths per minute) with less pressure and volume than for adults, the amount determined by the size of the child. (If hypothermia is present, half this rate.)

If vomiting occurs, quickly turn the victim on his side, wipe out the mouth, and then reposition him.

MOUTH-TO-NOSE METHOD

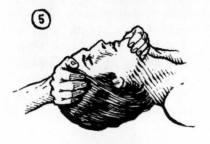

5. For the mouth-to-nose method, maintain the backward head-tilt position by placing the heel of the hand on the forehead. Use the other hand to close the mouth. Blow into the victim's nose. On the exhalation phase, open the victim's mouth to allow the air to escape.

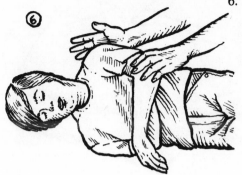

6. If a foreign body is prohibiting ventilation, as a last resort turn the victim on his side and administer sharp blows between the shoulder blades to jar the material free.

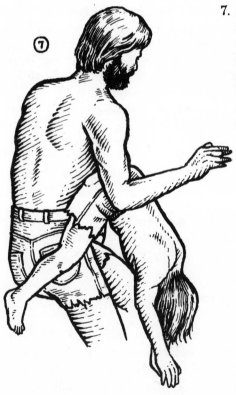

7. A child may be suspended momentarily by the ankles or turned upside down over one arm and given two or three sharp pats between the shoulder blades. Clear the mouth again, reposition, and repeat the blowing effort.

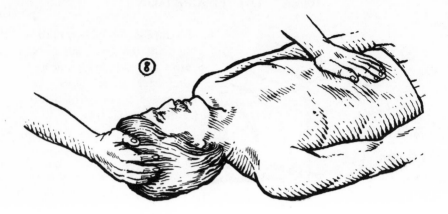

8. Air may get blown into the victim's stomach, particularly when the air passage is obstructed or the inflation pressure is excessive. Although inflation of the stomach is not dangerous, it may make lung ventilation more difficult and increase the likelihood of vomiting. When the victim's stomach is bulging, always turn the victim's head to one side and be prepared to clear his mouth before pressing your hand briefly over the stomach. This will force air out of the stomach but may cause vomiting.

When a victim is revived, keep him as quiet as possible until he is breathing regularly. Keep him from becoming chilled and otherwise treat him for shock. Continue artificial respiration until the victim begins to breathe for himself or a physician pronounces him dead or he appears to be dead beyond any doubt. (After the start of resuscitation, normal breathing, if it returns, usually resumes within 15 minutes, but revival can take as much as several hours.)

Because respiratory and other disturbances may develop as an aftermath, a doctor's care is necessary during the recovery period.

CLOSED-HEART MASSAGE *

If, in spite of mouth-to-mouth breathing, the injured person fails to respond, it may be because his heart has stopped. If no pulse is felt at the wrist, no sound heard with the ear to the chest, if the color is poor, or if the pupils are dilated, you can be fairly certain the heart has stopped. These steps taken promptly may save a life.

---

* This method of closed-heart massage is used by the U.S. Forest Service.

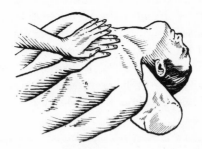

DRAWING 60   CLOSED-HEART MASSAGE

1. Place the victim on his back on a firm surface and raise his legs to drain blood toward heart.

2. Place support under shoulders to keep neck arched back.

3. Place the heel of one hand on the lower part of the breast-bone and the other hand directly on top of the first hand.

4. Press down firmly with both hands, then raise both hands from the chest to allow it to expand.

5. Repeat every second.

6. If alone, stop every 30 seconds to do mouth-to-mouth breathing three or four times.

7. With two persons, one does the heart massage five times, then the other does mouth-to-mouth once. Repeat.

8. Check the pulse periodically. Some hearts will start to beat on their own in a few seconds; others won't until treated by a doctor with electricity.

9. If you have access to a phone or radio, summon help and alert the rescuers to the fact that the heart is stopped so that preparations can be made.

SNAKEBITE

River country is snake country: Be alert and watch your step. Most of the poisonous snakes in the United States are pit vipers —rattlesnakes, moccasins, copperheads. These snakes have a pit between the eye and the nostril on each side of the head, ellip-tical pupils, two large fangs, and a single row of plates beneath the tail. Although some varieties of pit viper grow to be 8 feet long, most are between 3 and 4 feet long. The venom of pit vipers attacks the circulatory system. Their bites, which can be identified by one or more puncture wounds created by fangs (Drawing 61) usually cause extreme pain, rapid swelling, and discoloration of the skin. These symptoms are often accompanied by general weakness, rapid pulse, nausea and vomiting, shortness of breath, dimness of vision, and shock. Fortunately, recovery from the bites of pit vipers is usually complete, although the victim may be rather ill for several days to a week.

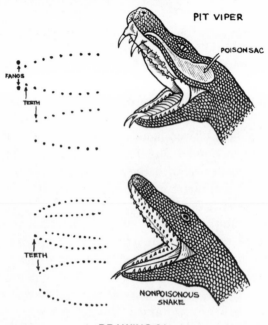

DRAWING 61

The only other poisonous snake of note in the United States is the coral snake. A variety of cobra, the coral snake is relatively thin and small, ranging in length up to 39 inches. This snake has tubular fangs, with teeth behind the fangs, and, like nonpoisonous snakes, it has round pupils and a double row of plates beneath the tail. The coral snake is strikingly colorful, with red, yellow, and black rings around its body. The nose is always black. The coral snake's extremely toxic venom attacks the nervous system with usually devastating effect. Although the bite causes only a slight burning pain and mild swelling at the wound, other symptoms include blurring vision, drooping eyelids, slurred speech, drowsiness, increased saliva and sweating, perhaps nausea, breathing difficulty, paralysis, convulsions, and possible coma. Happily, coral snakes are rarely encountered in whitewater country. They live along the coast and lowlands of the southeast and south, up the Mississippi to Indiana, and in the desert regions of southern Arizona and New Mexico.

Nonpoisonous snakes have round pupils, no fangs or pits, and a double row of plates beneath the tail.

The severity of reaction to poisonous snakebite varies greatly from case to case and is influenced by such things as the location of the bite, the thickness of the clothing worn, the size of the victim, the amount of venom injected, the speed with which the venom is absorbed into the victim's system, and the sensitivity of the victim to the venom. Naturally, the danger is highest for small people, particularly children. But in 20 percent of all bites by poisonous snakes, not a single drop of venom is injected. The most crucial factor in snakebite treatment is often the speed with which specific antivenin therapy is administered. Carry antivenin, know how to use it, and administer it as fast as possible after a poisonous snakebite. Unfortunately, reactions to snakebite are often aggravated by acute fear and anxiety. If you are bitten, try to be at ease, for the reassuring fact is that only ten to twenty deaths per year are caused by snakebite, and only 2 percent of all poisonous bites are fatal.

FIRST AID FOR POISONOUS SNAKEBITE *

Objectives

1. To reduce the circulation of blood through the bite area.

2. To delay absorption of venom.

3. To prevent aggravation of the local wound and to sustain respiration.

Procedure

Keep the victim quiet and reassure him. Transport the victim to a source of medical assistance as quickly as possible.

1. Immobilize the arm or leg in a lowered position, keeping the involved area *below* the level of the victim's heart.

2. If the bite is on an arm or leg, apply a constricting band from 2 to 4 inches above the bite, between the wound and

---

* Reprinted with permission of the American National Red Cross from *Standard First Aid and Personal Safety,* pp. 118-119.

the victim's heart [Drawing 62]. The constricting band should *not* be tight; if it is properly adjusted, there will be some oozing from the wound. You should be able to slip your index finger under the band when it is in place.

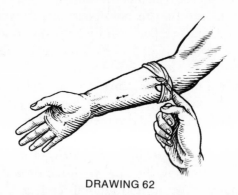

DRAWING 62

3. Use the blade in a snakebite kit, if available; otherwise, sterilize a knife blade with a flame, and make incisions through the skin at each fang mark and over the suspected venom deposit point. (The snake strikes downward, and the deposit point will be lower than the fang marks.) Be very careful to make the incisions through the skin only and in the long axis of the limb. Do *not* make cross-cut incisions. The incisions must not be deeper than the skin because of the danger of severing muscles and nerves. Special care is necessary in making incisions on the hand, wrist, or foot, because muscles, nerves, and tendons lie close to the surface, and their injury may cause considerable disability. Do not make incisions more than one-half inch long.

4. Apply suction with the suction cup contained in the snakebite kit, if available; otherwise, use your mouth. Snake venom is not a stomach poison but it should not be swallowed, and you should rinse it from your mouth. Continue suction for from 30 to 60 minutes. If swelling extends up to the constricting band, apply another band a few inches above the first, but leave the first band in place.

5. Wash the wound thoroughly with soap and water and blot dry. Apply a sterile or clean dressing and bandage it in place.

6. You may place a cold, wet cloth or ice wrapped in a

cloth, if available, over the wound to slow absorption but do not pack the wound in ice.

7. *Do not* give alcohol in any form.

8. Treat the victim for shock. Unless nausea and vomiting develop, sips of fluid may be given if the victim is conscious and can swallow without difficulty.

9. Give artificial respiration if indicated.

10. Consult a physician with regard to antibiotic therapy and prevention of tetanus, even if the bite has been inflicted by a nonpoisonous snake.

11. If the victim must walk, make sure that he moves slowly.

12. Telephone ahead to the nearest hospital or doctor so that antivenin can be made available quickly.

PLANT POISONING

Poison ivy, oak, and sumac are plentiful along rivers; learn to recognize and avoid them (Drawing 63). If you do contact one of these plants, wash the affected area immediately and repeatedly in thick soapsuds; also wash clothes and shoes in thick hot suds. If you still react with red, swollen, itching skin and small blisters, apply Surfadil cream, calamine lotion, or some other commercial lotion. If available, the extract of the plant "jewel weed," sometimes called "touch-me-not," may be used as a treatment. For a severe reaction take Prednisone (cortisone tablets) or apply a hydrocortisone ointment.

SUNBURN

The sun is extremely intense on most rivers, so use common sense. Expose yourself gradually. Make frequent use of sun cream. And when you feel that first mild burning, promptly put on trousers and a long-sleeved shirt. Because the nose always burns first, protect it with a thick coating of cream like zinc oxide or Glacier Cream. In hot climates, wide-brimmed hats have literally saved lives. If you do burn, use burn spray and a soothing ointment such as Surfadil cream. Cover blistered or raw burns with a dressing, and keep your burned parts out of the sun.

DRAWING 63   POISON PLANTS*

Common Poison Ivy
(Rhus Radicans)
—Grows as a small plant, a vine, and a shrub.
—Found everywhere in the United States except in California and parts of adjacent states.
—Leaves always made up of three leaf clusters.
—Also called three-leaf ivy, climbing sumac, poison creeper, poison oak, markweed, and mercury.

Western Poison Oak
(Rhus Diversiloba)
—Grows as a shrub and sometimes as a vine.
—Found in California and parts of adjacent states.
—Occasionally called poison ivy or yeara.
—Leaves always consist of three leaflets.

Poison Sumac
(Rhus Vernix)
—Grows as a woody shrub or small tree from 5 to 25 feet high.
—Found in most of eastern third of United States.
—Also called swamp sumac, poison elder, poison ash, poison dogwood, and thunderwood.

*Based on the American National Red Cross *Standard First Aid and Personal Safety.*

BLISTERS

Blisters on the hands frequently plague paddlers and oarsmen. Unless you have tough, leatherlike hands, wear gloves. Even with gloves, a long voyage may produce blisters. At the first sign of soreness, tape sensitive areas with cloth medical tape (Drawing 64). Some oarsmen have been forced to row on day after day in agonizing pain with bloody palms because they ignored the early signs of oncoming blisters.

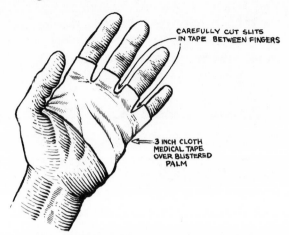

CAREFULLY CUT SLITS
IN TAPE BETWEEN FINGERS

3 INCH CLOTH
MEDICAL TAPE
OVER BLISTERED
PALM

DRAWING 64   TAPING A BLISTERED PALM

The tape ends should overlap a bit on the back of the hand.

When blisters do develop, stop *all* rowing and paddling if that is possible; blisters are best left unbroken. But when, as is usually the case, you must go on stroking with those blades, wash the entire area with soap and water and carefully make a small puncture hole at the edge of the blister with a needle that has been sterilized over an open flame. With a sterile pad gently press out the water or blood. Wash again with soap and water, apply antibiotic ointment to the puncture, and cover the entire area with sterile cloth medical tape. Do not put gauze or cotton between the tape and the blister; put the tape directly over the blister. Leave the tape in place—to pull it off would strip off the loose skin, leaving an open wound. Wait five days for the blister to heal completely; then remove tape. If the blister has popped, trim off the dead skin, wash with soap and water, apply antibiotic ointment, and keep dressed with a sterile gauze pad until new skin grows over.

Never wash open blisters with merthiolate or alcohol; these are skin disinfectants, not wound disinfectants. When used on the delicate tissue of an open wound, they kill tissue and actually cause infection.

Prevent foot blisters by protecting sore spots with tape or moleskin foam and by changing to dry socks and shoes for long side hikes. Treat foot blisters as indicated above.

TETANUS

As danger of tetanus (lockjaw) is high in accidents occurring where stock animals have been, boaters should have a series of antitetanus injections or, if appropriate, a booster shot. Tetanus immunizations require roughly two months to become fully effective.

CHAPTER FIVE

Food on the Flood

The range of foods for river trips can be as broad or as narrow as you wish. Meals may be simple, one-pot brews or elaborate gourmet affairs of many courses. For extreme lightness and compactness food can be freeze-dried, while for extravagant luxury it can be deliciously fresh. But only whitewater fanatics, in their zeal to keep their rafts as light as possible, are willing to pay the sky-high prices charged for freeze-dried food, and only epicures, in their utter devotion to the palate, are willing to tote and heave cumbersome ice chests packed with fresh foods and dry ice. Most rafters settle for foods somewhere in between.

GUIDELINES FOR FOOD SELECTION

Guided primarily by *ease of preparation* and *moderate cost* and achieving lightness and compactness where possible, do your shopping in a typical supermarket. Instant and dehydrated foods such as powdered milk and instant rice, oatmeal, and potatoes are chosen for their lightness and easy preparation. Fresh meat is eaten only on the first night, and the only fresh foods taken for subsequent days are durable fruits and vegetables like apples and carrots which keep for a while without refrigeration. Canned food is used widely; though bulky, it is relatively cheap, a snap to prepare, and waterproof. Liquid margarine is used because it is handy and requires no refrigeration. Soft bread is inevitably crushed into crumbs, so all bread is solid buns, biscuits, or rolls. (If bread becomes hard, fry it French-toast style in a batter of powdered milk, eggs, and water.)

An effort should be made to balance each meal with proper amounts of protein, fat, carbohydrates, vitamins, and minerals. Lemon and orange concentrates ensure adequate vitamin C. Powdered health drinks like Hemo and Tiger's Milk are fortified with vitamins and minerals and guarantee sufficient levels of key vitamins like thiamine (vitamin B_1) and riboflavin (vitamin B_2) needed for energy conversion.

The fare is kept zesty and alive through imaginative use of spices and condiments. Onions, garlic, salt, pepper, chili powder, and curry powder put taste into eggs, vegetables, soups, stews, etc. Condiments like pickles, chutney, pickled cauliflower, and cranberry sauce provide lively contrast. Fruit, whether fresh, canned, or dehydrated, is always a welcome item. Indulge your fantasies.

One good way to decide what food to buy for a trip is to plan menus and purchase supplies while en route to the put-in. As the group drives down the highway or eats breakfast in a cafe, work together on a menu (see menu at the end of this chapter). While evaluating meal ideas, try to take into account everyone's preferences, loathings, and unique cooking skills. If a devout cook shows himself, indulge his desires; otherwise select simple, quick dishes. When planning trip food, allow from 3 to 6 pounds of food per man-day. If the voyage is down an isolated river, consider taking at least one extra day's supply of food. Go through the supermarket as a group and choose the food together. If your companions have some new ideas as you move down the aisles, try to be flexible and work them in. This group approach makes menu planning and food buying part of the social adventure. Much is revealed in this simple interaction, especially if the people are new to one another.

A 12-foot raft with a frame that allows storage on top of the buoyancy tubes can carry enough canned food to last three people 14 days. A 16-foot raft with similar frame can carry enough food to feed four people for 21 days.

FOOD PACKING

Simplify food handling by organizing the food right at the super-market checkout stand. Set up an array of cardboard boxes and divide the food in one of the following ways: by *meal* with all breakfast food together, all lunch food together, and all dinner food together; by *separate meal* with breakfast 1 together, lunch 1 together, and so on; or by *food type* with crushables together, cold cans like beer and pop together, all other cans together, lunch food together, things to keep cool like eggs and cheese together, etc.

Later, put all gooey foodstuffs like honey, jam, and syrup into squeeze tubes. Prevent gigantic messes by sealing all breakables and messables such as eggs, pancake mix, flour, sugar, and to-matoes inside plastic bags. Canned drinks may go into a sturdy cloth sack which is cooled in the river. When you carry cans with paper labels in sacks that are not watertight, write the contents of each can on its top with a felt pen; this will allow you to identify the cans if the labels soak off. Pack all spices, staples, and basics in the kitchen box. Put crushables in a crush-proof box or in a separate bag for careful handling. A good way to preserve fragile perishables like eggs is to pack them carefully into a large silver-painted ammo box; keep this box cool by draping it with a thick, wet cloth.

MEALS

Even on a short rafting trip, the outdoor air and day-long expen-diture of energy combine to make appetites keen. Eating becomes both a necessity and a pleasure in a way not experienced off the river. In addition to the suggested menus at the end of the chap-ter, here are some notes on the three major meals of the day that should help make them both nourishing and satisfying.

Breakfast

Lavish breakfasts are possible on the river. Fresh eggs, canned sausage, bacon and ham, pancake mix, dried and canned fruit, powdered fruit juices, instant hot cereals, plus the broad array of instant beverages including coffee, cocoa, tea, milk, Tiger's Milk, and Hemo—all may make river breakfasts varied and tasty.

Here are a few tidbits of breakfast-cooking lore:

EGGS AND PANCAKES: Grease frying pan or aluminum plate thickly with cooking fat or margarine, and use low, steady fire.

SYRUP: To make syrup, boil two parts white or brown sugar with one part water. For a fancy touch add a few drops of maple flavoring.

TOAST: To make toast, make a level place in the hot coals of the fire , set your piece of bread directly onto the coals; roast each side for an instant and, voila, toast!

HOT CEREAL: Get oatmeal, cream of wheat, cream of rice, etc., in the instant, individual envelopes; add raisins, dates, or dried apples, pour in hot water, and eat.

FRUIT: Add fruit to your breakfast for a balanced meal.

STEWED PRUNES: Pour boiling water over dried prunes, cover and let soak all night, and next morning you have stewed prunes.

COOKING DRIED FRUIT: To cook dried fruit, add water and let simmer until soft. At first put in just enough water to cover the fruit, then add more as the fruit swells. Just before you are ready to stop boiling, stir in some sugar.

Lunch

A casual meal, lunch is pulled from the lunch sack like a big snack and devoured in handsful. It should consist of tasty, high-energy foods that require no cooking and can be eaten at some picturesque spot along the river. A good lunch site offers good swimming, an intriguing cave, or, on hot days, a shady rock overhang.

The mainstay of river lunches is a delicious blend of nuts, raisins, and M&Ms called gorp. At the outset of each trip, make a large bag of gorp by mixing equal parts of the three ingredients. For lunch, the squeeze cheese that comes in sausage-shaped tubes is best because it is easy to spread and does not require refrigeration. Powdered drinks with vitamin C and sugar, such as those manufactured by Wyler, make refreshing beverages.

Also, a pinch of citric-acid powder in cold water makes a fine thirst quencher.

Dinner

The end of the day is when appetites are keenest. There are many ways to make dinner a memorable meal.

Soup: The most appetizing soups are concocted on the spot. For body, put in powdered milk, pea flour, soy-bean flour, pre-cooked mashed potatoes, or instant soup mix. For flavor, put in tomato paste, bouillon cubes, onion, pepper, garlic, chili powder, salt, butter, bacon fat, etc.

One-Pot Meals: Rice, macaroni, spaghetti, and noodle dishes make simple, tasty meals. First, cook the rice (use instant rice) or pasta, then add flavor and protein by putting in things like tomato sauce, grated cheese, dried chipped beef, diced lunch meat, bacon squares, corned beef, cream sauce, onion, margarine, and milk.

Mulligan Stew: Mulligan, or hobo, stew makes an easy, full-flavored meal. The meat (any kind) is chopped into one-inch squares, browned and braised over hot coals, and then put into a big stew pot. Sprinkle in salt and pepper, and pour in just enough water to keep the meat from sticking. When the meat has cooked a while, drop in things like peas, onions, carrots, white potatoes, rice, soybean, and flour. Also, if you wish, add soup mix, bouillon cubes, noodles, and diced lunch meat. Simmer slowly. Keep water to a minimum, adding just enough to replace what boils away. Let simmer for 20 to 30 minutes, then serve proudly.

COOKING METHODS

Cooking in Cans

Save pot washing by heating canned food right in the cans. After removing the labels, immerse cans *unopened* in a kettle of cold water. Put over heat; when the water boils, the food in the cans is ready to eat. Be careful when opening hot cans. Hold with a cloth to protect hand and puncture a small hole in one end of the can. When the bubbling stops, open the entire end of the can in the usual way. Use the hot water in which cans were heated to wash cups and utensils.

Cooking Fish

Eating fresh-caught fish cooked over an open fire is, say some, one of the finest experiences to be found on earth. The fresher the fish, the richer the taste. So scale, clean, and cook fish as soon as possible after catching them. After cleaning, wipe the fresh dry; washing reduces flavor. If you're not going to eat the fish for a while, put it on ice if possible. Use a low fire or hot coals for cooking and cook until the fish meat is just flaky. Be careful not to overcook, for this will dry out the sweet flavor. Season with salt, pepper, lemon, or whatever you like.

PAN-FRY SMALL FISH: Roll panfish in cornmeal or fry deliciously plain. Put big chunks of margarine in the skillet and in and on the fish, or use plenty of bacon fat, olive oil, or salad oil. Have the pan hot, but not smoking, and fry slowly.

SKEWER SMALL OR MEDIUM FISH: Use forked green sticks. After cutting the fish, prong the sharpened fork ends into opposite sides, one near the backbone, the other in the ribs—the prong ends hold better when jabbed near bones. Then cover the fish with margarine, season it, and hold it over the fire.

SLICE LARGE FISH INTO STEAKS AND GRILL: Baste with margarine. If you have no grill, use a skillet.

Foil Cookery

Aluminum foil is very handy around a campfire. When used to bake, broil, line skillets, and serve food, foil simplifies cooking and minimizes dish and pot washing. Unfortunately, though, food sealed in foil neither browns nor absorbs the smoky campfire flavor. When cooking with foil never use a blazing fire; instead, use steady low flame or hot coals. For best results choose heavy foil and fold double. All foil and other unburnable garbage, of course, must be carried out of the wilderness in your garbage sack.

CORN ON THE COB: Thickly butter husked corn, and wrap each ear individually in many thicknesses of foil. Rotate the ears on a grill or work them in among the hot coals of the campfire. The timing here, as with all foil cooking, is critical; peek inside the foil occasionally until you are adept at judging heat and time.

BROILED MEAT: Put meat on a sheet of foil. Don't spread or seal foil over meat. Set foil right on the coals and turn the meat over when half-done. Cook until done to your liking.

BAKED POTATOES: Wrap potatoes individually in many thicknesses of foil and bury under the fire's hot coals. Bake for 1½ to 2 hours, depending on size of spuds. Use a toothpick or fork to test for doneness.

BAKED APPLES: Cut a slice off the top of each apple and cut out the core. Put a tablespoon of brown sugar and a few raisins or small marshmallows in the hollow. Set each apple on a square of foil, fold the corners up around the apple, and twist them together at the top. Bake about 30 minutes over low flame or hot coals.

BLUEBERRY MUFFIN BREADS: Prepare one package of blueberry muffin mix according to directions on the box. Tear off a sheet of foil roughly 1 foot wide and 2 feet long. Thoroughly grease one side of this sheet with margarine. Put mix on the greased side, and fold the sheet to form a sealed envelope around the mix about 10 inches square and 2 inches high. Place on a grill over low flame or coals. Cook 15 minutes on each side, turning the envelope occasionally for even baking. Then open, cut, and serve with margarine.

THE ART OF DUTCH OVEN COOKERY

by Bill Center *

Newly-baked breads and pastries are a real joy at any time, but by the tenth day of a river trip, when the fresh produce and meats are all gone, a steaming-hot blueberry pie tran-

---

* The author is an instructor in the American Whitewater School.

scends joy and becomes magic. Nothing completes a meal quite as well as a fresh-baked pastry from the dutch oven, and the successful production of a fully cooked but unburned batch of brownies is nearly as satisfying as a good run of Lava. But how hard is cooking with the dutch oven? (Or, as it is more commonly known, the D.O.) Is it as magic as we sometimes lead observers to believe?

The answers will be as varied as the boatmen you ask. No subject, except perhaps the tying down of loads, is so endlessly debated by boatmen as is the art of dutch oven cookery. I have found a few areas of agreement, however, that seem to indicate that almost anyone with a little patience can become a gourmet pastry-maker. Or, at the very least, you can manage a successful Bisquik shortcake, drown it in strawberries and whipped cream, and have a fail-safe, rave-reviewed, ego-boosting dessert.

A dutch oven is a heavy cast-iron or cast-alumnium pot. They come in various sizes and types; you should make sure that yours has three little legs and a lid with a raised lip for holding coals. A 12″ to 14″ D.O. seems the best size for river trips up to 20 people, and a 10″ is more efficient for smaller groups up to 10 or so. Recently aluminum D.O.'s are available which have the advantages of being lighter, rust-proof, and needing less heat, and the disadvantages of being more sensitive to heat variations and harder to cook with, and warping or even melting when exposed to excessive heat. Any cast-iron pot, including a D.O., must be kept dry and well oiled to keep it from rusting, and it can break if dropped. A cracked D.O. is nearly worthless.

The first step in using a D.O. is the preparation of coals. If you are unable to use charcoal briquets, try to prepare coals from a hardwood like oak, manzanita, or madrone. With briquets, 2 to 3 pounds per D.O. are needed; with hardwood, a couple of 4′-long, 2″-diameter limbs will usually do. Whatever you use, heating the coals on a grate *above* the fire makes transfer to the D.O. much easier. It also avoids getting sand and ash mixed in with the coals; it is necessary to keep sand and ash away from coals because they will keep the coals' heat away from the oven, and will keep air away from the coals, preventing them from burning hot. Heat the coals or wood only until they are just glowing or burning on their own; don't cook them. Also preheat the lid for five to ten minutes, and time your preparation so the batter will be ready when the coals are.

The first step in making any batter is gathering ingredients. Bisquik is a good base for almost anything and keeps you from having to carry many ingredients, but everything starts to taste the same before long if you use Bisquik exclusively. Making breads and cakes from scratch is amazingly easy if you carry flour, sugar or honey, baking powder and soda, dried milk, eggs, shortening or oil, and spices; most of these are part of a staples box anyway. Canned or fresh fruits, nuts, cheeses, etc., add variety, and Eagle brand milk is a great frosting base or topping just as it comes from the can. Make a very simple bread cookbook part of your commissary; be creative and eat well. When you get good you'll be eating pies, brownies, and even yeast breads —they will rise and get knocked down quite well on a raft during the day.

I believe in mixing the ingredients exactly as if you were cooking in a normal oven; however, a drier, thicker batter is preferred by many as it cuts the cooking time, although it also results in a heavier bread. Mixing the eggs thoroughly with the dry ingredients before adding water or milk will make a bread as light as possible. You should make enough batter to fill the D.O. ¼ to ⅓ full; grease the D.O. well and pour in the batter. In layered pastries like pineapple upside-down cake put the fruit, or whatever needs the least amount of cooking, on the bottom, and the batter on the top.

Next, find or make a level and flat spot for the D.O. to sit on. It must be in rocks or sand, not in grass or anything else that can catch fire. It should also be out of the wind or sheltered from it. Make sure the D.O. is level, then get the coals.

Heat is the most important thing in cooking. Two general principles about D.O. heat are that it should be concentrated on the top and around the outside edge of the D.O., and it should be evenly distributed in those areas. I use only about 20 to 25 percent of my coals beneath the D.O., close to but not touching the bottom and about an inch in from the outside edge. The rest I use on the top, right next to the lip of the lid all around the lid nearly touching each other. The hotter the oven needs to be, the more coals you use. Using charcoal, I've found that about 6 to 8 briquets on the bottom

and about 20 briquets on top is roughly equivalent to a 375°
oven. The most important thing is to keep most of the heat
on the top and almost all the heat right against the outside
lip; the only places I've seen a D.O. really burned are in
the middle and on the bottom. Taking a little time and care
in placement of the coals is essential to successful D.O.
cooking.

Periodically blowing the ashes off the coals will keep the
oven hot, and rotating (without lifting) the lid will even
out the heat. You can check the heat by rapidly and gently
lowering your hand (make sure it's dry and hasn't been near
the fire, so it's sensitive) from a couple of feet above to
within an inch of the lid. You should feel a sudden increase
in heat about 3 to 6 inches above the lid; with practice you'll
be able to tell just exactly the right heat level with your
hand, which is particularly important when you are using
hardwood coals rather than briquets.

Avoid lifting the lid and looking into the D.O. Every time
you look you lose 5 to 10 minutes of cooking time. The time
needed to cook will be close to whatever the recipe says,
from 15 minutes for biscuits up to an hour or more for pies
and brownies. I usually wait until about five minutes after
I first smell the ingredients cooking, and sometimes even
longer, before checking them. Check by lifting the lid and
quickly inserting a dry fork or stick in several places. If it
comes out clean, the cooking is done. Let the D.O. cool
some before serving and the pastry won't crumble badly.

Make sure you return the coals to the fire and put something over the spot where the D.O. was, because the ground
there will stay hot for quite a while. If at all possible, avoid
using soap to clean the D.O. Usually just wiping it out with
an oily paper towel will suffice, but if you have to use hot
water dry it well and re-oil it before putting it away.

The D.O. can also be used to cook roasts, stews, and
casseroles. Usually they are cooked for longer periods of
time with lower heat. Anything you cook in an oven you can
cook in a dutch oven. I've even known people to cook
Baked Alaska in a D.O. The hardest part of that is to keep
the ice cream hard-frozen up to the time when you put it in
the D.O.

The dutch oven has become an essential part of most
rafters' commissaries just as a century ago it was an essential

part of most miners' mule packs. Even today ancient, rusting D.O.'s are sometimes found at old abandoned camps and shacks along the Gold Rush rivers. So they have been around a long time and around rivers a long time. I cannot say that a D.O. is quite as magical as a river, but they do complement each other, and I would guess that rivers, rafters, and dutch ovens will be found together for many years to come.

WATER PURIFICATION

Many of our rivers are polluted. Countless towns and factories callously, stupidly dump waste into their neighboring rivers and streams. If you are downstream from any factories or towns, assume that the water is unfit to drink without purification. *Beware: Some rivers are so polluted that they are absolutely undrinkable under any circumstances; ask local people about water quality.*

When running a river with unpotable water, it is best either to carry your own water or to draw water from pristine sidestreams. If it is necessary to use water from the river, treat it with one of the following methods:

1. Use halazone tablets, closely following the directions on the label. Tablets are available from most drugstores.

2. Boil water vigorously for 3 minutes, aerate by pouring back and forth between two containers and let cool. If you wish, add a pinch of salt for improved taste.

3. Add 8 drops of undiluted chlorine bleach (5.25 percent sodium hypochlorite, i.e., straight Clorox or Purex) to each gallon of raw water. Double this dosage if water is cloudy:

Raw Water		*Chlorine*
Clear water	1 gallon	8 drops
Cloudy water	1 gallon	16 drops

Mix thoroughly by stirring or shaking and let stand a full 30 minutes before drinking or adding drink mixes. This half-hour waiting period is essential for complete disinfection and *improved* taste; chlorine is naturally a gas and, after its job is done, will dissipate considerably if given enough time, leaving little or no taste.

When added according to the above ratios, one fluid ounce of chlorine bleach purifies 30 gallons of cloudy or 60 gallons of clear water. Likewise, one pint of chlorine bleach purifies 480 gallons of cloudy or 960 gallons of clear water.

4. Add 1 drop of iodine from the first-aid kit (2-percent tincture of iodine) to each quart of raw water. Double this dosage if water is cloudy:

Raw Water		*Iodine*
Clear water	1 quart	1 drop
Cloudy water	1 quart	2 drops

Mix thoroughly by stirring or shaking and let stand a full 30 minutes before either drinking or adding drink mix. When used in these proportions, one fluid ounce of 2-percent tincture of iodine will disinfect 60 gallons of cloudy or 120 gallons of clear water.

5. In tropical or semitropical areas, do not rely on chlorine or chlorine-releasing compounds such as halazone. Instead, boil water, or when boiling is not feasible, use iodine water-purification tablets, following instructions on the label. Tablets of this sort are manufactured by Maltbie Laboratories Division of Wallace and Tierman, Inc., of Belleville, New Jersey.

DISHWASHING

As though animated with a will of their own, dirty pots seem to multiply prolifically in river camps, tormenting campers, causing even the brave to quake and jibber. There is only one way to tackle a problem of this wetness: Devise a dishwashing technique that is smooth and swift. In this method, above all, *be thorough.* For dirty dishware can transmit disease, and soap residue on dishes causes diarrhea, the great enemy of human happiness.

Use as few pots and cups as possible. Heat cans in water (see above). Take care not to burn food to pots, and pour water into pots as they are emptied. Have plenty of pot scrubbers, rubber gloves, and two or three big dishwashing pots or basins.

When working with pure water, wash dishes in the standard manner, i.e., with soap and hot water and rinse thoroughly. But when washing dishes in polluted water be aware that all dishes, cookware, and other utensils must be sanitized in a strong chlorine solution. To sanitize dishware, follow the three steps outlined below: *

1. *Wash* dishes, etc., in soap solution in hot water.
2. *Rinse* dishes, etc., in clean water (chlorine is not effective in soapy water or on surfaces with a soap film).
3. *Sanitize* dishes, etc., in chlorine sloution.
   a. For each gallon of water, add 2 teaspoons or 1 capful of chlorine bleach (Clorox, Purex).
   b. Completely immerse articles for 60 seconds in this solution and allow air to dry. DO NOT wipe dry unless articles have been fully immersed for at least 2 minutes, and then use only clean paper towels.
   c. Store in a clean, dry place, free from flies, etc. Dump soapy water at least 100 feet away from and well above the river.

GENERAL SANITATION

This is as good a place as any to mention that good general sanitation is extremely important on river trips. During the summer of 1972 there were serious outbreaks of shigellosis (a type of dysentery) on the Salmon and Colorado Rivers. Fortunately, no one died, but many people had to be flown out of the wilderness by helicopter and hospitalized, and hundreds suffered symptoms of severe abdominal cramps, fever, nausea, and so on. As it happened, only commercial rafting outfitters and their passengers were affected, but the dangers exist for private and commercial rafters alike. We must all exercise every precaution. Not only the disinfection of impure water, but other basic health practices, like washing hands after "using the bathroom," are vitally important. It is up to the seasoned people in every group to set a good example, for newcomers adopt a "monkey-see, monkey-do" attitude concerning basic sanitation. (See section on human waste in Chapter Six.)

---

* These steps have been endorsed by the Colorado River Health Committee.

NOTES ON FOOD

Here are a few additional tips on proper food handling and preparation:

• With the exception of canned and prepackaged food, wrap all food in suitable nonabsorbent material. This applies particularly to foods like lettuce, which, because they are not cooked, can readily harbor and transmit disease.

• Be especially wary when using fresh meat, the most spoilable of foods. Beef is least likely to spoil, while chicken and pork are the most susceptible.

• Food-service gear should be easily cleanable and should be kept clean.

• Single-service items like paper plates and cups reduce the risk of spreading disease.

• Do not use sheath knives or folding knives when preparing food.

• Food preparation surfaces should be smooth and clean.

• If you carry an ice chest, also carry a thermometer to check perishable-food temperatures inside the chest. Temperatures should be either below 45° or above 140° F, not in between. Bacteria multiply rapidly between these temperatures.

• Always sanitize dishes in a strong chlorine solution after washing them in polluted water (see above).

MENU FOR TEN-DAY TRIP

Day	Breakfast	Lunch	Dinner
1	fruit juice	sardines	steak
	eggs	crackers	corn on cob
	sausage	gorp	bread
	toast	drink	beverage
	beverage		pudding
2	hot cereal w/	squeeze cheese	canned ham
	raisins & dates	honey	pineapple
	French toast	Rye Krisp	buns
	beverage	gorp	beverage
		drink	
3	fruit juice	tuna	Mulligan stew
	cheese omelet	bread	cranberry sauce
	toast & jam	oranges	bread
	beverage	drink	beverage

Day	Breakfast	Lunch	Dinner
4	fruit pancakes sausage beverage	salami rye bread cookies gorp drink	pork & beans Boston brown bread baked potato beverage pudding
5	fruit juice bacon & eggs toast beverage	peanut butter cheese biscuits gorp drink	pea soup fish diced potatoes fruit beverage

6	Granola w/milk,
	  raisins, &
	  dates
	beverage
		canned lunch-
		  meat
		bread
		apples
		gorp
		drink
			tuna casserole
			  w/peas &
			  shredded
			  cheese
			bread
			beverage

7	fruit juice
	eggs
	hash-browned
	  potatoes
	beverage
		precooked
		  sausage
		jam
		crackers
		dried figs
		chocolate bar
		drink
			roast beef hash
			bean salad
			bread
			beverage

8	fruit
	bacon
	biscuits w/
	  honey
	beverage
		dried beef
		bread
		olives
		gorp
		drink
			spaghetti w/
			  tomato-sauce,
			  meat balls, &
			  shredded
			  cheese
			vegetable
			bread
			beverage

9	fruit
	mushroom
	  omelet
	toast
	beverage
		smoked oysters
		fig newtons
		gorp
		drink
			chicken noodle
			  soup
			creamed chipped
			  beef
			cranberry sauce
			beverage
			fruit cocktail

Day	Breakfast	Lunch	Dinner
10	fruit bacon biscuits w/ honey	deviled ham bread dates gorp drink	beef tamales refried beans corn chips beverage

LIST OF FOODS

Breakfast

eggs (fresh, dehy-
    drated, freeze
    dried)
canned sausage
canned bacon
Granola
wheat germ
hot cereal (instant
    oatmeal, cream of
    wheat, etc.)
pancake mix
instant hashed-brown
    potatoes
corn fritter mix
syrup

Lunch

nuts ⎫
raisins ⎬ gorp
M&Ms ⎭
non-melt chocolate
hard candy
cookies
fig newtons
salami
sardines
tuna
smoked oysters
salmon
jerky
canned lunch meat
precooked sausage
dates

dried figs
spreads
jam
peanut butter
jelly
malted milk tablets
shelled seeds
crackers
Ry-Krisp
wafers (rye, wheat)
melba toast
pretzels

Dinner

canned roast beef
canned chicken
meat (fresh, canned,
    smoked, dried,
    freeze-dried)
steak
chicken
fish
canned ham
pineapple
pork & beans
Boston brown bread
tuna
noodles
macaroni
rice, quick-cooking
roast beef hash
bean salad
spaghetti & meat
    balls

tomato sauce, paste
cream sauce
gravy and sauce
    mixes
onions (fresh, dried)
potatoes (fresh,
    instant; diced,
    mashed)
corn on the cob
vegetables (canned,
    fresh, dehydrated,
    dried, freeze-
    dried)
beef tamales
refried beans
corn chips
freeze-dried, one-dish
    meals
cranberry sauce

Desserts

instant pudding
marshmallows
popcorn (kernels)
date & nut bread
canned blackberries,
    raspberries

Beverages

coffee
tea
powdered milk
instant cocoa

chocolate drinks
Tiger's Milk
Hemo
Instant Breakfast
Wyler's lemonade,
    orangeade, etc.
Tang
instant iced tea
citric acid powder
canned tomato juice
orange juice mix
wine (carry in col-
    lapsible jug)
beer
pop

General

sugar (white, brown)
salt pork
cooking oil
cornmeal
margarine (liquid,
    cube)
catsup
relish
mustard
pickles
olives

mushrooms (fresh,
    canned, dried)
cheese (squeeze,
    hard)
jam
honey
bread (rolls, buns,
    biscuits, rye,
    pumpernickel)
biscuit mix
muffin mix
cornbread mix
breadsticks

Supplies

paper towels &
    napkins
paper plates, cups,
    etc.
dish soap
pot scrubber pads
aluminum foil
plastic bags

Fruit: fresh, canned,
    dried, dehydrated,
    freeze-dried

apple sauce

figs
prunes
dates
raisins
peaches
fruit cocktail
pears
apricots
apples
oranges
orange segments
tangerines
bananas

Flavorings

salt
pepper
onion flakes
garlic powder
celery flakes
parsley flakes
vegetable flakes
bacon flavored
    seasoning
maple flavoring
chicken and beef
    bouillon cubes
seasoning mixes

CHAPTER SIX

River Camping

CARE OF THE ENVIRONMENT

With more and more people journeying into the wilderness each year, it is imperative that all of us minimize our impact on the natural environment. A raft, by its very nature, leaves no trace of its passage down a river. But in those temporary toeholds, lunchsites and campsites, we must behave with intelligence and care if we are to preserve the Edenlike beauty of our wilderness rivers. Our goal must always be to leave each place pure and clean. To achieve this end every man, woman, and child among us must be particularly careful in dealing with four things: soap, garbage, human waste, and fire. Nature is delicate; let us treat it tenderly.

Soap

When bathing in a river or a tributary stream, *use only biodegradable soaps and shampoos*. When brushing teeth or using regular hand soap, use a bowl filled with water as a wash basin, and after brushing or washing, dump the water at least 100 feet

PHOTOGRAPH 25 Sunrise on the Rogue. (*Bob Krips Photo, courtesy of the American River Touring Association.*)

away from and well above the river. Beware: A single bar of soap can fill miles of river with suds.

Garbage

Burn all flammable trash and carry all unburnable garbage out of the wilderness in sturdy canvas bags. Do *not* bury cans; animals will dig them up and scatter them. Women should wrap sanitary napkins and tampons in plastic bags and place them in the garbage sack, for they will not burn or decompose in any reasonable amount of time.

Everyone in the wilderness should devote a pocket to litter: Whenever you see a bit of litter or have something to throw away, put it in the pocket. Later, use the flammable bits, things like wrappers, matches, and cigarette butts, to start your fire, and put the rest of the trash, things like tin foil and caps, into the garbage sack. If your provisions include pop and beer, keep a garbage bag handy during the day to receive the empty cans. Incidentally, unless garbage bags are made of tight-weave, heavy-duty canvas, they will develop holes through which small items like soda-can pulltabs may drop to the floor of the raft, perhaps resulting in a puncture.

Always leave each campsite as clean as, or, if possible, *cleaner* than you found it. Just before pushing off each morning, after everything is packed aboard the rafts, make a final search of your camp, checking for stray bits of paper, forgotten gear, and so on. *Remember:* Cigarette butts and soda- and beer-can pull-tabs *are litter.*

Human Waste

Bury human waste, after burning toilet paper, in holes which are 6 inches deep and 100 or, preferably, 200 feet from the river's high-water line. (Food scraps can also be buried in this manner.) This shallow depth is best because most of the soil elements that cause rapid decomposition of organic matter lie within 6 inches of the surface. Waste buried deeper disintegrates very slowly. Placing the hole at least 100 feet from the high-water line ensures that the waste will not be scooped up in the next spring flood to pollute the river.

In the Grand Canyon, where sheer cliffs often make it impossible to get beyond the high-water line and where the heavy foot traffic of large commercial groups on some of the small beaches tends to uncover shallow waste holes, park regulations require that holes be at least 2 feet deep, at least 6 feet above the average high-water line, at least 50 feet from the river bank, and at least 200 feet from any area normally used for camping. Extremely large groups, such as those travelling on pontoons in the Grand Canyon, carry chemical toilets.

If yours is a moderately large group, it may be wise to dig a long, shallow slit trench in a secluded spot that is an appropriate distance from the river. After each person makes his contribution and burns the toilet paper, he or she covers it over, and gradually the trench is filled in.

When done without haste, in a meditative mood, a good crap in the wilds can be a deeply satisfying, even spiritual experience, reaffirming one's oneness with the earth and with the cycles of life.

Fire

Fire should always be used with extreme care. Besides presenting the terrible danger of forest fire, campfires offer a more subtle threat: they can pollute river beaches with ash, charcoal, and soot scars on rocks. On free-flowing rivers, where the beaches are cleansed by each spring flood, it is all right to leave a fire's ashes so long as the fire has been thoroughly doused with water and buried under sand, gravel, or mineral earth. But on dam-controlled rivers, where there are usually no purifying annual floods, the beaches must be treated with utmost care and no trace of a fire should be left behind. This means that fires should be built in fire pans or on fireproof blankets of asbestos which will contain the ash and charcoal (see Chapter One). On large rivers this ash and charcoal—after being thoroughly burned and sifted for unburnable trash like pieces of tin foil—will have no impact on water quality or on the river banks if dumped into the swift midstream current. But on small rivers it is best to carry out all fire ash in the garbage bag. For a discussion of fire building, see below.

CHOOSING CAMPSITES

Any level area on the riverbank with a good docking place for rafts will serve as a campsite. If level places are scarce, you will have to accept what there is. But if they are plentiful, you can be choosy; the following is written with the latter case in mind.

Look for picturesque sandy beaches for lounging, hot springs for soaking, deep pools for swimming and diving, and caves for exploring. Avoid long carries of gear and water by picking sites close to the river. Consider availability of firewood. If the river water is not potable, try to camp at the mouths of pure side-streams.

In hot climates, choose campsites that provide shade protection from the morning sun. Otherwise, especially in the south-west, the temperature can shoot up to 90° F soon after the sun climbs above the horizon. When laying over for a day in a hot zone, camp in the cool of thick forest.

Reduce mosquito problems by staying upwind of swamps and thick brush where insects breed—bear in mind that winds blow upriver by day, and downriver by night. Also, if necessary, camp on high ground, where breezes keep insects away. When there is strong wind, though, select a sheltered site.

If rain seems likely, don't camp under trees; they will drip long after the rain stops. Also, when rain is a possibility, choose ground that slopes slightly to drain off rainwater; the slope should be moderate, however, for a steep pitch makes for bad sleeping. The ideal campsite in a rainstorm is inside a cave or under a rock overhang. There is nothing so delightful, so deeply transfixing as cuddling in a cave by a warm fire looking out at wind-blown rain strafing the river.

Avoid high grass; it is damp. Do not camp under dead, leaning trees or delicately balanced boulders that might topple in a strong wind. Because of the danger of tetanus, do not camp near the watering places of livestock. If severe cold is a problem, you'll find that it is warmer at night a little way up from the river. Beware of hollows; they attract mosquitoes, mist, and cold air. And if you like things to flow in a smooth and relaxed way, make camp early.

FIRE BUILDING

Build your campfire early, preferably right after unpacking, so that it can burn down to hot coals in time for cooking. For safety, always place the fire on bare sand, gravel, or mineral earth, and never on duff, moss, or against a tree or log. For convenience, locate the fire near a broad, flat rock to use as a table for pots and utensils. And for comfort, situate the campfire about 6 feet from some comfortable-looking rocks or logs to serve as backrests. In cool weather build the fire in the open, but in hot weather place it in the shade. To avoid smoke problems, place the fire off to one side of the campsite in such a way that neither the upstream day wind nor the downstream night wind will blow smoke through camp. If there is an old fire scar in a safe location, use it.

Once the site has been chosen, gather an adequate supply of dead wood: There is usually plenty. Look for fallen trees and for flood deposits, those natural caches of wood stacked neatly by past floods on the upstream side of rocks and trees along the river bank. Break long pieces of wood into usable chunks by striking them over rocks; no axe is necessary. Make a stack of wood big enough for both the evening and morning fires. If there is a chance of rain, cover this stack with a tarp before turning in for the night. If there is a cache of wood at a campsite when you arrive, river etiquette requires that you leave a similar cache when you depart. To come dragging into a camp late, tired, wet, and hungry, and find a neat stack of firewood is a heart-warming experience. When possible, leave these caches under the shelter of trees or overhanging rocks.

To start a fire, build a little pyramid of thin, dry twigs close over several fist-sized wads of paper. Light the paper in two or three places, and as the fire grows, add larger and larger sticks until the fire's size suits your fancy. If you have no paper, light a tiny bundle of dry twigs, leaves, or shavings, and as the delicate flame gains strength, quickly and deftly add twigs of increasing size until you have a crackling campfire of suitable dimension. When adding wood, by the way, put it on loosely so air can reach the flames.

Keep cooking fires small. For a hot fire, steadily add small pieces of wood, but for slow cooking use larger pieces. To keep the wilderness clean and prevent forest fires, never throw away used matches; either burn them in the fire or put them in the garbage sack. If you choose to use lighter fluid for starting fires, exercise great caution.

Be careful with that fire. Keep kerosene and other flammable liquids well away, and never leave the fire unattended, not even for a moment. If your fire does ever begin to spread, fight it immediately with shovels, water, and wet ponchos or tarps. Above all, extinguish fires thoroughly, stirring in water until *all* the ashes are cold to the touch. Then, as described above, deal with the ashes in a manner that does not harm the environment: On dam-controlled rivers, where fires are generally built in fire pans or on fireproof blankets, either pour the ashes into the swift midstream current or carry them out in the garbage bag. On free-flowing rivers, cover the water-soaked ashes with sand, gravel, or mineral earth. But in much-used campsites, regardless of the type of river, do not disturb established fire pits.

WET-WEATHER FIRE BUILDING: Wet-weather fires must be hot enough to dry out and ignite damp wood. The trick is getting the fire started. Use this strategy: Always carry plenty of wooden matches in a waterproof container. Whenever rain threatens, cover your stack of firewood with a poncho or tarp, and put some dry kindling, small sticks for fire building, in your tent. But if caught unaware or if pitching a new camp in wet weather, obtain dry wood by breaking the dead, lower branches off thickly needled conifer trees. In even the worst rainstorms dry wood can be found by looking under fallen trees and by breaking open dead logs.

All fire problems can be eliminated, by the way, with a couple of lightweight gas stoves. Stoves have zero impact on the environment.

RIVERBANK BATHING

On rivers too cold for swimming, line a pit with plastic sheeting, fill it with warm water, and settle in to soak. Or have someone pour bucketfuls of warm water over you. Have the water poured against the back of your neck in such a way that it divides evenly and slides smoothly down front and back—an unforgettable sensation!

THE RIVER SAUNA

Nothing warms and loosens a group in the evening like a river sauna. In the course of the close sharing of heat and the refreshing dip in the river that follows, even the stiffest group plunges into intimacy. A sauna tent is made by suspending a large tarp (at least 12 by 14 feet) between rocks, trees, or upright oars in the manner shown in Drawing 65. The tie-off points at the four corners may be grommets or makeshift tufts. To make a tuft, press a golfball-sized stone against the underside of the tarp just where you want a corner to be, fold the tarp down around and pinch in below the stone, and then tie your line around this pinched neck, trapping the stone in such a way that the line cannot pull free. To prevent heat loss, hang the tarp so that the edges drag slightly on the ground all around.

The heat source is a metal bucket of hot rocks—these are heated until glowing red and are plucked from the fire with care so that no ash or charcoal get into the bucket. A bucket of water and a dipper cup provide steam. When everything is ready, get your group in under the tarp; etiquette dictates that everyone be

DRAWING 65 A RIVER SAUNA

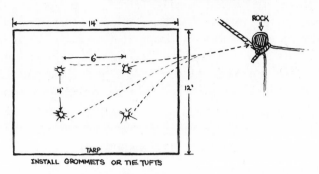

nude except for a wrap-around towel. Under the tarp splash water on the rocks for steam. If the tarp edges lift up, pin them down with your fanny. Things will warm up fast. When the time comes, dash out and jump in the river. *Note:* Always check out the place where you will dive beforehand during daylight. Make sure there are no rocks, snags, strong currents, or other hazards. Also, make sure just before entering the sauna that the water level has not suddenly dropped. One poor rafter once burst from a sauna on the banks of the Stanislaus, dove into a pool that he had checked out previously, and broke his neck on a submerged rock: The river had dropped 3 feet since sunset.

A FEW TIPS FOR SAFETY

HIKING: Never hike alone. Always leave word with those in camp as to where you are going, and always carry a snakebite kit. *Be careful:* The walls of river canyons are generally composed of loose, crumbling rock, and delicately balanced boulders are common. The best and safest hikes are usually up side canyons.

SWIMMING: Swim only in lakelike calms or eddies, and never, without good reason, just above rapids. River currents are often stronger than is apparent, and can sweep a swimmer off and away. Do not swim near whirlpools, but if you are caught in one, it is generally best to relax and let it flush you through to the surface. Always check depth before diving.

WATER SCOOPING: When drawing water from the river, take care not to scoop up any mud puppies, a type of water salamander. These reddish-brown water lizards are common in warm-water rivers and are quite harmless—except when cooked in your food or boiled in the tea or coffee water, in which case they are fatally poisonous.

BEARS

Bears are rarely encountered, but if you do meet one, treat it with great caution and respect. It can be dangerous and unpredictable.

Most bears will sprint away at the first sight of man. But if, on a side hike, you come across a bear that stands his ground, don't panic and run, for this may excite the bear and invite pursuit. Slowly put down any food or candy you might be carrying and retreat, keeping downhill from the bear and glancing around for escape routes and nearby trees to climb. If the bear advances in a threatening manner, either scoot up a tree or lie still on the ground, with knees drawn up and hands protecting the back of your head. In either case, stay put until you are certain the bear has gone.

In bear country, never keep anything in your tent that a bear might consider food. Burn out all tin cans and burn all food scraps after each meal. Make bear caches by suspending food at least 10 feet above the ground and well away from tree trunks. Never feed or get too close to a bear. Avoid pitching camp near bear droppings. Choose campsites with handy trees to climb. If a bear does enter your camp, frighten it away by banging pots, blowing a whistle, yelling, and, at night, flashing lights.

Be aware that female bears with cubs are particularly dangerous. Never approach a cub, even if it seems to be alone, for the mother may attack suddenly. Evidence suggests that bears are most likely to attack women wearing scented cosmetics, hair spray, or deodorant, and women in menstrual period. Fortunately, most bears are far more afraid of man than we are of them.

DRAWING 66   BLACK BEAR (Ursus Americanus)

The black bear is the native U.S. bear and is common in our wild areas. Generally mild, it attacks only when startled or when it thinks you are withholding food. Black bears weigh up to 600 pounds and are up to 5 feet long. Their color varies from black to brown to cinnamon, and they often have a white patch at the throat. Their claws are short and well-adapted to climbing. Like the grizzly, the black bear eats practically everything, including berries, grass, roots, herbs, fish, carrion, and whatever mammals it can catch. The nose of the black bear is longer than that of the grizzly, and black bears have no shoulder hump.

DRAWING 67   GRIZZLY BEAR (Ursus arctos horribilis)

Grizzly bears are an endangered species and are found only in the Yellowstone area, Glacier National Park, Alaska, and the Canadian wilderness. Grizzlies are big, mean, and unpredictable, and sometimes attack without warning or provocation. Though they sometimes may weigh as much 1100 pounds, the average size ranges from 450 to 800 pounds. Their color varies greatly, but each hair is usually white-tipped. Their claws are long and ill-suited to climbing. Grizzlies may be distinguished from other bears by their concave or dished faces and prominent shoulder humps. Both black bears and grizzlies have a keen sense of smell and will search single-mindedly for food and candy once they pick up its scent.

PART II

The Rivers:
A Guidebook

Introduction

Described here are some of the finest rafting rivers in North America. Long, rugged, isolated, and intensely beautiful, these runs should be worked up to gradually and should be attempted only by those who are experienced, well-equipped, and cautious. The novice, unless he goes with an experienced friend or a white-water school, should begin on easier streams. Excellent easier rivers can be located by consulting the guidebooks mentioned in the individual river bibliographies below. Most of the river guidebooks listed are regional, and cover not only the particular river included here but also a host of the finer runs of all levels of difficulty in their areas.

Everyone who runs rivers should understand the difficulty-rating scales and what is meant by river gradient and water volume.

DIFFICULTY-RATING SCALES

Two scales are now being used to rate the difficulty of both rivers and individual rapids. One, the International Scale, ranges from I to VI; I is easy and VI unrunnable.* This scale is used not only throughout most of North America but also in Europe and

---

* There is some disagreement on whether VI is flatly unrunnable or "almost" unrunnable. See following footnote.

elsewhere. The other scale, called by some the Western Scale, ranges from 1 to 10; 1 is easy and 10 almost unrunnable. Invented by Grand Canyon authority Doc Marston, this latter scale is used on a number of Western rivers, foremost among which is the Colorado. The International Scale is used in almost all river guidebooks, while the Western Scale is used only on the scroll maps of Leslie Jones and in a few other guides to certain Western rivers. In the river descriptions that follow the International Scale is used. Although I personally favor the 1-to-10 scale, the point is to create a single, universal scale understood by all, and the International Scale, which is also called the International River Classification System, is obviously it.

Respect these scales. Even a class II rapid requires skill and can cause serious trouble. For instance, a class II rapid on the Middle Fork of the Salmon called Velvet Falls (a #3 on the Western Scale) once flipped an entire party of rafts, terrorizing the group to such an extent that rather than continue down the river they packed their gear miles back to the nearest road. The accompanying chart explains these scales and shows how they relate to one another.

RAPID AND RIVER RATING SYSTEM

This chart is based in part on a similar chart by Leslie Jones and in part on the American Whitewater Association River Classification System.

International Scale		Western Scale
	Flat water	0
I	Easy. Waves small; passages clear; no serious obstacles.	1,2
II	Medium. Rapids of moderate difficulty with passages clear. Requires experience plus fair outfit and boat.	3,4
III	Difficult. Waves numerous, high, irregular; rocks; eddies; rapids with passages clear though narrow, requiring expertise in maneuver; scouting usually needed. Requires good operator and boat.	5,6

IV	Very difficult. Long rapids; waves powerful, irregular; dangerous rocks; boiling eddies; passages difficult to scout; scouting mandatory first time; powerful and precise maneuvering required. Demands expert boatman and excellent boat and outfit.	7,8
V	Extremely difficult. Exceedingly difficult, long and violent rapids, following each other almost without interruption; riverbed extremely obstructed; big drops; violent current; very steep gradient; close study essential but often difficult. Requires best man, boat, and outfit suited to the situation. All possible precautions must be taken.	9,10
VI or U	Unrunnable *	U

A river's difficulty rating is usually based upon the ratings of its most difficult rapids. Exceptions to this occur when single rapids far exceed the general level of difficulty. In such cases the overall rating may be based on the lower, general level of difficulty, and the individual tough rapids are indicated by a little notation under the main rating; for example, II_4 signifies that a stretch of river is generally of medium difficulty but has one or two very difficult rapids.

Because rapid and river ratings are determined by experts who slip with ease down difficult rivers, some ratings are lower than they should be. What an expert considers "medium difficulty" may be extremely tough for an intermediate or novice boater. So be careful. Bear in mind that all ratings, at best, provide only a rough estimate of difficulty, and remember that high water levels, cold water, and poor equipment greatly increase ratings. Do not attempt a river or rapid you are not ready to

---

* Some boaters, particularly those in the East, define a class VI as almost unrunnable but navigable by experts *at risk of life*. Other river people, including many boaters in the West, who view class V water as, sanely speaking, unrunnable, regard class VI as absolutely unrunnable. Thus, in some instances, a Western V is equivalent to an Eastern VI. This disagreement, it seems to me, is largely academic. Before a boater gets anywhere near class V water he should have acquired years of experience and should have developed a sound judgment for what he can and cannot handle.

handle, and, if you have no experience, make your way in the company of experienced people.*

GRADIENT

Measured in foot drop per mile, a river's gradient, or slope, provides a rough indication of its speed and level of difficulty. Rivers with gradients less than 10 feet per mile are usually slow and easy, while rivers with gradients of more than 20 feet per mile are usually fast, difficult, and dangerous. However, this is not always true. The Colorado of the Grand Canyon, for instance, though it has a gradient of less than 10 feet per mile, is an extremely challenging piece of water because it alternately pools up in long calms and crashes down in gigantic rapids. Some of its calms are 10 miles long, and the rapids are correspondingly difficult. An exception in the other extreme is the East Fork of the Carson, which has a gradient of 27 feet per mile and yet is relatively easy because it flows smoothly with little turbulence. Although there is no definite cut-off line, rivers with gradients steeper than 50 feet per mile generally have so many rocks and falls that they are, for all practical purposes, unrunnable for rafters. Kayakers paddle and portage to a different tune, though, and sometimes run streams that drop as much as 100 feet per mile.

VOLUME

Just as the skier is concerned with snow depth and the sailor with wind speed, the rafter focuses on river volume. Water volume is the crucial variable in his life: Too little turns a river into a long, narrow rock patch; too much creates a rampaging monster. To measure this ever-flowing variable, river people use the volume/time unit of cubic feet per second (cfs). Casually referred to as "second feet," cfs indicate the amount of water flowing past any given point along a river in one second. Most of the better rafting rivers have between 800 and 10,000 cfs; 800 cfs is small, 5000 cfs large, and 10,000 cfs somewhat gigantic.

---

* I take a number of trips each rafting season and welcome letters from people interested in coming along. Write my outfit: Whitewater Expeditions, 1811 Tulare St., Richmond, Calif. 94805.

Some rivers are runnable when as low as 350 cfs and others when as high as 400,000, but these are freak extremes.

The volume of a free-flowing river fluctuates greatly in the course of a year. In general, peak flow occurs during spring run-off, gradually decreasing flows follow through summer and early fall, and then water levels pick up somewhat during the rain and cold of late fall and winter. Of course, flows always increase for a while whenever it rains. Cold weather alone, unaccompanied by rain, may also cause a slight rise in flow rates by decreasing evaporation and plant transpiration, called, collectively, evapo-transpiration.

Good flows and weather for rafting are found anywhere from April to November, depending on the river and the climate. Of free-flowing rivers, some are runnable throughout this time, but many are runnable only during either spring or summer. Those raftable only in the spring often resemble rocky creeks during the drier months, and those raftable only in the summer are, in the spring, surging floods sown with gargantuan holes and dotted with deadly strainers in the form of half-submerged trees and brush. Clearly, a river's character can alter drastically with changes in water level. As a river's volume fluctuates, to quote river sage Carl Trost, "Rapids can appear and vanish in a meta-morphosis that may give the river entirely different personalities, from boulder dodging, to big-water maneuvering, to flood condi-tions."

Above all else, *beware of spring floods.* Do not attempt any river in spring flood unless you know for a fact that it is runnable at this time. And even if it is navigable, approach it with great caution, for its difficulty rating will generally be at least one or two points higher than normal. This also goes for small rivers. Even though a creek suddenly seems large enough to run, do not shoot it without thoroughly scouting it first. Creeks in flood often spell red, muddy death; many seasoned river people have drowned, ironically, in their local, flood-swollen creeks. The safest way to locate rivers runnable in the spring is through reliable river guidebooks.

Dam-controlled rivers are a somewhat different story. Although they are usually higher in spring than in summer, they are rarely in flood. Their volume fluctuates not so much with nature as with the demand for electricity. Electrical need is generally greater during the week and lower on weekends, and flows vary accordingly. By distributing high spring flows out over the summer, many dams do extend the rafting season on their rivers (provided they do not, as they often do, flood the runnable stretch), but there is something disturbing about these giant spigots. On the Saturdays and Sundays of middle and late summer, the dam-controlled Tuolumne River in California, for example, is a trickle among the rocks with a flow of 100 cfs, just enough to keep the fish alive. But on Monday mornings, within the space of a half hour, the flow picks up to 1000 cfs, the rocks submerge, and the Tuolumne becomes a river. This sparkling stream, like almost everyone and everything else between Wall Street and Waikiki, keeps regular hours and works a five-day week.

Volume largely determines power. A small river of 1000 cfs simply does not have the speed or force possessed by a large river of 4000 cfs or more. Although it may have rock-strewn channels and other difficulties, the small, weak river tends to be easier to run because it allows greater maneuvering and is more forgiving of mistakes. The large river, on the other hand, is generally more difficult because its power and speed minimize control and make obstacles, even though fewer in number, harder to avoid. And once hit, big-river obstacles tend to be devastating. As a general rule, then, rivers are easier to run at moderate rather than high volume.

RIVER TRIP PERMITS

Within the last few years, some of the most popular rivers have been threatened by overuse. As a result, permit systems have ben instituted on these rivers that require boaters to write for permits well in advance of their intended launch dates. Use is thereby limited, because only a certain number of permits is issued each season.

As this is written, private rafters are required to have permits on about a half-dozen rivers; commercial rafters must have permits on far more rivers. But in the future, permits for private trips will probably be required on additional rivers, so when you are planning a trip, write ahead asking if permits are needed. The names and addresses of the agencies managing the rivers covered here that now require permits or are likely to require permits in the future are given in the guides that follow. To check the permit policy on rivers not mentioned in this book, do as follows: If the river flows through a national park, forest or monument, write that park, forest, or monument headquarters; if the river is on undesignated government land, write the presiding district office of the Bureau of Land Management.

Although they may seem incongruous with the wilderness, permits can actually be beneficial. When handled correctly, permits do more than prevent overcrowding. They make a purer wilderness experience possible by excluding things that do not belong in the wilds, like jet boats, and they generally help to preserve rivers in their pristine state so that the unborn generations of our children will be able to enjoy the same wilderness adventures available to us. After all, who wouldn't prefer to write ahead and perhaps wait a while to run that big river, if he and his companions can thereby be assured of a wild and solitary experience?

But these permit systems must be managed wisely. Permits should remain free. They should not be used to legislate all risk out of the sport, although they probably should be used to prevent or at least warn against sure suicide. And they should distinguish the private rafter from the commercial outfitter. Private groups of from four to eight people simply do not have the environmental impact of large commercial groups of twenty, thirty, or more. As a consequence, the private rafter should neither be subject to the same restrictions, nor should he be forced to stay in established campsites, provided he has the means, as outlined in Chapter Six, to camp in an ecologically sound manner.

The private rafter has the dedication to acquire gear and skill; he has the courage to meet the river on its own terms. For him and for everyone else who yearns to someday shoot wildwater on his own, our rivers are a last frontier, a raw place of elemental living and real adventure. Since the time of Huck Finn, our rivers have haunted and beckoned to the American imagination, and we the private rafters, the true sons and daughters of the pioneers, must get to those rivers. Our style has changed: Today we do not come to conquer and we are careful to leave no mark, no trace of our passage. But we must be able to taste, to have access to those waves, to those deep pools; they are special to us, they live in our minds, and we must see for ourselves, again and again, that they are real.

ON SHUTTLES

To "set up the shuttle" is to arrange to have a vehicle waiting for you at the take-out at the end of a trip. To do this many rafters drop people and gear off at the put-in, drive to and park at the take-out, and then return to the put-in via bicycle, motorbike, plane, or a second car. Yet another way to set up the shuttle is to hire local people to drive your vehicle(s) around to the take-out. Waitresses and gas station attendants in nearby towns are often willing to drive shuttle for a reasonable fee. Also, rafting companies operating in the area can generally put one in touch with reliable local drivers. Reaching an agreement with a prospective driver about what constitutes a reasonable fee can be an interesting experience. The encounter inevitably smacks of the ancient rivalry between city slicker and country yokel, and each participant, to feel successful, must believe that he has gotten the best of the other.

ABOUT THIS GUIDE

This is not in any sense a mile-by-mile or rapid-by-rapid guide to rivers. Most of the runs discussed are far too long and have far too many complex rapids to permit such detailed coverage here. Rather, for each river this guide provides an overview, a summary of facts important to the river runner and a bibliography of maps, detailed, mile-by-mile guidebooks, and other literature treating the river and surrounding area. Thus, this material is not complete in itself; rather, it is a guide to guides. True, in places it does go into lengthy detail about certain particular rapids; but where this occurs, count the description as over and above the normal, and please do not consider the river less worthy, where such detail is not given.

The number of days suggested for each trip is based on an average progress of from 10 to 20 miles per day. Although it is possible to do 30 or more miles each day by pushing off early and staying on the river until late afternoon, a slower pace adds greatly to a trip by allowing time for fishing, swimming, exploring caves and side canyons, writing, carousing, and just lazing under the open sky. Although most of the runs covered here are long, many may be done in sections. Where this is possible, mention is made of midway access points. The raft sizes appropriate for a particular river may vary with different water levels and, in any case, are often subject to differences of opinion. The lengths suggested merely indicate the sizes commonly used with success. The flow figures cited are based on long-term U.S. Geological Survey surface-flow records; hence, they reflect averages and may not encompass extreme fluctuations caused by variations in rainfall or snow melt. For information on how to obtain U.S.G.S. quadrangle maps and Leslie Jones's fine scroll maps, see Chapter One. Because road directions are sometimes unobtainable from other sources, I include them here. If you want to avoid becoming hopelessly lost, I suggest you use these directions in conjunction with state and county road maps. Finally, the words right and left refer to the right and left banks as seen by the boater looking downstream.

I have personally run most of the rivers covered in this guide. With those rivers I have not run myself, I have been generously helped by veteran river people closely familiar with the runs. Several of these people are themselves the authors of river guidebooks. In this regard I would like to again thank Bob Burrell, co-author with Paul Davidson of *Wildwater West Virginia*, Eben Thomas, author of *No Horns Blowing* and *Hot Blood and Wet Paddles*, and Bob Palzer, co-author with his wife Jody of *Whitewater; Quietwater*. In addition, I would like to thank Tim Lawton, Mike Rettie, Jerry Meral, and Harry Chest, intrepid rivermen all.

A WORD OF CAUTION

When planning a run down one of these rivers, it is essential that you not only obtain the maps and guides mentioned but also inquire of local rangers, residents, or water-resource agencies about current conditions—particularly volume—on the river. *If you are a novice, do not rush out onto these rivers; you may kill yourself.* Most of the rivers covered here should be attempted only by seasoned rafters who have perfected their whitewater skills in the course of many trips on less treacherous streams.

Due to changing river conditions and the widely varying levels of individual skill, neither this author nor the publisher assumes any responsibility for those using this guide. Be careful and always use good judgment.

Eastern Rivers

YOUGHIOGHENY

Friendly, lovely, clean, the Youghiogheny (pronounced yŏk a GAY nee) is the delight of the East. Dam-controlled and full-bodied, it is not only runnable but downright feisty throughout summer and fall, and as a result it has become popular and crowded. The Youghiogheny, particularly in the Loop, is turbulent and powerful, dropping fast down a bed of rugged boulders and ledges.

This river runs through the heart of George Washington country. In fact, George was one of the Youghiogheny's first paddlers. In 1754 he ran the upper stretch from Confluence down to Ohiopyle, where he sensibly declined to tackle the boiling Loop.

LOCATION: Laurel Highlands of southwestern Pennsylvania about 45 miles south of Pittsburgh

PUT-IN AND TAKE-OUT: Ohiopyle to Stewarton

FAVORABLE SEASON: Late spring through late fall, excluding periods of high water

DIFFICULTY AT NORMAL SUMMER FLOW: III–IV

DIFFICULTY AT HIGH WATER: V to U

VOLUME: 600–10,000 cfs

GRADIENT: Overall 26 feet per mile. In the mile-long Loop at the head of the run, the river drops an astounding 100 feet. In the remaining 6 miles the drop is 13 feet per mile.

LENGTH: 7 river miles

TIME: 1 day (A longer run is possible if you continue on downstream.)

RAFT SIZE: 12 to 16 feet

WEATHER: Generally warm and sunny in midsummer. Cooler and variable in spring and fall. Wildflowers in spring; rich colors in fall. The Yough's water is *always* cold by Eastern standards.

WATER CONDITIONS: The Youghiogheny is controlled by the dam at Confluence and is generally runnable all year, except during high water. The Army Corps of Engineers tries to gauge releases from the dam so as to minimize dangerously high water and provide adequate flow when the level would otherwise be too low. U.S.G.S. records show that from December through May the flow averages from 2000 to 4000 cfs and sometimes surges to a murderous 10,000 cfs. From June through November the flow generally averages from 800 to 1000 cfs and sometimes swings higher or lower depending on rainy and dry spells.

There are two gauges. One is located on the downstream side of the center pier of the Route 381 bridge at Ohiopyle. This gauge reads in feet and can be interpreted as follows:

Reading	Flow	Comment
0.9'		low but OK. (The river rarely drops below the 1 foot mark.)
1.3'	750 cfs	maximum for open canoes
2.5'	2,300 cfs	River changes character, from rocky to powerful, heavy water.
4.0'	5,600 cfs	very powerful, almost continuous rapids in some stretches

This chart is from the Penn State Outing Club's *Select Rivers of Central Pennsylvania* mentioned in "Guidebooks and Literature" for the Youghiogheny.

A recorded gauge reading can be heard by phoning (412) 644-2890. This reading is taken at Confluence and is roughly 0.9′ higher than the gauge above. The information on these gauges is from *Wildwater West Virginia,* cited below.

In addition to these gauges, check the levels of the Meadow and Cucumber runs. These tributaries below the falls at Ohiopyle sometimes add enormously to the river's volume.

When the Youghiogheny is too high, many rafters in this area run nearby tributaries, the Casselman or the Laurel Hill, both in Pennsylvania. For detailed information about these small but challenging rivers, consult *Select Rivers of Central Pennsylvania.*

RIVER HAZARDS: This is a run for the experienced intermediate. The Yough is heavy, has many complicated rapids, and requires much scouting.

At the head of the run is the famous Loop, where the river cascades downward 100 feet in a single mile. Although an expert familiar with the run can shoot the Loop in about 12 minutes, newcomers should plan to spend a few hours here, carefully scout-

PHOTOGRAPH 26   Running the Youghiogheny, the most popular river in the East. (*Photo by Michael Fedison, courtesy of Wilderness Voyageurs.*)

ing each tough rapid. Entrance Rapid, the Loop's first rapid, is a long, winding course of tricky currents with a giant rock, called Sugarloaf Boulder, hunkering in midstream waiting to undo the unskilled boater. Next is Cucumber Drop; scout this on the left bank. Continue through the Loop cautiously, always scouting when in doubt. The Loop's final rapid, Railroad, is mean.

Below the Loop, the next 2 miles are open and easily read. Then, roughly 3 miles below the Loop's railroad bridge, is Dimples Rapid, which should be scouted. Here the river narrows against the left bank and crashes into a midstream boulder. A mile below Dimples is Pipe Stem Rapid, where the river again presses against the left bank and disappears behind a large boulder. For a detailed account of this river, see *Wildwater West Virginia.*

An East-West comparison: The Youghiogheny is similar to but a bit more difficult than California's upper Stanislaus.

Road directions: Put in at the Ohiopyle boat-launch area just below the falls. Take care to leave your car in a regular parking area, not along the busy road.

To reach the Stewarton take-out, go 6 miles north on Route 381. Then go left at the Route 589 crossing located at the top of a hill with a church on the left. Go left again at the cemetery onto Route 804. Descend along this steep road, go left at the fork, and continue to the take-out at the end. Take care to park your shuttle car where it will neither block driveways nor hamper traffic. While you are at the take-out, walk down to the river and study the place closely, so that you will be able to recognize it when you come floating down the river. Otherwise, it is easy to miss.

Camping: Campsites are available in Ohiopyle State Park. For information about the park, write Park Superintendent, Park Office, Ohiopyle State Park, Ohiopyle, Pa. 15470.

An intriguing local spot: Just a few miles from Ohiopyle is Frank Lloyd Wright's Fallingwater, an enchanting home built around an idyllic waterfall. Fallingwater may be visited from April 1st through November. Tickets and reservations are necessary. Call the Western Pennsylvania Conservancy at (412) 329-4603 for information.

MAPS

U.S.G.S. quadrangles: The entire run is covered by 15' Conflu-
ence (Penn.), or, for more detailed coverage, get 7½' Ohiopyle
(Penn.), 7½' Fort Necessity (Penn.), and 7½' Mill Run (Penn.).
For information on how to order these maps, see Chapter One.

To make the shuttle easier, send for a free Fayette County
Highway Map. Write to PennDOT Publications Sales Section,
Room #117, A,T&S Bldg., Commonwealth and Forester Sts., Har-
risburg, Pa. 17120. Or call (717) 787-5967.

GUIDEBOOKS AND LITERATURE

Canoeing Whitewater River Guide by Randy Carter. A good
guide. Describes the access points, gradient, difficulty, length,
scenery, and other aspects of 95 whitewater rivers in the Virginia,
West Virginia, and Great Smokey Mtn. areas. 1967, revised 1974.
$5.25 postpaid. Available from Appalachian Books, Box 248, 2938
Chainbridge Rd., Oakton, Va. 22124.

Select Rivers of Central Pennsylvania by the Penn State Outing
Club. Available from President, Canoe Division, Penn State Outing Club, Recreation Building, University Park, Pa. 16802.

Wildwater West Virginia by Bob Burrell and Paul Davidson.
The finest, most readable, most literate river guide I have ever
seen. Covers the Youghiogheny and 58 whitewater rivers in West
Virginia. Includes difficulty classification, gradient, time, etc. Provides thorough, fascinating discussions of the rivers and their
surrounding areas, and covers in detail the shuttle, water-level information, and hazards for each run. This guide was written from
the viewpoint of kayakers and decked canoeists, but so long as one
bears this in mind and makes allowances here and there, the guide
applies also to rafting. 1972. $5.25 postpaid. Available from Bob
Burrell, 1412 Western Ave., Morgantown, W.Va. 26505.

Whiskey Rebels: The Story of a Frontier Uprising by Leland
Dewitt Baldwin. Pittsburgh, Pa.: University of Pittsburgh Press,
1939. Map on end papers.

CHEAT

Moving through a steep-walled canyon strewn with boulders and
ledges, the free-flowing Cheat offers a nearly continuous series of
rapids that demand intricate maneuvering in heavy water. Even

though the water is lightly polluted with mine waste, this is a canyon of striking beauty.

LOCATION: Allegheny Mountains in northeastern corner of West Virginia, roughly 25 miles east of Morgantown, Preston County

PUT-IN AND TAKE-OUT: Albright, Route 26 bridge, to Jenkinsburg bridge

FAVORABLE SEASON: Generally, mid-April to early June. Too high in early spring; too low after first or second week in June, unless rainy weather predominates. Comes up again in mid-October.

DIFFICULTY AT MODERATE WATER: IV

DIFFICULTY AT HIGH WATER: V to U

VOLUME: 100–8000+ cfs

GRADIENT: 25 feet per mile

LENGTH: 11 river miles

TIME: 1 day

RAFT SIZE: 12 to 16 feet

WATER CONDITIONS: During winter and spring, this free-flowing river averages from 2000 to 3000 cfs and occasionally rises to 8000 cfs or more. During summer and fall, the flow averages from 350 to 700 cfs, with occasional radical variations due to rainfall. The best flows and weather for rafting occur from April until sometime in June. The river is generally too low through the summer, except during periods following heavy rain in the headwaters. Then, late in the fall, the flow picks up, and the river again becomes runnable. Throughout the year, the flow is subject to sudden change and on occasion fluctuates 2 feet or more within a few hours.

There is a boater's gauge on the Albright bridge. Current readings from this gauge may be obtained by calling Marvin Morgan's gas station in Albright; call (304) 329-1748. Because this gauge is located at a wide spot and some of the canyon's chutes are extremely narrow, a 2-inch change on the gauge can indicate a 2-foot difference in some of the narrow chutes downriver. Readings from 1½ to 2½ feet make for good rafting. Above 3 feet, the river undergoes a vast transformation: The waves and holes become larger, the rapids run into each other, and the current gains massive power. In short, extremely dangerous class V conditions are created. Even expert boaters stay off the river above 4 feet.

Up-to-date flow information for the Cheat can also be obtained by calling the Weather Service in Pittsburgh. Either ask for or listen to the *Parsons* reading by dialing (412) 644-2890. The Albright boater's gauge reading can be calculated by subtracting 2.3 from the Parsons reading and then multiplying by 4/3. The Weather Service will also give an Albright reading, but it is *not* the same as the boater's gauge and I don't know how the two correlate.

One of the few fatalities involving a person wearing a lifejacket occurred on the Cheat when an inexperienced rafter attempted the run during high water. High water generally occurs in the early spring; stay out of the canyon at this time. *Note:* When this section is too high, go just upstream and try the stretch from Rowlesburg to the Albright power dam. For details, see *Wildwater West Virginia*.

RIVER HAZARDS: The Cheat is dangerous and powerful, and should be attempted only by experts and those in the company of experts. The intricate, heavy rapids are nearly continuous; each is separated from the next by only a short calm. Because boulders often block the rafter's view, many of these rapids cannot be read from upstream and so must be scouted. Be prepared to devote several hours to scouting. Because of the sheer number and complexity of the rapids, even a rough account is not feasible here. For a discussion of some of the more difficult rapids, see *Wildwater West Virginia*.

As with any very difficult river, the Cheat is best approached in the company of experienced people *already familiar with the run*. One outfit that runs paddle-raft trips through the canyon is Mountain Streams & Trails Outfitters, Box 106, Ohiopyle, Pa. 15470. Phone (412) 329-8810.

ROAD DIRECTIONS: Put in at the Albright bridge, found where W.Va. Route 26 crosses the river. The shuttle is long and subtle. Drive south on Route 26 to Kingwood, and then west on Route

7 to Masontown. In Masontown turn right at the drugstore at the corner of Main and Depot Streets. When you come to the fork, go left toward Bull Run and a second fork. Go right at this second fork, down the steep, narrow road to Jenkinsburg. The take-out, which consists of a steep, muddy bank, a trail, and a parking area, is about 100 yards downstream from the bridge.

MAPS

U.S.G.S. quadrangles: The run is covered by 7½′ Kingwood (W.Va.) and 7½′ Valley Point (W.Va.).

To make the shuttle easier, send for a road map of Preston County. Maps are available for a nominal fee from West Virginia Department of Highways, Advanced Planning Division, Charleston, W.Va. 25311.

GUIDEBOOKS AND LITERATURE

Canoeing Whitewater River Guide by Randy Carter. $5.25 postpaid. Available from Appalachian Books, Box 248, 2938 Chainbridge Rd., Oakton, Va. 22124.

Wildwater West Virginia by Bob Burrell and Paul Davidson. $5.25 postpaid. Available from Bob Burrell, 1412 Western Ave., Morgantown, W.Va. 26505.

NEW

Known to the Indians as the River of Death, the New impresses all who run it. Now yawning calm, now gnashing wild, it offers the very best in daring river adventure. The 29-mile stretch discussed here can be split into two one-day trips, or can be run in one continuous voyage lasting two or three days. The water is warm and the thickly wooded riverbanks afford excellent camping.

LOCATION: Allegheny Mountains of West Virginia about 40 miles southeast of Charleston

UPPER SECTION

PUT-IN AND TAKE-OUT: McCreery beach, near Prince, to Thurmond

DIFFICULTY AT NORMAL SUMMER FLOW: III

DIFFICULTY AT HIGH WATER: IV

GRADIENT: 10 feet per mile

LENGTH: 15 river miles

TIME: 1 day

LOWER SECTION

PUT-IN AND TAKE-OUT: Thurmond to Fayette Station Bridge

DIFFICULTY AT NORMAL SUMMER FLOW: V

DIFFICULTY AT HIGH WATER: V to U

GRADIENT: 12 feet per mile

LENGTH: 14 river miles

TIME: 1 day

BOTH SECTIONS

FAVORABLE SEASON: Late May to mid-November, excluding periods of high water due to heavy rain

VOLUME: 2000–20,000 cfs

RAFT SIZE: 12 to 24 feet

WEATHER: During summer, daytime temperatures are 80° to 90° and the water temperature is a warm 70°. Cooler temperatures in May and October. Wet suits necessary during cold weather.

WATER CONDITIONS: Large and dam-controlled, the New is runnable from late May until well into November, except when heavy rain hits the area. In winter and spring, the flow is dangerously high, averaging from 7000 to 14,000 cfs. In summer and fall, the flow is usually more manageable, averaging from 2000 to 5000 cfs, with occasional dramatic variations due to rain.

For water conditions on the upper section, call Bluestone Dam at (304) 466-1234 and ask for the current reading for the Hinton gauge. The water level rarely drops below 1.75 feet. Above 2.5 feet the run becomes dangerous and should be approached with extreme care.

For water conditions on the lower section, call Jon Dragan at (304) 469-2551. Jon and his brothers, who operate a commercial rafting outfit on the river called Wildwater Expeditions Unlimited, are prepared to aid any New River boater, whether they are their customers or boaters on their own. The gauge is found just below the Fayette Station bridge.

RIVER HAZARDS: On the upper section, intermediate rafters can handle the lively ride from McCreery to Thurmond. The rapids here are long, river-wide zones of big waves with few obstructions. Big curlers and souse holes are encountered now and then, but all are easily avoided.

The lower section is for experts only. Be very, very adept on the Cheat before attempting this run. Many of the rapids are big and tough, and can be killers. Much scouting is necessary. Even the professional guides who run this stretch scout these rapids time after time. One recent rafting fatality occurred here on a trip conducted by a professional outfitting firm—a firm fully cognizant of the dangers and fully equipped to handle almost all emergencies. Yet still the death occurred.

This lower leg begins with an 8-mile calm interrupted by only one rapid of note, Surprise Rapid. Found about 5 miles below Thurmond, Surprise begins as an easy riffle and then, presto, pinches funnel-fashion into two big waves, the second of which is a curling stopper in high water. Prudent rafters can usually sneak Surprise on the left.

Three miles below Surprise is a railroad trestle. The big rapids begin just above this trestle and, interspersed with calms, continue on through the run in hell-roaring style. From here on scout often and well: Your life hangs in the balance. Six miles below the railroad bridge are the treacherous Keeney Brothers, three tough rapids that flow into each other at high water. Upper Keeney, the first of the three, is marked by a boulder resembling a whale in size and shape. Upper and Middle Keeney are mean, but Lower Keeney is meaner; scout all three with care. Other death-dealers downstream are Double Z, Undercut Rock, and Greyhound Bus Stopper, all of which should be approached with extreme caution. Persons attempting the New should first consult *Wildwater West Virginia* for a detailed, rapid-by-rapid account of the river. Also, local inquiry with experienced rafters is essential.

Road directions: The McCreery put-in is at the sandy beach on the west bank two rapids downstream from the U.S. 19 bridge. Just where U.S. 19 turns to climb the valley wall, a dirt road goes north along the river to the put-in.

Regardles of whether you plan to take out at Thurmond or Fayette Station, do not use the dirt road running from Prince to Thurmond. Instead, take U.S. 19 toward Beckley, go right on W.Va. Route 61 to Mount Hope, and turn right onto U.S. 21. To reach Thurmond, turn right onto secondary road #25 after going just 1 mile on U.S. 21. To travel on to Fayette Station, follow U.S. 21 to Fayetteville and turn right onto Route 82.

Intriguing local spots: The riverside town of Thurmond, found midway in the run, has a wild and illicit history. Around the turn of the century, to quote *Wildwater West Virginia*, "it was a lawless town somewhat akin to the Dodge City of the Old West. Its infamous 100-room Dunglen Hotel was host to the longest continuous poker game in history, some 14 years! Women, booze, dice, and cards were brought in fresh every day while unlucky losers of arguments over same were quietly disposed of in the New. Two old sayings survive that describe the town colorfully: 'No Sunday west of Clifton Forge and no God west of Hinton' and 'The only difference between Hell and Thurmond was in that a river ran through Thurmond.'"

On summer evenings the Hatfield and McCoy feud is brought to life in an outdoor drama at nearby Grandview State Park. It is best to make advance reservations by calling (304) 253-8313.

Other points of interest in the area are the Exhibition Coal Mine at Beckley, the tram ride at Hawks Nest, and Bluestone Lake near Hinton.

Fishing: Smallmouth bass, rock bass, white bass, walleye in spring, also catfish. Just below the Bluestone Dam, which lies 26 miles upstream from McCreery, is one of the finest warm-water fishing areas in the United States. Here the New is broad and shallow, and one can wade out to hook bass, redeye, bluegill, catfish, and suckers. Muskies lurk a short distance downriver. Although heavily fished, this stretch of river continues to deliver handsomely.

MAPS

U.S.G.S. quadrangles: The run is covered by 15′ Beckley (W.Va.) and 15′ Fayetteville (W.Va.).

To make the shuttle easier, send for road maps of Fayette and Raleigh Counties. Maps are available for a nominal fee. Write to West Virginia Department of Highways, Advanced Planning Division, Charleston, W.Va. 25311.

GUIDEBOOKS AND LITERATURE

Canoeing Whitewater River Guide by Randy Carter. $5.25 postpaid. Available from Appalachian Books, Box 248, Oakton, 2938 Chainbridge Rd., Va. 22124.

Wildwater West Virginia by Bob Burrell and Paul Davidson. $5.25 postpaid. Available from Bob Burrell, 1412 Western Ave., Morgantown, W.Va. 26505.

"Beating the New River," *Time,* July 16, 1973.

"Grand Canyon of the East; raft trip on the New River gorge in West Virginia" by Bob Burrell. *Field & Stream,* vol. 78 (March, 1974), p. 62–3+.

"Hawk's Nest" by H. Skidmore. *West Virginia Heritage* series, vol. 4 (1970). Richwood, W.Va.: Bronson McClung, publisher.

History of Summers County by J.H. Miller. McClain Printing Co., Parsons, W.Va. 26287, 1908 (reprint 1970).

Thurmond: Dodge City of West Virginia: Believe It or Not City by E. Scott. Available in stores around southern West Virginia. Publisher unknown.

"Tragedy on the New" by Bob Burrell. *American Whitewater,* vol. 18, no. 4 (Winter, 1973), p. 132.

"U.S. House of Representatives Hearings on Hawk's Nest Tunnel Construction." *West Virginia Heritage* series, vol. 8. Richwood, W.Va.: Bronson McClung, publisher.

"The Very Old New River" by M. Brooks. *Wonderful West Virginia,* vol. 34, no. 1.

GAULEY

Deep in the Appalachians of West Virginia, the big-toothed Gauley gnaws at the foundations of 1000-foot cliffs and awesome wooded inclines. The relentless flow shifts great boulders, and snaps logs like twigs. Man ventures into the Gauley Canyon at great risk; meeting the challenge of that risk can provide an intense experience.

The Gauley is without doubt one of America's finest whitewater rivers; yet, like Hell's Canyon and the Grand Canyon, this natural wonder has attracted the deadly eye of the dam builder. Perhaps out of an inane desire to outdo the Russians by building an 875-foot dam (four feet higher than a recent Russian dam), the Army Corps of Engineers is planning to flood this incomparable, irreplaceable waterway.*

LOCATION: Allegheny Plateau of West Virginia about 40 miles west of Charleston

PUT-IN AND TAKE-OUT: Foot of Summersville Dam to Swiss

FAVORABLE SEASON: Fall

DIFFICULTY AT MODERATE FLOW: V_6

DIFFICULTY AT HIGH WATER: U

VOLUME: 500–10,000 cfs

GRADIENT: 27 feet per mile

LENGTH: 24 river miles

TIME: 2 days

RAFT SIZE: 12 to 18 feet

WATER CONDITIONS: After Labor Day and on through most of the fall an adequate water level is assured by the release schedule of Summersville Dam. Summer flows are generally too low. The Gauley is raftable between 1000 and about 4000 cfs. High water on the Gauley is absolutely unrunnable.

The flow at the put-in may be obtained from the dam keeper's office. The flow for the lower 18 miles of the run, often a bit higher than at the put-in if the Meadow is high, is obtainable from the Weather Service as the Belva gauge. Flow information

---

* It is important that we who enjoy and care about rivers work to defend and preserve them. Write to American Rivers Conservation Council, 324 C St. SE, Washington, D.C. 20003.

for rivers in the Kanawha basin (Gauley is part of the Kanawha system) may be obtained by calling (304) 529-2318, extension 604.

RIVER HAZARDS: With over sixty rapids rated III or higher, including at least two of class V, the Gauley is considered by many to be the most difficult stretch of whitewater in West Virginia. It is powerful, treacherous, and intoxicating. Long, intricate rapids follow upon one another in wonderful, terrible succession. Ledges, stopper waves, house boulders, souse holes, and undercut rock join forces with devastating effect, often causing even veteran rafters to falter.

An ultimate challenge, this perilous, fascinating voyage should be attempted only by expert boaters *in the company of others who have previously made the run.* One such individual, who guides expeditions through the canyon, is Jon Dragan, of Wildwater Expeditions Unlimited, P.O. Box 55, Thurmond, W.Va. 25936. Mr. Dragan requires that anyone rafting the Gauley with him have previously rafted the lower leg of the New at least twice.

ROAD DIRECTIONS: To reach the put-in at the base of Summersville Dam, drive south from Summersville on U.S. 19, then west on Hwy 129. To shuttle to the take-out near Swiss, go northwest on Hwy 129, then west on Hwy 39. The take-out is 1 mile upriver from Swiss along secondary road #19/25. After paralleling a railroad siding for several hundred yards, this road turns up Laurel Creek. Stop just before the turn. The sandy peninsula across the tracks is the take-out beach.

MAPS

U.S.G.S. quadrangles: Two maps are needed: 15′ Winona (W.Va.) and 15′ Fayetteville (W.Va.).

To make the shuttle easier, get road maps of Nicholas and Fayette Counties. Write to West Virginia Department of Highways, Advanced Planning Division, Charleston, W.Va. 25311. A small fee is charged for the maps.

GUIDEBOOKS AND LITERATURE

Wildwater West Virginia by Bob Burrell and Paul Davidson. 1972. $5.25 postpaid. Available from Bob Burrell, 1412 Western Ave., Morgantown, W.Va., 26505.

"Golly, That's Falling Water" by Charlie Walbridge. *American Whitewater,* vol. 18, no. 2 (Summer, 1973). Includes a map showing the major rapids in the upper half of the run. Send $1.00 to George Larsen, Box 1584, San Bruno, Calif. 94066.

"Rafting the Gauley" by Sayre Rodman. *Wildwater Splashes; Newsletter of the West Virginia Wildwater Association,* vol. 7, no. 9 (Sept., 1972). For a copy write Idair Smookler, 2737 Daniels Ave., South Charleston, W.Va. 25303. Sayre was the first to run the Gauley back in 1961.

Tumult on the Mountains by R.B. Clarkson. Parsons, W.Va., McClain Printing Co., 1964.

ST. JOHN

The St. John offers an extended voyage through the woods of Maine on soothing current and tantalizing whitewater. This run begins easy and gradually builds to a crescendo of spirited foam.

LOCATION: Northern Maine about 150 miles north and slightly west of Bangor. The river flows northwest paralleling the U.S.–Canada border.

PUT-IN AND TAKE-OUT: Red Pine Camp near Daaquam to the village of Allagash

FAVORABLE SEASON: Mid-May to first week in June

DIFFICULTY AT MODERATE WATER: I–II except for Big Black and Big Rapids, which are III–IV.

DIFFICULTY AT HIGH WATER: III–IV

VOLUME: 700–15,000 cfs

GRADIENT: 7 feet per mile

LENGTH: 83 river miles

TIME: 5 to 8 days

RAFT SIZE: 11 to 16 feet

Plan to do some rowing or paddling in the Seven Islands stretch; the river is flat and sluggish through there.

WATER CONDITIONS: Because no large lakes feed the St. John, this run can become a long, narrow rock patch by late June. To check the current water level, call the district forest ranger in Daaquam at (418) 244-6501.

The best time to raft the St. John is generally from mid-May to early June, for during this time an adequate water level is assured. Spring run-off, which occurs from April to June, averages, at the put-in, 7000 cfs in April, 5000 cfs in May, and 2000 cfs in June. Through the rest of the summer the flow averages about 1000 cfs. All these flow figures apply to the river at the put-in. Due to the many tributaries entering the river along the run, the flow at Dickey, down near the take-out, is generally twice the flow at the put-in.

At low water, the river alternates between shallow rapids and pools. At high water, particularly in April, the small rapids tend to fill in, the current becomes smooth and swift, and the large rapids mentioned below become markedly more powerful and difficult.

RIVER HAZARDS: For the most part this is a run of easy rapids and gentle current. However, there are two rapids that can be heavy in high water and that always require scouting.

The first major rapid is Big Black Rapid. Found midway through the run just above the mouth of Big Black River, Big Black is 1½ miles long and is the steepest rapid on the run. In the high water of spring it has haystacks, rocks, and holes. As with all the rapids on this run, Big Black's exact location is shown on the U.S.G.S. quadrangle maps. At the head of this rapid, pull over to the left bank above the sharp left turn to scout.

Big Rapid, the other major rapid, is located near the end of the run about a mile below Campbell Brook. This is a splendid class III where for two miles the river courses downward among large boulders. Big Rapid can be very dangerous and has been the scene of several drownings, so scout it carefully. Because of its length, many boaters scout and run Big Rapid in sections. Because the better channels are generally on the left, it is wise to use the left bank for scouting. Exercise particular caution toward the end;

there is an especially tricky place near the bottom where the rapid makes a slight bend to the left.

ROAD DIRECTION: The put-in near Daaquam lies 65 miles east and slightly south of the city of Quebec, Canada. Daaquam, also in Canada, may be reached from the south by taking Interstate 95 and the Maine Turnpike northeast to Waterville, Maine, and then U.S. 201 north to Canada. At the border explain that you are on your way to float the St. John and will reenter the U.S. at Daaquam. After crossing into Canada, follow Route 23 northwest to St. Georges, then go right on Route 24 to Daaquam. In Daaquam turn right, asking at the cafe for directions if necessary, and recross the border. Just beyond the border is the gate to the International Paper Company road, commonly known as the "American Realty Road." Time your arrival here to coincide with the hours mentioned on your permit (see below). On the right just before the gate is the fire warden's house; current fire conditions may be checked here. Beyond the gate, drive east about 12 miles. After the road crosses the St. John, watch for Red Pine Camp, an authorized Maine campsite, on the left side of the road on a bluff over the river. A road suitable for vehicles with four-wheel drive drops down to the river, or you can carry your gear down.

Some people shuttle back down U.S. 201 to Waterville, up Interstate 95 to Houlton, up U.S. 1 to Caribou, and then along Route 161 through Fort Kent to Allagash. A shorter but rougher shuttle route runs around through Canada: Take Route 24 from Daaquam northeast to St. Pamphile, then northwest to St. Jean Port Joli. Follow Trans-Canadian Hwy. 2 northeast to Riviere du Loup and then southeast to Edmundston. Here cross the border to Madawaska, and take U.S. 1 to Fort Kent, then Route 161 to Allagash village.

ROAD PERMITS: A permit is required to use the private road leading from Daaquam to the put-in at Red Pine Camp. To obtain a permit, write well in advance to International Paper Company, Androscoggin Mill, Department of Woodlands, Chisholm, Maine 04222. In your letter mention that you want to use the road running east from Daaquam to Red Pine Camp. Also indicate the date and time you plan to enter, the number of people in your group, and the number and type of vehicles you will use. A fee is charged for each vehicle. No trailers are allowed. The gate at the head of this road is open only during the hours noted on the permit. (For general information about the use of private roads in the backcountry of Maine, contact the Executive Secretary, Paper Company Information Office, 133 State Street, Augusta, Maine 04330. Phone (207) 622-3166.)

CAMPSITES AND FIRE PERMITS: Along the banks of the St. John and throughout most of Maine, camping is allowed only in designated campsites. In some of these campsites fire permits are required, while in others they are not. Sites where no fire permits are needed, called "authorized Maine campsites," tend to be, at least on the St. John, open, nude patches of ground, often with roads and cabins nearby. There are eight of these sites spaced out along this run (see list below). The other campsites, called "fire-permit campsites," are usually more wooded, isolated, and beautiful. But due to these very assets, fires are unsafe in these sites during periods of prolonged dry weather; hence, fire permits are required and are issued only when recent rain has reduced the danger of forest fire. But stoves may be used at these sites *without* a permit.

Fire permits for the St. John may be obtained by writing or phoning the District Forest Ranger, Daaquam, County of Montmagny, Province of Quebec, Canada. Phone (418) 244-6501. When requesting permits, mention the dates of trip, number of people in group, and name of leader. If you obtain your permit well in advance, be sure, as you drive to the put-in, to check at the fire warden's home at the road gate east of Daaquam about current fire conditions. If there has been a drought, your permit may have been revoked. For details on the locations of the attractive, secluded, fire-permit sites, see *No Horns Blowing* or the *A.M.C. New England Canoeing Guide*.

As stated above, fire permits are not necessary at authorized Maine campsites. Each site is marked by a sign visible from the river; some camps look like authorized sites but are not, so be sure there is a sign. The notes in the righthand column below plus the U.S.G.S. quadrangle maps will make these camps easy to find. For use on the river, transpose these notes onto the appropriate spots on your maps.

AUTHORIZED MAINE CAMPSITES ON THE ST. JOHN

Red Pine (put-in) — Right bank on bluff over river (see "Road Directions" above)

Ninemile bridge
(This is the setting for
Helen Hamlin's novel—see
below.) — Left bank behind the fire warden's cabin, near mouth of Ninemile Creek

Seven Islands — Left bank in open meadow near California Road

Priestly Brook — Left bank just upstream from logging bridge (not secluded—bridge plus various camps nearby are heavily used)

Black River — Left bank at mouth of Big Black River in clearing close by Forest Service cabin

Long Rapid — Left bank below rapid

Ouellette Farm — Left bank in field at mouth of Ouellette Brook

Fox Brooks Rapid — Left bank above rapid near mouth of Fox Brook

MAPS

U.S.G.S. quadrangles: Six maps are needed—15′ Beaver Pond (Me.), 15′ Clayton Lake (Me.), 15′ Seven Islands (Me.), 15′ Round Pond (Me.), 15′ Rocky Mountain (Me.), and 15′ Allagash (Me.).

GUIDEBOOKS AND LITERATURE

Appalachian Mountain Club New England Canoeing Guide. 1971. $6.00 An excellent, mile-by-mile guide to New England water trails. Available from Appalachian Mountain Club, 5 Joy St., Boston, Mass. 02108.

Nine Mile Bridge by Helen Hamlin. New York: W. W. Norton, 1945. (Out of print.)

No Horns Blowing: Canoeing 10 Great Rivers in Maine by Eben Thomas. 1973. $3.95 plus 30¢ handling. Very useful. Includes a map of the run and much detailed information on the river, campsites, fire permits, etc. Also provides an interesting account of a voyage down the river. Available from Hallowell Printing Co., 145 Water St., Hallowell, Maine 04347.

ST. CROIX

With the United States on one bank and Canada on the other, the St. Croix glides in lively fashion through lush forests of hemlock and maple.

LOCATION: Maine–New Brunswick border 80 miles northeast of Bangor

PUT-IN AND TAKE-OUT: Vanceboro to Loon Bay

FAVORABLE SEASON: May to mid-June

DIFFICULTY: II$_4$

VOLUME: 300–1000 cfs

GRADIENT: 7 feet per mile

LENGTH: 21 river miles

TIME: 2 days

RAFT SIZE: 9 to 16 feet

WATER CONDITIONS: The dam at Vanceboro backs up Spednic Lake and generally provides an adequate flow into late summer. On the average, according to U.S.G.S. records, the flow is 1000 cfs in March and gradually diminishes to roughly 700 cfs in August. Minimum runnable flow is about 700 cfs. During fall and winter, the St. Croix is generally quite low with a volume averaging between 300 and 500 cfs.

RIVER HAZARDS: Except for Little Falls, which is rated IV, this is a run of easy class I and II rapids. At Little Falls, the river divides around a small island and drops over two ledges. Scout. There is a straight-shot run down the right channel in high water. In low water, some boaters carry around the right side. Little

Falls and all of the other rapids on this run are shown on the U.S.G.S. quadrangle maps.

ROAD DIRECTIONS: The township of Vanceboro is situated 85 miles northeast of Bangor where Maine Route 6 and New Brunswick Route 4 meet at the U.S.–Canada border. The put-in is on the west bank just below the dam.

A number of gravel logging roads run in to the take-out points at Loon Bay and Spednic Falls. One runs south from Route 6 near Lambert Lake. Another bumps west from Waite on Route 1. Check with the forest ranger in Topsfield (located on Route 6 about 23 miles southwest of Vanceboro) for precise directions.

CAMPSITES AND FIRE PERMITS: There are two authorized campsites where no fire permits are required. One is an attractive, forested site at Little Falls midway through the trip. The other is in an open field on the shore of Loon Bay right at the take-out. Both are on the right bank. Fire permits for other sites may be obtained from the District Forest Ranger, Topsfield, Maine 04490. Phone (207) 766-2643.

MAPS

U.S.G.S. quadrangle maps cover the river and western bank, while Canadian maps cover the river and the eastern bank. Although it is possible to get by with just the U.S.G.S. maps, it is best to have both.

U.S.G.S. quadrangles: 15′ Vanceboro (Maine), 15′ Kellyland (Maine), 15′ Waite (Maine), and 15′ Forest (Maine). These last two maps will help with the shuttle roads.

Canadian maps: 21 G/11 West McAdam and 21 G/6 West Rolling Dam. These two half-sheet Canadian topo maps are available for 50¢ each from Map Distribution Office, Department of Energy, Mines, and Resources, 615 Booth St., Ottawa, Ont., Canada. Make checks payable to Receiver General of Canada.

GUIDEBOOKS AND LITERATURE

Appalachian Mountain Club New England Canoeing Guide. 1971. $6.00. Available from Appalachian Mountain Club, 5 Joy St., Boston, Mass. 02108.

No Horns Blowing: Canoeing 10 Great Rivers in Maine by

Eben Thomas. 1973. $3.95 plus 30¢ handling. Available from Hallowell Printing Co., 145 Water St., Hallowell, Maine 04347.

OTHER EASTERN RIVERS

Among the many other fine rafting rivers in the East, here are a few favorites. The guidebooks referred to are listed in the Selected Bibliography at the back of this book.

Shenandoah Staircase

Located in the Blue Ridge Mountains of West Virginia's eastern panhandle, the legendary Shenandoah Staircase plunges over drop after drop in exciting yet fairly safe fashion. This popular 7-mile run begins at Millville, W.Va., and ends at Sandy Hook, Md. Flows are generally good from spring through midsummer. For details see *Wildwater West Virginia* and *Canoeing Whitewater River Guide*.

Potomac Needles

Close by the Shenandoah Staircase is the 3-mile stretch of the Potomac called the Needles. Here, beginning at Dam Number Three and coursing down past historic Harper's Ferry to Sandy Hook, George Washington's Potomac runs through continuous class I and II rapids. As with the Staircase, flows are usually good from spring through midsummer. But avoid high water. For the full story consult *Wildwater West Virginia* and *Canoeing Whitewater River Guide*. *Note:* The Shenandoah Staircase and the Potomac Needles form two arms of a Y, and both are often run in the same day.

Bluestone

During March and early April the Bluestone offers a rollicking ride through a dazzling West Virginia canyon with numerous 200-foot sidestream waterfalls. For 25 sweet bumping miles, from Spanishburg to Bluestone State Park, this stream runs through continuous intermediate rapids. See *Wildwater West Virginia* for further information.

Chatooga

Famous as the setting for the film *Deliverance*, the Chatooga crashes through the Great Smokey Mountains to form the north-ernmost jog in the border between Georgia and South Carolina. The fierce 22-mile run from Earl's Ford down to Lake Tugaloo, with a gradient many times that of the Grand Canyon and dozens of blistering falls and rapids, is both dangerous and thrilling in the extreme. Adequate flows occur throughout the year, except during periods of drought or high water. *Warning:* This is a class V run, and some of the falls are *unrunnable* at any water level. For more information see *Canoeing Whitewater River Guide* and "Chatooga!" by Donald Wilson in *American Whitewater*, vol. 18, no. 3 (Autumn, 1973). For a complete river runner's map and guide get the *Chatooga River Map;* coated enamel $4.00, water-proof paper $5.00 postpaid. River Runners, Box 1231, Charlotte, North Carolina 28230. Also see Claude Terry's articles on the Chatooga in Brown's guide to Georgia.

Carrabassett

Prancing smartly through a mountain valley just north of King-field, Maine, the Carrabassett is well known as the scene of white-water races early each spring, usually on Easter weekend. The 10-mile run from Carrabassett Village to Kingfield drops through nearly continuous rapids, offering a wet and rousing ride. For details see *Hot Blood and Wet Paddles* by Eben Thomas (available for $4.95 plus 30¢ handling).

Lower Dead

Deep in the Longfellow Mountains of Maine, from Long Falls Dam, which backs up Flagstaff Lake, to West Forks, the lower Dead River offers a 6-mile flat stretch, a ½-mile portage, and then 16 electrifying miles of continuous class III–IV rapids. Said to be the best rafting river in New England, this plunging, rock-strewn run is navigable only when Long Falls Dam releases flows of from 900 to 1200 cfs. For information, consult Eben Thomas, *Hot Blood and Wet Paddles,* and the *Appalachian Mountain Club New England Canoeing Guide.*

Midwestern Rivers

FLAMBEAU

As it winds through wild, scenic Flambeau State Forest, this river offers peaceful calms and a sprinkling of mild, easily negotiated rapids. In this region of thick forest, eagles float on high while deer step through the shallows. When French explorers first came upon this river in the night, they found Indians fishing with the aid of torches, hence the name Flambeau, or "flaming torch."

LOCATION: Superior Upland in north-central Wisconsin about 80 miles northeast of Eau Claire

PUT-IN AND TAKE-OUT: Nine Mile Creek to Flambeau Lodge

FAVORABLE SEASON: April through September

DIFFICULTY AT NORMAL SUMMER FLOW: I–II

DIFFICULTY AT HIGH WATER: II

VOLUME: 500–5000 cfs

GRADIENT: 4 feet per mile

LENGTH: 45 river miles

Time: 3 to 4 days

Raft size: 9 to 16 feet

Water conditions: From April through September the flow ranges steadily between 1000 and 1400 cfs. A U.S.G.S. gauge is located at the Babbs Island Ranger Station near the county road W bridge. The river is runnable above 750 cfs, or 1.8′ on the Babbs Island gauge. Readings from this gauge are mailed weekly to Rice Lake Field Office, P.O. Box 151, Rice Lake, Wis. 54452. Phone (715) 234-4015.

River hazards: The Flambeau has a number of lively but moderate rapids. The rowdiest of these are Wannigan (I–II), Flambeau Falls (I–II,) Cedar (II), and Beaver Dam (II). All are covered in the guidebooks mentioned below. The place to approach with particular caution is Beaver Dam Rapid, where a dangerous reversal develops in high water.

Road directions: The put-in ramp at the mouth of Nine Mile Creek is beside Route 70, 6 miles east of Oxbo.
   For the shuttle, drive west on Route 70; at Ojibwa turn left onto Route 27; near Ladysmith turn left onto U.S. 8; in the village of Tony turn left again onto county road I. Road I runs due north, crossing Lake Flambeau at Tony bridge. One-and-a-quarter miles beyond the bridge, turn right toward Big Falls Dam. Follow this unpaved road 1 mile east and then 2 miles north as it passes the dam and skirts along the western shore of Big Falls Flowage. About 1½ miles north of the dam, a half-mile-long spur road cuts east to the take-out at the Flambeau Lodge. A fee is charged for parking at the lodge. *Note:* The proprietor of Flambeau Lodge will shuttle vehicles for a fee (contact Flambeau River Lodge, Route 2, Ladysmith, Wis. 54848. Phone (715) 532-5392).

Fishing: Good for muskie, walleye, and small-mouth bass. There are also trout in some sidestreams.

Campsites: One-night-only campsites are spaced every 2 to 4 miles along the route. Most have good water, usually a spring.

MAPS

U.S.G.S. quadrangles: Six maps cover the run—7½′ Lugerville (Wis.), 7½′ Oxbo (Wis.), 7½′ Kennedy (Wis.), 7½′ Draper SE (Wis.), 7½′ Ingram NE (Wis.), and 7½′ Ingram SW (Wis.). *Note:* These maps are not necessary if you get either of the guidebooks mentioned below.

GUIDEBOOKS AND LITERATURE

Canoe Trails of North-Central Wisconsin. 1973. $4.00. Provides detailed river maps and mile-by-mile narration covering rapids, access points, history, fishing, campsites, etc. Also includes blow-up maps of individual rapids. Unfortunately, this guide is flawed by its use of a naive 1-to-4 difficulty rating scale. Available from *Wisconsin Trails* Magazine, P.O. Box 5650, Madison, Wis. 53705.

Whitewater; Quietwater: A Guide to the Rivers of Wisconsin, Upper Michigan and NE Minnesota by Bob and Jody Palzer. 1973. $7.95. Provides flow data, detailed river maps, and mile-by-mile discussion of rapids, local history, campsites, fishing, scenery, geology, access points, and so on. Uses, like most sophisticated guidebooks, the International scale for rating rapids. Price includes free future supplements of up-to-date information on the rivers covered. Available from Evergreen Paddleways, 1416 21st St., Two Rivers, Wis. 54241.

"Deliverance—Flambeau Style" by Gary E. Myers. *American Whitewater,* vol. 18, no. 2 (Summer, 1973), pp. 74-77.

NAMEKAGON/ST. CROIX

Float serenely through cedar and balsam lowlands, swimming, fishing, lazing. Camp on sandy islands. Soak in the clear, clean water. The St. Croix has been set aside by Congress as a Wild and Scenic River, and it deserves this consideration well. The feeling here is one of seclusion; the quiet is almost tangible. Though this is largely a smooth run, there are a few mild rapids to teach the beginner a few tricks. Whitetail deer, bald eagle, and great blue heron drink from these rivers. Namekagon, an Ojibwa Indian word, means "where the sturgeon are beautiful." This is not a true whitewater river, but peaceful drifting through paradise is also a part of rafting. There are a number of access points along the run, so a trip may be shortened as desired. See the guidebooks mentioned below for information on alternate take-outs.

LOCATION: Northwestern Wisconsin—the lower portion of the St. Croix forms the border between Minnesota and Wisconsin

PUT-IN AND TAKE-OUT: Route 77 Bridge on the Namekagon to Soderbeck Landing on the St. Croix

FAVORABLE SEASON: April through September (lovely colors in the fall)

DIFFICULTY AT NORMAL FLOW: I

DIFFICULTY AT HIGH WATER: II

VOLUME: Namekagon: 300-800 cfs   St. Croix: 600-2500 cfs

GRADIENT: 2½ feet per mile

LENGTH: 56 river miles

TIME: 4 to 7 days

RAFT SIZE: Use rafts 6 to 16 feet long. Rafts 9 feet long or shorter are best when the Namekagon is low.

WATER CONDITIONS: Both the Namekagon and the St. Croix are generally runnable throughout the summer. To learn the current flow of the Namekagon, call Trego Dam—(715) 635-2846—between 7 A.M. and 3 P.M. on weekdays only. Minimum runnable flow for the Namekagon is 350 cfs. The St. Croix, though almost always runnable, does occasionally drop too low during a few days in July, August, and September.

A U.S.G.S. gauge is located at Riverside on the left bank of the St. Croix near the Highway 35 bridge. Eight hundred cfs, or 0.9 feet on this gauge, is the minimum runnable flow, while 1500 cfs, or 1.5 feet on the gauge, marks high water, which makes the run class II.

U.S.G.S. records show that, on the average, the Namekagon flows 700 cfs in April and gradually diminishes to 400 cfs in

September. The St. Croix averages 2000 cfs in April and steadily recedes to roughly 1500 cfs in September.

RIVER HAZARDS: This is an excellent novice float with no particular hazards. The only significant rapids are found toward the end of the run near the mouth of Kettle River. Here the river divides around an island to pour through Big Beef Rapid in the left channel and Lower Kettle Rapid in the right. Where the two channels reunite, August Olson Rapid sets the river boiling. All three of these rapids are rated II in high water and I in low.

ROAD DIRECTIONS: The put-in at the Route 77 bridge is 50 miles due south of Duluth. For the shuttle, go west on Route 77, south on Route 35, and then west on Route 70 to Grantsburg. At Grantsburg go due north 3 miles, then west 4 miles to the take-out at Soderbeck Landing.

FISHING: Superb for smallmouth bass, muskie, northern pike, walleye, catfish, and sturgeon. There are trout in some side-streams.

MAPS

U.S.G.S. quadrangles: 15′ Webb Lake (Wis.), 15′ Danbury (Wis.), 15′ Webster (Wis.), 15′ Grantsburg (Wis./Minn.), 15′ Pine City (Wis./Minn.). These maps are unnecessary with the guidebooks below.

GUIDEBOOKS AND LITERATURE

Canoeing the Wild Rivers of Northwestern Wisconsin. 1969. $3.50. A fine, waterproof guide providing detailed maps and mile-by-mile information on rapids, campsites, fishing, wildlife, local history, etc. Unfortunately, some of the maps do not show the shuttle roads clearly. Available from Wisconsin Indian Head Country, Route 1, Box 313, Chippewa Falls, Wisc. 54729.

Minnesota Voyageur Trails. 1970. $2.00. Provides maps and mile-by-mile log of St. Croix where it borders Minnesota. Also covers other Minnesota rivers. Available from Minnesota Department of Natural Resources, Division of Parks and Recreation, 320 Centennial Building, St. Paul, Minn. 55155.

Whitewater; Quietwater: A Guide to the Rivers of Wisconsin, Upper Michigan and NE Minnesota by Bob and Jody Palzer.

1973. $7.95. Available from Evergreen Paddleways, 1416 21st St., Two Rivers, Wis. 54241.

PESHTIGO

The Peshtigo is a delightful little river with two runnable sections, one long and exciting, the other short and hair raising. The upper, longer stretch lies entirely within Nicolet National Forest and tumbles in lively style between thickly forested shores. The lower portion, well known to river people far and wide as the Roaring Rapids section of the Peshtigo, has some of the most extraordinary whitewater in the entire Midwest. The Peshtigo deserves protection as a wild river.

LOCATION: Northeastern Wisconsin roughly 60 miles northwest of Green Bay and 35 miles east of Rhinelander

THE UPPER SECTION

PUT-IN AND TAKE-OUT: Forest Service road 2131 bridge to Forest Service road 2136 bridge (midway access point: Burnt Bridge)

FAVORABLE SEASON: Runnable during the high water of spring run-off or after heavy rains

DIFFICULTY AT NORMAL SUMMER FLOW: II

DIFFICULTY AT HIGH WATER: III

VOLUME: Because the nearest U.S.G.S. gauge is far downstream below several dams, exact flow data are not available.

GRADIENT: 14 feet per mile

LENGTH: 16 river miles

TIME: 1 or 2 days

RAFT SIZE: 9 feet recommended; 12 feet all right

WATER CONDITIONS: This stretch is runnable during the high water of spring run-off and after heavy rains. For many years there has been a stage marker on the downstream side of the county highway C bridge, and boaters have been able to obtain up-to-the-minute flow information by calling the little resort here. But as this is written the situation is in flux: The bridge is being rebuilt and the resort is changing hands. It is likely, though, that a new gauge will be painted on the new bridge and that the new owners of the resort will provide gauge readings over the phone. Consult *Whitewater; Quietwater* and its free updated supplements for the latest information on what number to call and how to interpret the readings.

RIVER HAZARDS: This run has numerous mild rapids spaced out along its length. One of the tougher rapids is Michigan Rapid, found 10 miles below the put-in. Michigan, which has a whirlpool near its end and develops large waves in high water, is rated II during normal summer flow and III during high water. Two and one half miles below Michigan is Ralton's Rip Rapid, the run's most challenging rapid. Here the river divides around an island; the left channel is too shallow and rocky to run, and the right is a narrow raceway 10 to 20 feet wide and 150 feet long. Rated II in low water and III in high water, Ralton's Rip (also known as the Dells) should be scouted from the island. Should you need it, there is a portage trail on the right bank. For a detailed account of all the rapids in this stretch, see *Whitewater; Quietwater.*

ROAD DIRECTIONS: The put-in is near the town of Laona, which lies at the meeting point of Route 32 and U.S. 8 about 25 miles east of Rhinelander. Three miles north of Laona, U.S. Forest Service road 2131 turns eastward from U.S. 8 and wends its unpaved way some 6 miles to the put-in bridge. This bridge was built by the Civilian Conservation Corps in 1936 and is known locally as the CCC bridge.

For the shuttle, continue along Forest Service road 2131, following it first northeast from the CCC bridge and then southeast as it parallels the river. About 7 miles from the CCC bridge, turn right onto Forest Service road 2134 and cross the Peshtigo near Burnt Bridge Campground. About 3 miles beyond Burnt Bridge, go left (east) on Forest Service road 2136. When, after another 3 miles, road 2136 hits road 2141, take the right fork toward the take-out bridge, where there is a landing and primitive campground. Because this area has numerous Forest Service roads, there are a number of alternate routes for reaching both the put-in and the take-out. *Whitewater; Quietwater* contains a map of these roads.

FISHING: Fine trout in rapids and some sidestreams.

MAPS

U.S.G.S. quadrangles: 15′ Laona (Planimetric—no contour lines) (Wis.), and 15′ Goodman (Planimetric) (Wis.).

Overview map: U.S.G.S. Special Map, Geodetic Control Diagram, *Iron Mountain* (scale 1:250,000).

The guidebooks mentioned below contain maps.

THE LOWER SECTION

PUT-IN AND TAKE-OUT: Farm Dam (Silver Cliff's baseball area) to county highway C bridge

FAVORABLE SEASON: Spring and summer

DIFFICULTY AT NORMAL SUMMER FLOW: II$_3$–III

DIFFICULTY AT HIGH WATER: III–IV

GRADIENT: 40 feet per mile

LENGTH: 4 river miles

TIME: 1 day

RAFT SIZE: 9 to 12 feet

WATER CONDITIONS: See "Water Conditions" for the upper section.

RIVER HAZARDS: This is the Roaring Rapids! For its entire length this run plunges relentlessly downward through one wild rapid after another. Only an occasional short calm interrupts the boiling whitewater. Challenging and thrilling, this run demands much careful scouting and skillful maneuvering.

The rapids begin 100 yards below the put-in. The first is 1½ miles of sustained class II whitewater. Next come the three Drops. The First Drop, recognized by a cleared swath for a pipeline crossing the river just above it, has an angled curling wave on the right side of the main channel that has flipped countless rafts. First Drop is rated II at normal summer flow and III during high water, and should be scouted on the left bank. A stone's throw below First Drop is Second Drop, which should also be scouted on the left. Second Drop is rated II during low and III during high water. Third Drop, also called Kussokavitch Rapid, earns a III rating because it has a broad, dangerous reversal in high water. Immediately above Third Drop there is first a small, wooded, midstream island and then a little rock island close to the left bank. Pull over *left* of this small rock island and scout along the left bank. If you pass the rock island on the right, you will be swept headlong into the rapid and have no opportunity to scout. *Note:* Five-Foot Falls follows hard on the heals of Third Drop, so scout both at once.

Five-Foot Falls is a tough III. A threatening boulder lurks on the left just below the drop. You may want to line this one. Immediately below Five-Foot Falls is Horserace Rapid, rated III in low and a nasty IV in high water. Horserace is marked by a cabin halfway down its length on the left bank. A narrow, 100-yard-long ribbon of speeding water, Horserace grows increasingly difficult as one approaches its end. Because downed trees sometimes block the narrow channel, portaging is occasionally required. Stop on the left bank well above the rapid to scout; be sure to pull over early, for a rock garden on the left just above the rapid hampers things if you delay too long. Just below here is S-curve Rapid, a II in low and III in high water. Scout on the left bank. The final rapid is a long, easy, splashy dash.

ROAD DIRECTIONS: The Farm Dam put-in is just off county highway C near the town of Silver Cliff and is marked by a sign on highway C which says "Silver Cliff Baseball." Farm Dam, now damless, was once the site of a sluice dam. There is a free campground here with toilets and tables but no water supply.

Shuttle southeast 3 miles along highway C to the take-out at the private landing on the east bank just below the highway C bridge. Before taking out here, check in the bar for permission, and, while you're at it, wet your whistle in this superb little pub. An alternate take-out on public land is located on the east bank about ½ mile downstream.

FISHING: Northern pike plentiful at Farm Dam.

MAPS

U.S.G.S. quadrangle: 16′ Thunder Mountain (Planimetric) (Wis.).

Overview map: U.S.G.S. Special Map, Geodetic Control Diagram, *Iron Mountain* (scale 1:250,000).

Guidebooks below contain maps.

GUIDEBOOKS AND LITERATURE

Canoe Trails of Northeastern Wisconsin. 1972. $4.75. Provides information on rapids, access points, fishing, history, campsites, etc., and detailed, sometimes spotty, river maps. For instance, this guide's map of the Roaring Rapids section shows only three rapids. Available from *Wisconsin Trails* Magazine, P.O. Box 5650, Madison, Wis. 53705.

Whitewater; Quietwater: A Guide to the Rivers of Wisconsin, Upper Michigan and NE Minnesota by Bob and Jody Palzer. 1973. $7.95. Available from Evergreen Paddleways, 1416 21st St., Two Rivers, Wis. 54241.

"Peshtigo Wildwater Race April 21-22," *American Whitewater,* vol. 18, no. 1 (Spring, 1973), pp. 12–14.

"We Run the Peshtigo," by Carl Bennet. *American Whitewater,* vol. 14, no. 4 (Spring, 1969), pp. 7–9.

WOLF

Boulder-strewn and narrow, the Wolf wends its way down a course of challenging drops interspersed with scenic stretches of quiet water. Although the road encroaches in places, the setting is generally wild and often stunning in its ruggedness. It is for good reason that the Wolf is renowned among whitewater enthusiasts throughout the United States. The trout fishing, too, is excellent.

LOCATION: Northeastern Wisconsin roughly 60 miles northwest of Green Bay

PUT-IN AND TAKE-OUT: Highway 55 bridge in Lily to Big Smoky Falls

FAVORABLE SEASON: Spring and early summer for upper section; spring, summer, and fall for lower section

DIFFICULTY AT NORMAL SUMMER FLOW: III

DIFFICULTY AT HIGH WATER: IV

VOLUME: 200–1200 cfs

GRADIENT: 14 feet per mile

LENGTH: 38 river miles

TIME: 4 days

RAFT SIZE: 9-foot rafts recommended; 12-foot rafts are all right; 16-foot rafts are good above 800 cfs.

FISHING: The Wolf is famous for its excellent and abundant brown, brook, and rainbow trout.

WATER CONDITIONS: A U.S.G.S. gauge is located just above the Highway 64 bridge at Langlade. Daily readings are sent at weekly intervals to the Rice Lake Field Office of the U.S.G.S., P.O. Box 506, Rice Lake, Wis. 54868. Phone: (715) 234-4015. There is also a stage marker a few hundred yards downstream from the U.S.G.S. gauge. Cap Buettner has generously agreed to read this gauge for boaters. Consult *Whitewater; Quietwater* and its free updated supplements for Cap's phone number.

The upper section (above Langlade) is runnable most of the time, except for a few low days during July, August, and September. The lower section of the run, happily, is almost always runnable. Minimum flow for the upper stretch is 300 cfs; this is 5 on Cap's gauge and 7.6 feet on the U.S.G.S. gauge. Above 800 cfs the Wolf is in high water and difficulty increases markedly; a flow of 800 cfs is indicated by 15 on Cap's gauge and 8.4 feet on the U.S.G.S. gauge. For more detailed flow data, consult *Whitewater; Quietwater.*

RIVER HAZARDS: A feisty stretch of water, this run on the Wolf has rapids spaced out along its entire length. Things begin easy and gradually build to a thrilling, end-over-end climax.

The upper 15-mile stretch from Lily to Langlade has numerous minor rapids, including several of class II. Though these rapids require alertness and skill, they are not particularly treacherous. Through here, in fact, the place to approach with extra care is not a rapid but a log jam. Located ½ mile below the Lily put-in, this permanent log jam usually has a navigable passage through its center.

Seven miles below Langlade, Boy Scout Rapid, rated II in low water and III in high, marks the beginning of the difficult stretch. Also called Gardner Dam and Garfield Rapid, Boy Scout Rapid can be identified by the footbridge crossing the river at its upper end. Although it presents no visibility problems, Boy Scout is quite long and as a result is generally scouted.

Two miles below Boy Scout is the constricted, charging mill-race called Gilmore's Mistake Rapid. Rated II in summer low water and III during spring run-off, Gilmore's Mistake is particularly turbulent in high water, when tall waves develop in its upper portion and holes appear near its lower ledge. Scout this one from the left bank, and be sure to walk clear to the rapid's foot, for the correct passage over the ledge can be hard to spot from upstream.

Two miles downstream from Gilmore's Mistake is the Wolf's longest rapid, Shotgun Rapid. Rated II, Shotgun is over ½ mile long and should be scouted on the left bank. Shotgun's most troublesome spot comes at its end, where an island bulges up from the river bottom, creating an unrunnable channel on the left and a passage on the right where big haystacks develop in high water and where tight maneuvering is required in low water.

About a half-mile below Shotgun comes Pissmire Falls. Rated II in low and III–IV in high water and marked by the WW bridge which crosses the river above it, Pissmire has a wicked final drop with a side curler that has flipped many rafts *and can trap swimmers and rafts for long periods.* Pull over on the left above the bridge to scout. When running the final drop of Pissmire, the goal is to avoid the curler by staying far right.

Now the tempo picks up and the difficulties mount dramatically in Sullivan and Evergreen, in Ducknest, Tea Kettle, and the Dalles. Four miles below Pissmire a quarter-mile-long island squats in midriver. Two hundred and fifty yards down the left channel is unrunnable Sullivan Falls, preceded by a 200-foot rapid. And in the right channel is Evergreen Rapid. Rated II and also known as Runaround Rapid, Evergreen is sometimes blocked by fallen trees and is often quite shallow—when Cap's gauge reads below 6, Evergreen is too low to run. It is wise here to stop on the right bank just upstream from the island. After scouting, you may decide to run or line Evergreen, or you may choose to go cautiously down the left channel and make the shorter portage around Sullivan Falls on the right bank.

Just downstream is Ducknest Rapid. Ducknest consists of two pitches with a boulder garden between. Rated III in medium and IV in extremely high water, this rapid is pocked with holes at all water levels. Scout carefully from the left bank.

One and a half miles below Ducknest is Tea Kettle Rapid, class III. Tea Kettle, called the Upper Dalles by some, has an Indian teepee on its left bank and is marked at its head by a small rocky island. There is raw beauty here. Steep cliffs hunker in to squeeze the river into a twisting sinew of wild, plunging foam. Ledges, boulders, and curlers, many hidden from upstream, cause the water to leap and tumble. Tea Kettle's final drop is just below an island; in high water both channels around the island are navigable, but in low water only the left channel can be run. Scout Tea Kettle along the left bank.

Just below Tea Kettle is the Dalles. Rated III in low and IV in high water, the Dalles makes all that has come before look small and pale. Sheer stone cliffs press in from either side of the river. The mood is uncanny. The toughest drop comes sudden and fast at the beginning of the gorge; a reversal develops here at high water that can trap boats and boaters. It has been reported that a rafter drowned there recently. Be careful. Scout along the left bank.

About 2 miles below the Dalles is Big Smoky Falls, where the river splits into two channels. The take-out, which has road access, is in the left channel just above the footbridge. Absolutely do not attempt to run this left channel below the foot bridge. The right channel of Big Smoky has been successfully run by experts, but it too is best avoided with a portage. It has a very steep chute ending in a 6-foot drop and has a bad reversal in the middle. For the lucky crazies who make it through here, there is an alternate take-out 1½ miles below at a highway wayside.

ROAD DIRECTIONS: The put-in is in Lily on the north bank of the Lily River just above the Highway 55 bridge. The first, short stretch along the Lily River to the confluence with the

Wolf is sometimes very shallow and often involves pushing and scraping over rocks.

For the shuttle, drive southeast along Highway 55 through Langlade and Markton. About 9 miles beyond Markton, turn right onto the unpaved road heading southwest to Big Smoky Falls.

If a shorter trip is desired or if the upper portion is too low to run, you may wish to use one of the many access points spread out along the run. These are located at Hollister, Langlade, Markton, and elsewhere. One alternate put-in used by many rafters is located just above Boy Scout Rapid. This launch site is on the land of the Valley Council Boy Scout Camp, so ask permission to use the site beforehand. To get there, take the Gardner Dam Road turnoff from highway 55 1½ miles northwest of Markton. The put-in is 1 mile in from the highway.

MAPS

U.S.G.S. quadrangles: 15′ Lily (Planimetric) (Wis.), 15′ White Lake (Planimetric) (Wis.), 15′ Langlade (Planimetric) (Wis.).

Overview Map: U.S.G.S. Special Map, Geodetic Control Diagram, *Iron Mountain* (scale 1:250,000).

The guidebooks below contain maps.

GUIDEBOOKS AND LITERATURE

Canoe Trails of Northeastern Wisconsin. 1972. $4.75. Available from *Wisconsin Trails* Magazine, P.O. Box 5650, Madison, Wisconsin 53705.

Whitewater; Quietwater: A Guide to the Rivers of Wisconsin, Upper Michigan and NE Minnesota by Bob and Jody Palzer. 1973. $7.95. Available from Evergreen Paddleways, 1416 21st St., Two Rivers, Wis. 54241.

Northwestern Rivers

MIDDLE FORK OF THE SALMON

Spritely and prancing, raucous and throbbing, the Middle Fork of the Salmon is the deep-throated sweetheart of all who love whitewater. Dip oars into the feisty brew; feel it slip and kick. Drink the water freely; it is pure. Soak in the warmth of wilderness hot springs.

The Middle Fork is a cold and clear stream, flowing first among forested slopes, then through sheer granite canyons dotted with caves. At the Dagger Falls put-in, it is little more than a rocky creek. But in the course of the mountain-dodging, 99-mile stretch described here, the Middle Fork builds into a rugged heavy-water demon, until, finally, it climaxes with the pounding rapids of Impassable Canyon.

LOCATION: Salmon River Mountains in north-central Idaho. The put-in is 80 miles as the crow flies northeast of Boise.

PUT-IN AND TAKE-OUT: Dagger Falls to Cache Bar

FAVORABLE SEASON: June through September (best month: July)

DIFFICULTY AT MOST WATER LEVELS: IV

DIFFICULTY AT EXTREME HIGH WATERS: IV to U

VOLUME: 400–10,000 cfs

GRADIENT: 27 feet per mile

LENGTH: 99 river miles

TIME: 5 to 7 days *

RAFT SIZE: 12 to 18 feet

WEATHER: Warm days, cool nights. July and August temperatures range by day between 65° and 85° and by night between
50° and 65°. Occasional thundershowers.

FISHING: Once touted as a fisherman's paradise, the Middle
Fork has long been overfished and now offers scant pickings.
The skilled angler can still land, in season, an occasional salmon
and steelhead, and can, with careful stalking up sidestreams,
sometimes hook cutthroat and rainbow. It is strongly recommended, however, that fishing on the Middle Fork be pursued
purely for fun, and that all catches be released. This will allow
the critically small fish population to rebuild itself, so that in a
few years the Middle Fork can again offer lusty, if more judicious,
fishing. Idaho license required.

RIVER TRIP PERMITS: Permits are required for private trips.
Write well ahead to Middle Fork District Ranger, Challis National Forest, Challis, Idaho 83226.

WATER CONDITIONS: Because the only gauge on the Middle
Fork is far upstream from Dagger Falls, exact flow information
is not available. However, it is estimated that the spring run-off
ranges between 3000 and 10,000 cfs, and that during the rest of
the year the flow varies from 400 to 3000 cfs. The heaviest run-
off is generally during late May and early June; during this peak
flow, the river becomes far more difficult, sometimes even unrunnable. Occasionally, these dangerously high flows continue
on through late June and early July but usually the mid-June

---

* A 10- to 15-day trip is possible if you continue on down the main Salmon
to Riggins. See "Main Salmon," the next section.

to mid-July period offers medium-high water ideal for rafting. As the summer progresses, the flow gradually recedes, and sometime during August the upper 20 miles become too low to run. At this time it is still possible to make the run by flying into the air strip at Indian Creek, below which there are usually adequate flows throughout summer and fall.

WARNING: The water levels of the Middle Fork and of other Idaho rivers can undergo sudden, drastic changes during the spring and early summer due to heavy snow melt caused by warm rain or hot spells. Almost overnight, the river can rise 5 feet, becoming, sanely speaking, unrunnable. Parties that have already begun the run have no choice but to continue—at enormous risk. So consider well all weather forecasts before making a spring run, and even then be prepared for extremely hazardous conditions.

RIVER HAZARDS: Fast, rock-strewn, and turbulent, the Middle Fork demands expertise in reading whitewater and in technical maneuvering. Of the 100 or so rapids, about 28 have names. The toughest of these should definitely be scouted; they are, in the order encountered, Velvet Falls, Power House, Pistol Creek, Tappan Falls, Haystack, Redside, and Hancock.

Velvet Falls deserves special mention because it tends to sneak up on boaters running the river for the first time; as a result, the newcomer may not have an opportunity to scout. Found just below the mouth of Velvet Creek, about 5 miles below the put-in, Velvet is a low, vertical fall knifing across the river at a right angle. Along its base is an almost riverwide reversal which, though it may appear harmless, is in fact extremely dangerous and can flip and trap rafts and rafters. Avoid this reversal by using a sharp ferry to tuck under the rock jutting out from the left bank just above the fall; this will allow you to hit the slide that slips around the left end of the fall and reversal.

Another rapid, House Rock, also deserves a note. At House Rock, which is located at the far end of the run just 2½ miles above the confluence with the main Salmon, the river is jumbled with house-sized boulders. House Rock is easy *if you run the left side*.

All of the Middle Fork's major rapids, along with running instructions for each, are included on Leslie Jones' scroll map. Be sure to carry several of these maps.

The Cache Bar take-out is on the north bank of the main Salmon 3 miles downstream from the mouth of the Middle Fork.

EQUIPMENT NOTE: Be sure to have at least 200 feet of strong line. Putting in at Dagger Falls involves lowering your inflated raft down a steep slide with long ropes.

ROAD DIRECTIONS: The put-in at the foot of Dagger Falls is about 36 miles northwest of Stanley, Idaho. To get there drive along U.S. 93 to Stanley, turn northwest on state highway 21, and then, near Banner Campground, turn right onto the gravel road to Dagger Falls. This gravel road is well marked with signs and is shown on the Forest Service river map mentioned below.

For the shuttle, return to Stanley, head north on U.S. 93, at North Fork turn left onto the road running through Shoup, and continue west to the take-out at Cache Bar, found 18 miles beyond Shoup. Cache Bar is on the north bank 3 miles downstream from the confluence of the Middle Fork and main Salmon.

MAPS

Leslie Jones scroll map: "Middle Fork of the Salmon." For information on how to obtain these superb maps, see Chapter One.

Forest Service river map: "Middle Fork of the Salmon." Available free from Challis National Forest, Stanley Ranger District, Stanley, Idaho 83278.

GUIDEBOOKS AND LITERATURE

Wildwater Touring by Scott Arighi and Margaret S. Arighi. New York: Macmillan, 1974. $8.95. 334 pp. This excellent guidebook not only treats the whole subject of river touring in kayak, canoe, raft, or drift boat—the equipment, river camping, and river running procedures—it also covers in superb detail nine long, isolated river runs ranging in difficulty from class I through class IV in Idaho and Oregon. The rivers covered include: Rogue, Grande Ronde, John Day, Owyhee, the Middle and Main Salmon, and the remote lower gorge where the Salmon tumbles into the Snake.

The Bonanza Trail by Muriel Sibell Wolle. Bloomington, Ind.: Indiana University Press, 1958.

"Hermit of the Middle Fork" by Charles Kelly. *True West*, February, 1970, pp. 26-27, 40.

Idaho Federal Writer's Project, New York: Oxford University Press, 1950.

"Middle Fork of the Salmon," *Oar and Paddle*, May-June 1974, vol. 1, no. 1. (*Oar and Paddle* is a fine magazine of interest to all whitewater boaters. Published quarterly. Subscription rates: 5 issues, $4.50; 9 issues, $8.00.) Send subscription requests to *Oar and Paddle*, P.O. Box 621, Idaho Falls, Idaho 83401.

My Wilderness by Justice William O. Douglas. New York: Pyramid Publications, 1968.

"River Rat Pioneer" by Ethel Kimball, *True West*, December, 1963, pp. 30-31, 50-53.

Sheepeater Indian Campaign. 1968. $3.00. Available from Idaho County Free Press, P.O. Box 267, Grangeville, Idaho 83530.

"That River Swallows People. Some It Gives Up; Some It Don't" by Tom Brokaw, *West (Los Angeles Times Sunday Magazine)*, November 1, 1970, pp. 12-19.

"White-Water Adventure on Wild Rivers of Idaho" by John and Frank Craighead, *National Geographic*, February, 1970, pp. 213-239.

Wild Rivers of North America by Michael Jenkinson. New York: Dutton, 1973.

MAIN SALMON

After scouting the upper main Salmon, Captain Clark of the Lewis and Clark expedition concluded that it was not navigable, declaring it the "River of No Return." Though the Salmon is certainly no place for birchbark canoes, it is spanking good water for inflatable boats. It is a big river of middling, playful rapids, long, lazy calms, broad, sandy beaches, and deep pools of warm water ideal for swimming. Sloping through the heart of the enormous, protected Idaho Primitive Area, which encompasses parts of four national forests, its shores are the habitat of elk, deer, bear, mountain goat, and bighorn sheep. The Salmon gorge is the second deepest canyon in North America; it is one-fifth of a mile deeper than the Grand Canyon and is outclassed only by Hell's Canyon on the Snake.

No voyage down the Salmon would be complete without a visit with the gregarious "hermit" Sylvan Hart. Hart, better known as Buckskin Bill, has lived in a cozy stone hut at the mouth of Five Mile Creek for over 35 years. Throughout this time he has poured his considerable ingenuity and strength into countless projects, including the mining and refining of copper and the construction of a stone fortress near his hut. Hart loves to talk, and with little urging will show you his rifle, which he bored by hand, and his skull and bible: "Everyone knows that to be a hermit," he says with a twinkle in his eye, "you got to have a skull and a bible, so here's mine." This run on the main Salmon can be combined with the Middle Fork for a two-week odyssey.

After a week of rough wilderness living, the Riggins Tavern and Cafe is a fine place to go for homespun hospitality, delicious food, and spirited, back-country talk.

LOCATION: North-central Idaho about 130 miles north and slightly east of Boise

PUT-IN AND TAKE-OUT: Cache Bar to Vinegar Creek near Riggins

FAVORABLE SEASON: June through September

DIFFICULTY AT NORMAL SUMMER FLOW: III

DIFFICULTY AT HIGH WATER: IV

VOLUME: 2000–20,000 cfs

GRADIENT: 12 feet per mile

LENGTH: 89 river miles

TIME: 5 to 8 days

RAFT SIZE: 12 to 22 feet

WEATHER: Hot days, warm nights, possible thunderstorms. Generally, during July and August temperatures range from 80° to 90° by day, and from 55° to 70° by night. In September, rain is more likely, and cooler temperatures prevail; days vary from 50° to 75° and nights from 35° to 50°.

FISHING: Although fishing is usually poor, some talented anglers still manage to take salmon, steelhead, Dolly Varden, whitefish, smallmouth bass, and, in tributaries, trout. Idaho license required.

RIVER TRIP PERMITS: Private boaters need permits. Write well in advance to Big Creek District Ranger, Salmon National Forest,

McCall, Idaho 83638. Or write to National Forest District Ranger, Salmon National Forest, North Fork, Idaho 83466.

WATER CONDITIONS: Adequate flows for rafting are found throughout the year. During the run-off, which occurs in May, June, and sometimes part of July, flows generally range between 5000 and 20,000 cfs. The rest of the year, flows vary from 5000 down to a low of 2000 cfs.

RIVER HAZARDS: Skilled intermediates with good equipment can make this run. Most of the 40 or so rapids are easily read and demand no tricky maneuvering. At high water, approach Gunbarrel Rapid and Salmon Falls with extra caution.

The rapid always to approach with care is Big Mallard, which has a gigantic hidden hole. Run it on the far left, after you have thoroughly scouted it from head to foot along the left bank.

The standard take-out is on the left bank opposite the mouth of Vinegar Creek. If you go beyond this point, carefully scout Vinegar Creek Rapid. Although it is no longer a class V, as it once was, Vinegar remains difficult. It contains towering haystacks but requires little maneuvering, other than keeping the bow in, if entered correctly.

Les Jones's scroll map covers all the Salmon's hazards in detail.

ROAD DIRECTIONS: The Cache Bar put-in is roughly 35 miles west of North Fork, Idaho. To get there, take U.S. 93 to North Fork, then follow the Forest Service road that runs westward along the river.

The shuttle is almost 400 miles long. If you can possibly afford to do so, hire shuttle drivers. Reliable drivers may usually be found by asking around town in Salmon, 22 miles south of North Fork. The shortest shuttle is around to the north. Take U.S. 93 north toward Missoula; at Lolo turn west onto U.S. 12, "The Lewis and Clark Trail," then swing southwest to Riggins via U.S. 12, State highway 13, and U.S. 95. Immediately south of Riggins, turn left onto the rough road that follows the river 27 miles to the take-out at Vinegar Creek boat ramp. (For a longer voyage, you can take out at Alison Creek boat ramp just 10 miles east of Riggins.)

MAPS

Leslie Jones scroll map: "Main Salmon River."

Forest Service river map: "The Salmon, The River of No Return." Available free from Salmon National Forest, Salmon, Idaho 83467.

GUIDEBOOKS AND LITERATURE

Wildwater Touring by Scott Arighi and Margaret S. Arighi. New York: Macmillan, 1974. 334 pp. $8.95. This fine guidebook not only treats the whole subject of river touring in kayak, canoe, raft, or drift boat, it also covers in superb detail nine long wilderness river runs in Idaho and Oregon. Includes general descriptions of country, wildlife, rapids, and changes in difficulty from the lowest to the highest flows, and provides maps, detailed flow data, and mile-by-mile notes on campsites, rapids, landmarks, and points of interest.

The Bonanza Trail by Muriel Sibell Wolle. Bloomington, Ind.: Indiana University Press, 1958.

Idaho Federal Writer's Project. New York: Oxford University Press, 1950.

Journals of Lewis and Clark, edited by Bernard DeVoto. Boston: Houghton Mifflin, 1953.

"River Rat Pioneer" by Ethel Kimball, *True West*, December, 1963, pp. 30-31, 50-53.

"Sylvan Hart Is Alive and Well in the Wilderness" by J. Randal, *Avant Garde*, January, 1969, pp. 46-49.

"That River Swallows People. Some It Gives Up; Some It Don't" by Tom Brokaw, *West* (*Los Angeles Times Sunday Magazine*), Nov. 1, 1970, pp. 12-19.

"White-Water Adventure on Wild Rivers of Idaho" by John and Frank Craighead, *National Geographic*, February, 1970, pp. 213-239.

Wild Rivers of North America by Michael Jenkinson. New York: Dutton, 1973.

SELWAY

With its pure, sparkling water and white, sandy beaches, the Selway is a river of exquisite beauty. Tumbling through the largest wilderness in the United States, it abounds with trout, bighorn sheep, and brown bear. My mountain tent still carries a constellation of toothmarks made by a curious Selway bear that was dissuaded from giving me the big hug only by my hooting and clapping. This entire run lies along the retreat route taken by the well-spoken Chief Joseph and the Nez Perce Indians. Some old-timers in the area claim that Joseph still hangs out along the river, loafing in the sun, fishing, and occasionally terrorizing river runners in his bear outfit.

LOCATION: Selway-Bitterroot wilderness, northern Idaho, about 120 miles southwest of Missoula, Mont.

PUT-IN AND TAKE-OUT: White Cap Creek to just above Selway Falls

FAVORABLE SEASON: July

DIFFICULTY AT MOST WATER LEVELS: IV

DIFFICULTY AT EXTREME HIGH WATER: IV to U

VOLUME: 500–20,000 cfs

GRADIENT: 22 feet per mile

LENGTH: 49 river miles

TIME: 4 to 6 days

RAFT SIZE: Optimum size is 12 feet, but boats up to 17 feet are all right.

WEATHER: Commonly fair and hot in July. Occasional thunderstorms. Summer daytime temperatures characteristically range from 85° to 100° F.

FISHING: Selway trout respond nicely to dry flies; lures are productive at the mouths of creeks and in the deep pools below the falls. There are also chinook salmon and steelhead. An Idaho fishing license is required and can be purchased for the length of your trip.

PERMITS: Private boaters must have permits. Write many months in advance to West Fork Ranger Station, Darby, Mont. 59829. Phone (406) 821-3269.

WATER CONDITIONS: The Selway has a very short season because it is generally too high (and occasionally snowed in) until sometime in June and too low by mid-August. During May and June the run-off generally fluctuates between 5000 and 15,000 cfs or more. During July, the best month for rafting, flows usually range between 1000 and 5000 cfs. By mid-August the upper half of the run generally drops below 1000 cfs and becomes unrunnable. At this time, it is still possible to raft the lower portion by arranging a flight in to the airstrip at the mouth of Moose Creek. For current water level information, contact U.S. Forest Service, Moose Creek Ranger District Office, Grangeville, Idaho 83530. Phone (208) 983-1950.

RIVER HAZARDS: One of the most technically difficult rivers in the United States, the Selway is laced with rocky, intricate rapids that require frequent scouting and supreme boat-maneuvering skill. It should be attempted only by whitewater experts.

Difficult rapids are spaced out along the entire run. A particularly challenging series of almost continuous rapids is found in the 5-mile stretch below Moose Creek, where the river drops at the rate of 40 feet per mile. Wolf Creek Rapid (mistakenly shown on Les Jones' scroll map as Jim's Creek Rapid) is the most difficult single rapid of the run. Here the river dives into a heaving, churning battlefield of smoking foam and holes almost impossible to avoid. Scout carefully along both banks. Warning: Be sure to take out *above* Selway Falls.

For detailed coverage of the Selway Rapids, see Les Jones's scroll map.

ROAD DIRECTIONS: A paved road, road 437, runs to the put-in from the Montana town of Conner, which is on U.S. 93 about 70 miles south of Missoula. Without four-wheel drive, and perhaps even with it, be wary of approaching via Elk City, because the pass between Elk City, population about 15, and the put-in is often snow-blocked until August. Put in either below the bridge or ¼ mile up White Cap Creek. Some vehicles with four-wheel drive shuttle to the Selway Falls take-out via Elk City over tortuous, slick, snow-covered, mud roads. Most vehicles, though, shuttle the long way around up U.S. 93 to Lolo, down U.S. 12 to Lowell, and then up along the river to the take-out just above the falls at Race Creek Campground.

MAPS

Leslie Jones scroll map: "Selway River"; shows rapids and provides detailed running instructions.

U.S. Forest Service map: "Selway-Bitterroot Wilderness." Available free from U.S. Forest Service, Clearwater National Forest, Orofino, Idaho 83544.

GUIDEBOOKS AND LITERATURE

"Across the Bitterroots with Lewis & Clark—by Snowmobile," *Popular Mechanics,* December, 1968.

Buckskin Brigade by James Arthur Kjelgaard. New York: Scholastic, 1947.

The Flight of the Nez Perce by Mark Herbert Brown. New York: Putman, 1967.

From Where the Sun Now Stands, I Will Fight No More Forever by Will Henry. New York: Bantam Books, 1972.

Indian Braves and Battles and *Nez Perce Indian War and Original Stories.* $1.25 each. Available from Idaho County Free Press, P.O. Box 267, Grangeville, Idaho 83530.

Journals of Lewis & Clark, edited by Bernard DeVoto. Boston: Houghton Mifflin, 1953.

The Lewis & Clark Expedition by Richard Lewis Neuberger. New York: Random House, 1957.

No Other White Men by Julia Davis. New York: E. P. Dutton & Co., 1938.

"Selway River Whitewater Management Plan," Bitterroot and Nez Perce National Forests, U.S. Department of Agriculture, April, 1974.

HELL'S CANYON

The true, majestic Snake River of Hell's Canyon lies dead behind three dams. Below these dams, though, a shadow of the old serpent survives. Briefly running wild, then settling in for a long, mysterious glide through North America's deepest gorge, the Snake offers a day of intense action and then a week of smooth drifting. The warm water makes delightful swimming. The towering canyon walls dwarf the imagination. Sometimes strong upriver winds make rowing a necessity. The quiet is broken by the cawing and rustling of wildlife such as mule deer, bighorn sheep, bear, golden eagle, and osprey, and, sad to say, by the scream of passing jet boats, which each day hustle sightseers 100 miles up-river from Lewiston and then back again.

This canyon and its neighboring valleys were once the home of the intellectual Nez Perce Indians. Inventive and outreaching, the Nez Perce developed the Appaloosa, domesticated animals, and on hunting trips roamed over a wide area, often venturing across the Great Plains to hunt buffalo. When, in 1805, they encountered two peculiar characters called Meriwether Lewis and William Clark,* the Nez Perce were boldly curious and sent a delegation into the East to research the extraordinary ways and religion of the strange palefaces. As time went on, relentless encroachment by the white men led to the Nez Perce Indian War in 1877. Today, remnants of the Nez Perce tribe live on a reservation not far from Hell's Canyon, and within the canyon, numerous archeological sites and petroglyphs bear witness to the Indians' past.

LOCATION: Hell's Canyon forms a portion of the border separating Idaho from Oregon and Washington. The put-in lies roughly 110 miles northwest of Boise, Idaho.

PUT-IN AND TAKE-OUT: Just below Hell's Canyon dam to mouth of Grande Ronde River

FAVORABLE SEASON: April through October

DIFFICULTY AT MODERATE WATER: IV

DIFFICULTY AT HIGH WATER: V

VOLUME: 3000–35,000 cfs

GRADIENT: 8 feet per mile

LENGTH: 78 river miles

TIME: 5 to 7 days

RAFT SIZE: Rafts 16 to 30 feet long commonly used; 12-foot boats expertly rowed may be all right at lower levels.

---

* This meeting took place opposite the present site of Lewiston, 30 miles down-river from the take-out.

WEATHER: Very hot July and August. Warm in spring, early summer, and fall. Dazzling cloud formations. Depending on the season, daytime temperatures range from 65° to 110° and night-time temperatures range from 45° to 70°. Thunderstorms are common. Swarms of yellowjackets in August.

FISHING: Trout, smallmouth bass, and channel catfish are usually plentiful. Some steelhead plus chinook and silver salmon can be had in season. In all the earth, this is the last bastion of the giant white sturgeon. The largest of all freshwater fish, these sturgeon weigh up to 300 pounds and require special deep-sea, heavyweight tackle. Because they are an endangered species, sturgeon are fished purely for sport and must be released when caught. Idaho and/or Oregon licenses required, depending on which shore you're fishing from.

PERMITS: Private trip permits are required. Write well in advance to Hornet District Ranger, Payette National Forest, Council, Idaho 83612. Or write to Supervisor, Wallowa-Whitman National Forest, Federal Office Bldg., Box 907, Baker, Oreg. 97814.

WATER CONDITIONS: This is an enormous river held in check by many dams. Generally, flows fluctuate broadly from 8000 to 35,000 cfs during the wet months and from 4000 to 20,000 cfs during the dry months. The dams minimize spring high water. This run is never too low.

RIVER HAZARDS: Most of the magnificent rapids that won this canyon its name are now under water. But two very challenging rapids remain: The first, Wild Sheep Rapid, rated IV–V and found 6 miles below Hell's Canyon dam, is best scouted on the west bank. The second, Cache Rapid, rated IV, lies 2 miles below Wild Sheep and should also be scouted. Except for the first 18 miles, which have, besides Wild Sheep and Cache, a number of lively rapids, this is a mild, easy run.

ROAD DIRECTIONS: To reach the put-in below Hell's Canyon dam, take U.S. 95 to the town of Cambridge, which lies 70 miles northwest as the crow flies from Boise. Then follow state highway 71 northwest to the put-in below the dam. The round-trip shuttle is a 9-hour drive. Take highway 71 to Cambridge, go north on U.S. 95 to Lewiston, cross the river to Clarkston, and follow the road running south up the west bank of the Snake 30 miles to the take-out at the mouth of the Grande Ronde.

MAPS

Leslie Jones scroll map: "Hell's Canyon." Like all of Jones's scroll maps, this shows rapids, access points, etc., and provides running and scouting information.

U.S.G.S. quadrangles: 15′ He Devil (Id.), 15′ Kerman Point (Id.), 7½′ Kirkwood Creek (Id.), 7½′ Grave Point (Id.), 7½′ Wolf Creek (Id.), 7½′ Cactus Mtn. (Id.), 7½′ Deadhorse Ridge (Id.), 7½′ Wapshilla Creek (Id.), 7½′ Jim Creek Butte (Id.), 7½′ Limekiln Rapids (Id.).

U.S.G.S. Overview Map: "Snake River Sheet" (NL-11), 1:1,000,000 series. Scale: 16 miles to 1 inch. Shows entire run, including roads, but large scale permits no river details.

Forest Service maps of the area are available from Wallowa-Whitman National Forest, P.O. Box 907, Baker, Oreg. 97814; Nez Perce National Forest, 319 E. Main St., Grangeville, Idaho 83630; and Payette National Forest, Forest Service Building, P.O. Box 1026, McCall, Idaho 83638.

GUIDEBOOKS AND LITERATURE

The Flight of the Nez Perce by Mark Herbert Brown. New York: Putnam, 1967.

From Where the Sun Now Stands, I Will Fight No More Forever by Will Henry. New York: Bantam Books, 1972.

Journals of Lewis and Clark, edited by Bernard DeVoto. Boston: Houghton Mifflin, 1953.

Lewis & Clark Expedition by Richard Lewis Neuberger. New York: Random House, 1957.

Lewis & Clark, Pioneering Naturalists by Paul Russel Cutright. Urbana, Ill.: University of Illinois Press, 1969.

Nez Perce Indian War and Original Stories. $1.25. Available from Idaho County Free Press, P.O. Box 267, Grangeville, Idaho, 83530.

No Other White Men by Julia Davis. New York: E. P. Dutton & Co., 1938.

Snake Country Journal, 1826-27 by Peter S. Ogden, edited by K.G. Davies. London: Hudson's Bay Record Society, 1961.

Upper Snake River Valley Historical Society Quarterly. Available in the Bancroft Library, University of California at Berkeley; dates back to the 1890s.

ROGUE

The Rogue River Canyon is a voodoo haunt. Its pounding whitewater and long, body-warm pools are not, outwardly, supernatural. Nor are the fern grottoes, thick conifer forests, and mossy stone cliffs markedly weird. The tantalizing sidecanyon waterfalls like Flora Dell and the countless talismanlike boulders, though spellbinding, are not enchanted in any definable sense. Yet in its total effect the Rogue works powerful magic on all who experience it, firing the imagination, deepening the sense of wonder.

Midway through this run, at Winkle Bar, Zane Grey wrote many of his books. Peering out curiously from the edge of the forest, then as now, were bear, bobcat, deer, and raccoon. Water ouzel,

PHOTOGRAPH 27   A tantalizing waterfall on a sidestream in the Rogue River Canyon. (*Bob Krips Photo*).

pileated woodpecker, and great blue heron fly near the water, and bald eagles soar easily over the canyon.

LOCATION: Siskiyou Mountains of southwestern Oregon just northwest of Grants Pass

PUT-IN AND TAKE-OUT: Alemeda Campground or Grave Creek bridge to Illahe or Agness

FAVORABLE SEASON: June to September

DIFFICULTY AT LOW WATER: III$_4$

DIFFICULTY AT MOST WATER LEVELS: IV

DIFFICULTY AT EXTREME HIGH WATER OR FLOOD: IV to U

VOLUME: 700–60,000 cfs

GRADIENT: 12 feet per mile

LENGTH AND TIME: The full run from Alemeda Campground to Agness is 45 river miles long and is usually done in from 4 to 6 days. The wild, roadless, middle portion from Grave Creek bridge to Illahe is 34 river miles long and is most often run in from 3 to 5 days.

RAFT SIZE: Rafts 12 to 17 feet long are commonly used. Boats up to 22 feet are all right in high water; boats as small as 9 feet may be used during low water of late summer.

WEATHER: Often cold and cloudy in the spring, but very pleasant during summer. In summer, daytime temperatures usually range from 70° to 90° while nighttime temperatures average 60°. Slight chance of rain in June.

FISHING: The Rogue is famous for its large salmon and steelhead runs in spring and fall. In the fall especially, the shallows at the mouths of sidestreams are packed solid with huge salmon; the concentration of dorsal fins resembles a small forest. During summer, however, fishing is generally poor, though some talented anglers hook fine trout. Oregon license required.

RIVER TRIP PERMITS: At the time this is written, permits are required for commercial but not private trips. It is likely, though, that private boaters will need permits in the near future. Check current permit requirements by contacting Bureau of Land Management, Medford District Office, 310 W. 6th St., Medford, Oreg. 97501. Phone (503) 779-2351, extension 328. Or contact Forest Supervisor, Siskiyou National Forest, P.O. Box 440, Grants Pass, Oreg. 97526.

WATER CONDITIONS: Although occasional wet-season floods drive the volume up to and above 60,000 cfs, the Rogue generally ranges between 3000 and 15,000 cfs in winter and spring and between 800 and 4000 cfs in summer and fall. Flows gradually decrease during early summer, level off by mid-August, and then gradually pick up from about September 1 on through the fall. Like all the flows cited in this book, these are averages; the week-to-week flows may fluctuate in a wider range depending on rainfall. Almost without exception, however, the Rogue is runnable throughout summer and fall.

The Medford field office of the U.S.G.S. Water Resources Division keeps a monthly tab on the water level of the Rogue and can usually provide an accurate estimate of current flow. Contact Field Office, Water Resources Division, U.S. Geological Survey, 1019 W. Riverside, Medford, Oreg. 97501. Phone (503) 779-2351.

RIVER HAZARDS: The Rogue is difficult and dangerous and should be attempted only by experienced boaters. This is a river of long calms and relatively abrupt rapids.

Of the many demanding rapids, thundering Rainie Falls is the most awesome. Located about 2 miles below Grave Creek bridge, Rainie is an almost sheer 10-foot drop (see Photograph 23). Although it can be run at enormous risk at some water levels, it is far better to run or line down the steep, narrow, "fish-ladder" chute on the right. Rafts attempting the nearly vertical face of the fall itself often flip, sending crew and loose gear deep into the foamy reversal below. Escapees from the reversal are sometimes flushed 200 feet downstream before their lifejackets and frantic swimming efforts bring them to the surface of the aerated water.

About 2½ miles below Rainie is Tyee Rapid, where an island divides the river. Rated IV, Tyee is just as treacherous as Rainie at certain water levels. The main channel is on the right; scout along the right bank. The steep drop that is Upper Black Bar Falls, rated III and found 4 miles below Tyee, should be scouted along the right bank and then run on the far right. Kelsey Falls, 5 miles down from Upper Black Bar, should also be thoroughly scouted.

Seven miles below Kelsey is monolithic Mule Creek Canyon, where 40- to 50-foot vertical cliffs pinch the river into a wild and speeding torrent at times only 18 feet wide. The trick here is to navigate the heavy, rebounding waves while keeping your boat away from the cliffs. Toward the end of Mule Creek Canyon is the Coffee Pot, a whirlpool cauldron scooped out of the lefthand cliff. Keep right here. Because logs can jam in this slotlike canyon, it is wise either to check with other boaters who have recently run the river (you will probably encounter many—this is a very popular river) or to scout the entire canyon from the rim.

A short distance below Mule Creek Canyon is Blossom Bar, a class IV, labyrinthine garden of giant boulders (see Photograph 20). Rafts entering Blossom Bar incorrectly become wedged between these boulders like food stuck between giant teeth. The one navigable channel through the bar begins on the right, jogs left, and then flushes down through the center. Scout on the right.

For detailed coverage of the Rogue's rapids, see Leslie Jones's scroll map and Scott and Margaret Arighi's guidebook.

ROAD DIRECTIONS: The put-ins lie about 25 miles northwest of Grants Pass and are best reached via the road that runs through Merlin and Galice. Alemeda Campground is located about 4 miles north (downriver) from Galice, and Grave Creek bridge lies another 4 miles north of Alemeda. Both of these launch sites have boat ramps.

Shuttle west via the Galice-Agness road, which juts sharply westward just upriver from Galice. Long, rough, and often muddy, this road sometimes requires tire chains as late as mid-June. Numerous roads split away from this road and the forks can be confusing, so be sure to have the Siskiyou Forest Service map mentioned below. When the Rogue comes into view, drive upriver a few miles and cross to the west bank. For an Agness take-out, turn left after crossing the bridge and go back downriver to the broad take-out beach opposite the mouth of the Illinois River. For an Illahe take-out, turn right and go 3 miles upriver. About 1 mile beyond the National Forest Service campground at Illahe, at the foot of the hill and about 100 yards short of Foster Creek bridge, turn right onto the short drive leading to the Illahe (also called the Foster Creek) boat ramp.

BEGINNER'S RUN UPSTREAM: The 11-mile stretch of the Rogue from Indian Mary campground (about 5 miles above Galice) to Grave Creek bridge, rated II, is a good beginner's run. Do not assume, though, that just because you can navigate this easy stretch, you are ready for the more dangerous run below the bridge.

INTRIGUING LOCAL SPOT: The Oregon Shakespearean Festival, America's oldest Elizabethan theater, stages indoor and outdoor performances daily throughout the summer at Ashland, found on Interstate Highway 5 about 45 miles southeast of Grants Pass. Information about the current program, which usually includes modern as well as Shakespearean plays, can be obtained by writing Shakespearean Festival, Ashland, Oreg. 97520. It is best to get tickets ahead of time.

MAPS

Leslie Jones scroll map: "Rogue River."

U.S.G.S. quadrangles: 15′ Galice (Oreg.), 15′ Marial (Oreg.), 15′ Agness (Oreg.).

An overview map, "Siskiyou National Forest," which shows the shuttle road, plus a good river map, "Rogue River Wild and Scenic," are available free from U.S. Forest Service, Siskiyou National Forest, P.O. Box 440, Grants Pass, Oreg. 97526.

GUIDEBOOKS AND LITERATURE

West Coast River Touring: Rogue River Canyon and South by Dick Schwind. 1974. $5.95. Provides maps, mile-by-mile description of rapids, and information on flows, access points, shuttle roads, etc. Covers the Rogue, the Illinois, and every coastal river from the Oregon border south to San Luis Obispo. Includes a special note on the appropriateness of each run for rafts. A must for all boaters in the area. Available from The Touchstone Press, P.O. Box 81, Beaverton, Oreg. 97005.

Wild Rivers of North America by Michael Jenkinson. New York: Dutton, 1973.

Wildwater Touring by Scott Arighi and Margaret S. Arighi. New York: Macmillan, 1974. $8.95.

Indian Wars of the Rogue River by Dorothy and Jack Sutton. Grants Pass, Oregon: Josephine County Historical Society, 1969.

Indian Wars of the West by Paul Wellman. Garden City, N.Y.: Doubleday, 1956.

"Master Plan for the Rogue River Component of the National Wild & Scenic Rivers System," Bureau of Land Management, Medford, Oreg. 1969.

"Old Reelfoot—Scourge of the Siskiyous," by Art Chapman. *Frontier Times*, August-September, 1966, pp. 32-60.

"The Rogue," *Sunset*, June, 1966, pp. 77-85.

"Rogue River and Tributaries." This booklet is available from river guide Glen Woolridge, 913 SW "H" St., Grants Pass, Oreg.

"The Rogue, Wild River," Bureau of Land Management, Medford, Oreg. (booklet)

Strange World by F. Edwards. New York: Bantam Books, 1973.

Tall Tales from Rogue River: The Yarns of Hathaway Jones, edited by Stephen D. Beckham. Bloomington, Ind., and London: Indiana University Press, 1974. 178 pp. illus.

BY ZANE GREY

Forlorn River. New York: Grosset & Dunlap, 1927. Fiction.

Roping Lions in the Grand Canyon. New York: Harper & Row, 1928. Photographs.

Tales of Freshwater Fishing. New York: Harper & Row, 1928. 100 photographs.

Tales of Southern Rivers. New York: Harper & Row, 1924. Photographs.

Zane Grey: The Man & His Work. Autobiographical sketch, photographs. New York: Harper & Row, 1928.

California Rivers

KLAMATH

This moderate, bouncy river moves through the land of Big Foot and the gold rushes of old. Its warm water is perfect for swimming, and, interspersed with larger rapids, there are many easy riffles to thrill the air mattress rider. Marred only by a road following its course, the Klamath is a fine river for the intermediate rafter.

If you listen carefully in the quiet of summer evenings, that shy behemoth, Big Foot, can be heard stomping across the timbered mountainsides. Often on the Klamath, food supplies run short—a sure sign that Big Foot has been raiding the grub box. Also, big boulders shift around from year to year in ways that indicate the tampering of some powerful brute. Living in harmony with and yet more visible than Big Foot are great blue heron, osprey, bald eagle, mink, beaver, killdeer, otter, and bear.

LOCATION: Klamath Mountains of northern California about 50 miles due east of Crescent City

PUT-IN AND TAKE-OUT: Horse Creek to Happy Camp to Upper Ti Bar. If you can only do one section, run the lower stretch from Happy Camp to Upper Ti Bar; it is more exciting.

FAVORABLE SEASON: June through October

DIFFICULTY AT AVERAGE SUMMER FLOW: III

VOLUME: 1300–50,000+ cfs

GRADIENT: 12 feet per mile

LENGTH AND TIME: The full run from Horse Creek to Ti Bar (pronounced tee bar) is 67 river miles and is usually done in 6 days. The lower section from Happy Camp to Ti Bar is 30 river miles and usually requires 3 days. Because there are numerous access points along the entire run, trips may be shortened as desired.

RAFT SIZE: 7 to 18 feet

WEATHER: See Rogue.

FISHING: The Klamath is famous for its outstanding steelhead and salmon. Fishing is also excellent for trout, sturgeon, striped bass, and shad. Best time is September and October. To pursue the Klamath's streamlined, hardfighting "steelies," which weigh from 3 to 6 pounds, use light spinning, fly, or bait gear and work the riffles and fast-water glides. For salmon, use a 6-foot rod with 15- to 20-pound test monofilament line, and probe the deeper, slower water, especially at the mouths of tributary streams.

WATER CONDITIONS: This is a long, large river with dams upstream and a runnable flow throughout summer and fall. During June the flow ranges anywhere from 2000 to 14,000 cfs. From July through October the flow generally ranges between 1500 and 6000 cfs. During winter and spring, though, the Klamath is often extremely high and dangerous, with flows occasionally surging into full flood.

The Eureka field office of the U.S.G.S. Water Resources Division checks its gauge at Orleans, located about 20 miles downstream from the Ti Bar take-out, once each month and can usually provide an accurate estimate of the current water level. Contact Field Office, Water Resources Division, U.S. Geological Survey, P.O. Box 1307, Eureka, Calif. 95501. Phone (707) 443-0668.

Winds: Prevailing winds out of the northwest tend to blow directly upstream along the stretch above Happy Camp. This can be bad news for rafts, which, unless heavily loaded, are greatly affected by wind. Below Happy Camp, fortunately, the river angles south and the winds generally offer little trouble.

River hazards: This is a run of intermediate difficulty. Its rapids, which include Hamburg Falls, Rattlesnake Creek Rapid, Swillup Creek Rapid, and King Creek Rapid, provide excitement and moderate challenge. Some scouting is necessary. The stretch between Happy Camp and Ti Bar offers the most action. If you continue downriver below Ti Bar, be aware that Ishi Pishi Falls is unrunnable. For a mile-by-mile account of the Klamath, consult Dick Schwind's guide mentioned below.

Road directions: The various access points for this run are all spaced out along the Klamath River Road, state highway 96, which follows along the winding river, sometimes creeping in close, sometimes veering well away. Horse Creek, a wide spot in the road with a tiny post office, a store, and a camping resort, lies 30 miles west of where highway 96 leaves Interstate 5. In Happy Camp best access is found where a dirt road drops down to the water just below the mouth of Indian Creek. The take-out at Upper Ti Bar is located 3½ miles below Dillon Creek near the Guard Station just above Ti Creek.

Intriguing local places: While you're in this region, you may want to explore the Mount Shasta Caverns, or, for a fascinating glimpse into the history of the entire Klamath area, you may visit the quaint little museum in Yreka. For a great kick, time your trip to coincide with the annual Big Foot celebration in Happy Camp; write ahead to the Happy Camp Chamber of Commerce for the festival dates. In the fall, watch the Klamath River Indians net fish in their ancient manner at Ishi Pishi Falls. After your voyage, if you live to the south and have sufficient time, meander home down U.S. 101 through the magnificent coastal redwoods.

MAPS

U.S.G.S. quadrangles: 15′ Seiad Valley (Cal.), 15′ Happy Camp (Cal.), 15′ Ukonom Lake (Cal.), 15′ Dillon Mountain (Cal.).

GUIDEBOOKS AND LITERATURE

"Angler's Guide to the Klamath" by Millard Coots. This interesting pamphlet is published by the California Department of Fish and Game, Sacramento, Calif.

Bigfoot: The Yeti and Sasquatch in Myth and Reality by John R. Napier. London: Jonathan Cape, 1972. Illustrations.

A *Chronicle Tackle-Box Guide to Klamath River Fishing* by Jim Freeman. San Francisco: Chronicle Books, 1971.

"Is There an American Abominable Snowman?" *Reader's Digest,* January, 1969, p. 179.

Lower Klamath Country by Francis Turner McBeth. Berkeley, Calif.: Anchor Books, 1950. Maps.

"The Monster Apes of Oregon," in *Strange World* by Frank Edwards. New York: Ace Books, 1973.

Snake Country Journal, 1826-7 by Peter S. Ogden, edited by K. G. Davies. London: Hudson's Bay Record Society, 1961.

West Coast River Touring: Rogue River Canyon and South by Dick Schwind. 1974. $5.95. Available from Touchstone Press, P.O. Box 81, Beaverton, Oreg. 97005.

EEL

Between Alderpoint and Fort Seward the Eel is not a whitewater river, nor is it well suited to rafts. I mention it here, frankly, because it possesses an idyllic beauty that has haunted me for many years. The setting for one of my earliest trips, this run is one of easy riffles, of warm water unsurpassed for swimming, of broad, white beaches, and of striking rock formations towering up from midriver. But just why it lives in my mind as a paradise, I don't exactly know. In the course of that run over a dozen years ago, the four of us squabbled and feuded the whole time, our nerves were continually on edge, and we became hoarse with yelling at each other. To top it off, our ridiculous, donut-shaped raft was actually blown *upriver* by the powerful, daily wind. Like idiots, we had left the paddles at home, so we had to tow the raft downstream after the fashion of Erie Canal mules. It took us 4 days to make the 8-mile run. I loved it.

Saner personalities can find more whitewater and less pain on other parts of the Eel. The stretch from Dos Rios to Alderpoint makes an excellent 4- or 5-day voyage in May and June, and the Middle Fork of the Eel, from the confluence of the Black Butte River to the Levi Ranch, makes a nice 2-day run in April and May. For more information on these stretches, see Dick Schwind's guidebook mentioned below. Definitely do get more information, certain water levels can be quite hazardous and there are some very dangerous places on this run.

LOCATION: Coastal Range of northern California about 50 miles southeast of Eureka and 10 miles east of Garberville

PUT-IN AND TAKE-OUT: Alderpoint to Fort Seward

FAVORABLE SEASON: April to June

DIFFICULTY: I

VOLUME: 20–150,000 cfs

GRADIENT: 7 feet per mile

LENGTH: 8 river miles

TIME: 1 to 4 days

RAFT SIZE: 4 to 18 feet

WEATHER: Windy and hot

FISHING: Steelhead

WATER CONDITIONS: This is a free-flowing river with outrageous fluctuations in volume in the course of the year. During the wet months the flows vary erratically between 2000 and 40,000 cfs and sometimes, because of heavy rain, explode to an incredible 100,000 cfs or more. Obviously, the Eel is to be avoided during these times of high water. From April until sometime in June, runnable flows of 4000 to 1000 cfs generally occur. But bear in mind that even during this period rains can drive the flow dangerously high. Sometime in June the flow usually recedes to an unrunnable low. Then, as the summer progresses, the Eel continues to drop until it is not even a creek, but an ooze of 20 cfs or less. Because of the powerful upriver winds, a strong flow of from 3000 to 4000 cfs is best for rafting.

The Eureka field office of the U.S.G.S. Water Resources Division checks its gauge at Fort Seward once each month and can usually provide an accurate estimate of current flow. Contact Field Office, Water Resources Division, U.S. Geological Survey, P.O. Box 1307, Eureka, Calif. 95501. Phone (707) 443-0668.

RIVER HAZARDS: None. Easy riffles.

ROAD DIRECTIONS: The best road to Alderpoint leaves U.S. 101 just north of Garberville, climbs the steep Mail Ridge, runs through Harris, and then descends into the scenic Eel River Valley. The put-in is on the west bank just upstream from the Alderpoint bridge. The winding shuttle road linking Alderpoint and Fort Seward is shown on both the state road map and the U.S.G.S. 15′ quadrangle Alderpoint. Find the take-out on the left or west bank just upstream from the Fort Seward bridge.

MAPS

U.S.G.S. quadrangle: 15′ Alderpoint (Cal.).

GUIDEBOOKS AND LITERATURE

West Coast River Touring: Rogue River Canyon and South by Dick Schwind. 1974. $5.95. Provides maps, mile-by-mile narration of rapids, and information on flows, access points, shuttle roads, etc. Covers the Rogue, the Illinois, and every coastal river from the Oregon border south to San Luis Obispo. Includes a special note on the appropriateness of each run for rafts. Available from Touchstone Press, P.O. Box 81, Beaverton, Oreg. 97005.

Geology of the Eel River Valley Area, Humboldt County, Calif. Unpublished thesis by Bernadette A. Ogle. University of California, 1951. Maps, diagrams, tables.

Report on 1938 Eel River Survey. Sacramento, Calif.: California Division of Fish & Game, 1939. Preliminary outline of suggested stream and lake improvement.

Report to Water Commission on Water Supply by Philip E. Harroun. California: East Bay Water Commission, 1920. Fold-out maps.

SACRAMENTO

From Redding to Red Bluff the Sacramento is an ideal river for the first-time rafter. Its broad, mild rapids provide a safe setting for learning the basic oar and paddle strokes and for practicing maneuvers like the ferry and the portegee. Occasional snags and other obstacles keep the voyage interesting by providing something to maneuver around. And Chinese Rapid near the end of the run provides an exciting but not too difficult test of new rafting skill.

This is not a wilderness river. The surrounding countryside is farmland and at times houses are visible along the banks. Fortunately, though, the banks are thick with trees and blackberry bushes, giving the river an isolated, almost junglelike feeling. Water fowl are abundant.

LOCATION: Northern end of the California Central Valley about 200 miles due north of San Francisco

PUT-IN AND TAKE-OUT: Redding to Red Bluff

FAVORABLE SEASON: May to October

DIFFICULTY: I

VOLUME: 5000–100,000 cfs

GRADIENT: 4 feet per mile

LENGTH: 56 river miles

TIME: 4 days

RAFT SIZE: 6 to 20 feet

WEATHER: Warm to hot

FISHING: Steelhead and salmon in season; also, plentiful native trout. Lures, worms, roe, and flies are good here.

WATER CONDITIONS: The Sacramento is a large river with a flow controlled by Shasta Dam. During the wet months, flows range widely from 10,000 to 70,000 cfs, and on rare occasions during extremely wet winters the flow soars above 100,000 cfs, flooding the banks and wreaking general havoc. But from May through October the flow is around 15,000 to 20,000 cfs, and, as summer and fall creep by, the flow gradually diminishes to about 7000 cfs.

The Redding field office of the U.S.G.S. Water Resources Division keeps a monthly tab on the water level of the Sacramento and can generally provide an accurate estimate of the current flow. Contact Field Office, Water Resources Division, U.S. Geological Survey, 640 Twin Rd., Redding, Calif. 96001. Phone (916) 246-5282.

RIVER HAZARDS: Snags are sometimes a serious hazard on this run. Most numerous in spring and early summer, snags in the form of uprooted trees often dot the river channel. Be alert and begin evasion early, for when hit these snags tend to draw pinned objects underwater and hold them there permanently.

Except for Chinese Rapid, where some maneuvering is required, most of the rapids are broad, choppy, and easy. Just below Chinese Rapid, in beautiful Iron Canyon, large whirlpools sometimes spin but rarely seriously threaten rafts.

ROAD DIRECTIONS: There is a low dam across the river in the middle of Redding, so put in at the south end of town. The city lagoon, on Marina Drive off state highway 44, makes a good launch site. Interstate 5 links the two towns. In Red Bluff, take out at the boat ramp on the west bank just south of the center of town.

For a shorter trip, possible take-outs upstream of Red Bluff are Ball's Ferry and Jelly's Ferry; see topo maps.

INTRIGUING LOCAL PLACE: A deepening experience awaits those who can spend a couple of days at the Trappist Monastery near Vina. Vina lies 20 miles south of Red Bluff, just off state highway 99; ask in town for directions to the monastery. The Trappist monks, after 300 years of quietude, have recently abandoned their vows of silence, and it seems that this was a wise move, for they do love to talk. To stay with and talk with these men is to perceive more clearly the broad range of human choice, and it is also to be reminded that a tree is a great deal more than just a tree.

MAPS

U.S.G.S. quadrangles: 15′ Redding (Cal.), 15′ Anderson (Cal.), 15′ Tucson Buttes (Cal.), and 15′ Red Bluff (Cal.).

For greater detail, the run is covered by five U.S.G.S. quadrangles of the 7½′ series: 7½′ Enterprise (Cal.), 7½′ Cottonwood (Cal.), 7½′ Ball's Ferry (Cal.), 7½′ Bend (Cal.), 7½′ Red Bluff East (Cal.).

GUIDEBOOKS AND LITERATURE

Gypsy Days on the Delta by Erle Stanley Gardner. Maps, photos, ports. Primarily houseboating but some up-river information as well.

Parks & Outdoor Recreation Plan and Program. Sacramento, 1971: "Regional General Plan." Sacramento Regional Planning Commission. Complete detailed maps.

The Sacramento, River of Gold by Julian Dana. New York: Farrar, Straus & Giroux, 1939.

Sacramento River Study, 1964. House resolution. California Department of Beaches and Parks. Illustrated, fold-out maps.

SOUTH FORK OF THE AMERICAN

The American River offers a blend of relaxing calms and thrilling rapids. Moving first among big, rounded foothills and later through steep granite canyon, it initially struts out quick and strong, then yawns serenely, and finally, with little warning, rushes headlong through the fabled American River Gorge, where one rapid follows the next in fast succession. In places, wildflowers blanket the shore.

Six miles downstream from the put-in, the river flows past the township of Coloma. It was here that James Marshal discovered gold, thereby starting the California gold rush. A lunch stop here will give you time to examine the many relics and monuments, which include a reconstructed Sutter's Mill.

LOCATION: Western slope of the Sierra Nevada Range about 30 miles due east of Sacramento

PUT-IN AND TAKE-OUT: Highway 193 bridge (Chili Bar) to Salmon Bar bridge on Folsom Lake

FAVORABLE SEASON: May through September

DIFFICULTY AT NORMAL SUMMER FLOW: III

DIFFICULTY AT HIGH WATER: IV

VOLUME: 100–8000 cfs

GRADIENT: 24 feet per mile

LENGTH: 20 river miles

TIME: 1 or 2 days

RAFT SIZE: 12 to 18 feet

WATER CONDITIONS: In May and June, the flow generally ranges from 1500 to 3000 cfs and occasionally floods up to 8000 cfs or more. *Warning:* This river is very cold and dangerous above 4000 cfs. In July the flow is usually adequate, averaging from 800 to 1000 cfs. During August and September, dams upstream usually provide an adequate flow on weekdays and Saturday afternoons but not on Sundays. Flow information is difficult to obtain in advance because both S.M.U.D. and P.G.&E. control the dam gates and neither seems to know what the other is going to do.

RIVER HAZARDS: This run has over 50 rapids. The first section, from Chili Bar to Coloma, drops at 30 feet per mile, is continuously swift, and has several long rapids rated III–IV. Most of these rapids can be surveyed from upstream. The first long rapid, found about ½ mile below Chili Bar, is called Meatgrinder. What appears from upstream as Meatgrinder's final haystack is not a haystack but a *rock*. This pointed rock has slashed the bottoms of countless rafts, but if you know about it ahead of time, it is easy to avoid on the left. The most difficult rapid in this section, called Troublemaker, lies ½ mile above Coloma; it should be scouted. An S-shaped rapid in which the water is forced right then left, Troublemaker is runnable down the left side at most water levels.

The second section, between Coloma and Lotus, is fairly easy. The only excitement is provided by Old Scary: beforehand there are two sharp, short drops and then, around the bend, Old Scary suddenly presents itself, causing faint hearts to skip a beat. But relax, Old Scary's two souse holes offer some fun but no serious danger.

The third section, from Lotus to Folsom Lake, starts off, after one rapid just below Lotus, with several miles of calm. Then, as the riverbed turns to granite, the canyon walls grow jagged, and boulder formations rise from the water, the river plunges into the Gorge, where one rapid follows another almost without interruption for 8 miles. Near the beginning of these rocky drops is Satan's John, where the river pinches, spins, and drops like an enormous, diabolic toilet. Once in the Gorge, just take each rapid as it comes and, if necessary, keep some people bailing so the boat doesn't become swamped. Stopping places are scarce.

When Folsom Reservoir is up, one must cross almost a mile of flatwater to reach the take-out at the bridge, but when the reservoir is down the current takes you clear to the bridge. The take-out involves an arduous carry up a steep slope.

ROAD DIRECTIONS: Near the highway 193 bridge (located 4 miles north of Placerville), there are at least two possible launch sites. Both are privately owned and a fee is charged at each. One, Chili Bar, is immediately downstream from the bridge on the right bank. The other, Golden Nugget Campground, is on the right bank a short distance upstream from the bridge, and is raeched by a well-marked drive that turns right from highway 193 a bit north of the bridge. A fully developed campground operated by John Hood, the Golden Nugget allows you to drive right down to the water's edge and launch in calm water. At Chili Bar, on the other hand, rafts and gear must be carried down a steep bank, and the run must be begun in the middle of a rapid.

Shuttle south on highway 193 to Placerville, northwest on highway 49 to Pilot Hill, then south on the Folsom/Pilot Hill road to Folsom Lake. The take-out is on the north bank where Salmon Bar bridge crosses the Folsom Lake backwater at the mouth of Skunk Canyon.

MAPS

U.S.G.S. quadrangles: For detailed coverage, get 7½′ Garden Valley (Cal.), 7½′ Coloma (Cal.), and 7½′ Pilot Hill (Cal.). The U.S.G.S. quadrangles 15′ Georgetown (Cal.) and 15′ Auburn (Cal.) also cover the run but offer less detail.

GUIDEBOOKS AND LITERATURE

Sierra Whitewater by Charles Martin. 1974. $5.95 plus 50¢

postage and 36¢ sales tax in California. A fine, thorough guide to the rivers of California's Sierra Nevada Range. Describes 74 runs of all levels of difficulty. Includes 52 detailed maps showing acces points, etc. Covers mileage, gradient, shuttle, and time. Although the difficulty ratings are specified for whitewater kayak and covered canoe, they give the rafter a fair idea of what to expect. A final chapter on conservation issues discusses the many threats to these superb but fragile whitewater rivers. Available from Fiddleneck Press, P.O. Box 114, Sunnyvale, Calif. 94088.

Anybody's Gold: The Story of California's Mining Towns by Joseph Henry Jackson. San Francisco: Chronicle Books, 1970.

California Department of Beaches & Parks. "American River Study, 1964," requested by House Resolution. Illustrated, fold-out maps.

California Department of Public Works. "Supplemental Report with Reference to Size of Folsom Reservoir of American River Development." 1947. Fold-out maps.

Gold Rush Country: A Guide to California's Mother Lode and Northern Mines by the editors of *Sunset* Magazine. Menlo Park, Calif.: Lane Publishers, 1968.

STANISLAUS

Cutting through a wild canyon deep in the Mother Lode, the Stanislaus moves past sandy beaches, caves, and occasional limestone cliffs. Along its banks are abandoned gold mines, and a short climb up Rose Creek brings one to swimming holes and slick-rock water slides. Its dependable, summer-long flow, lively yet moderate rapids, and proximity to urban centers have made the Stanislaus the most popular whitewater river in California. Because of this intense popularity, the Stanislaus does not offer a solitary wilderness experience, but it can provide good whitewater.

However, the Stanislaus is gravely threatened: The New Melones Dam, unless modified, will flood the entire run. A dam of high cost and dubious benefit, the New Melones, at the time this is written, is being strongly resisted by river people and conservationists all over California. Please support this effort. For more information write the Environmental Defense Fund, 2728 Durant, Berkeley, Calif. 94704, or call (415) 548-8906.

PHOTOGRAPH 28 A 7-man paddle raft on the Stanislaus, a lively but forgiving river. (*Photo courtesy of the American River Touring Association.*)

LOCATION: Western slope of the Sierra Nevada Range about
100 miles, as the crow flies, west and slightly south of San Francisco. Roughly 5 miles north of Sonora.

This run consists of two sections that can be done separately
or together. The 9-mile upper section from Camp Nine to Parrot's
Ferry is racy and rather difficult and is best attempted by people
with some experience, while the 5-mile lower section from Parrot's Ferry to the Route 49 bridge is mild and easy and makes a
fine maiden voyage for novice rafters. Together the two sections
make a choice 2-day adventure.

UPPER SECTION

PUT-IN AND TAKE-OUT: Camp Nine to Parrot's Ferry bridge

DIFFICULTY AT NORMAL SUMMER FLOW: III

DIFFICULTY AT HIGH WATER: IV to U

GRADIENT: 26 feet per mile

LENGTH: 9 river miles

TIME: 1 day

LOWER SECTION

PUT-IN AND TAKE-OUT: Parrot's Ferry bridge to Route 49 bridge at Melones

DIFFICULTY AT NORMAL SUMMER FLOW: II

DIFFICULTY AT HIGH WATER: III

GRADIENT: 10 feet per mile

LENGTH: 5 river miles

TIME: 1 day

BOTH SECTIONS

FAVORABLE SEASON: April to October

VOLUME: 200–5000 cfs

RAFT SIZE: During high water, use boats 16 to 22 feet long. During normal summer flow, rafts 10 to 18 feet long are best.

WEATHER: Usually good but unpredictable in spring. Warm throughout summer.

FISHING: Trout.

PERMITS: At the time this is written, private boaters do not need permits. But this may change in the near future. For information on current permit requirements, contact Outdoor Recreation Planner, Folsom District Office, Bureau of Land Management, 63 Natoma St., Folsom, Calif. 95630.

WATER CONDITIONS: The P.G.&E. powerhouse at Camp Nine generally releases runnable flows all year. Most of the time the volume ranges between 600 and 1500 cfs, but from March through

June the flow fluctuates erratically between 1500 and a murderous 5000 cfs. *During high water, the Stanislaus is extremely cold and dangerous.* In the course of the first hot spells and warm rains of spring, melting Sierra snow can transform this river into an icy killer.

RIVER HAZARDS: The 16 major rapids of the upper Stanislaus tend to be forgiving and often allow even beginners to scoot through all right. At times, though, these rapids impose severe penalties on the inexperienced and ill-prepared. Each season dozens of canoes and ill-guided rafts become wrapped around Stanislaus rocks, and their crews are either drowned or forced to climb the steep canyon walls. Years ago, I arrived at the Camp Nine put-in to find four nearly naked men trying to hot wire their Volkswagen. They had lost everything in the river, their rafts, gear, clothing, even their car keys. But they did not complain. They were glad just to be alive. Clearly, the upper Stanislaus is best attempted by people with some experience and with proper equipment. Beginners should be accompanied by experienced people.

ROAD DIRECTIONS: To reach the Camp Nine put-in, drive north from Sonora through Columbia toward Vallecito. Pass Moaning Cave and, ½ mile before Vallecito, turn right onto the Camp Nine (Stanislaus Powerhouse) road. This road is easy to miss because the sign faces Vallecito. If you read Vallecito, you've gone too far; double back ½ mile. The Camp Nine road drops down to the river after 9 miles of wandering and winding; the put-in is on the north bank a bit downstream from where the road crosses the river.

Parrot's Ferry bridge is found where the Columbia-Vallecito road crosses the river. Convenient access to the water lies on the north bank just upstream from the bridge.

The Melones take-out is on the north bank immediately upstream from the state route 49 bridge. Long ago this was the site of Robinson's Ferry. For a small fee, a car may be left here for the duration of a trip.

INTRIGUING LOCAL PLACES: Nestled within a few miles of the Stanislaus are the historic gold-rush towns of Angel's Camp, Murphys, and Columbia. The area also has many caves.

MAPS

U.S.G.S. quadrangle (one map covers all but the first half mile): 7½' Columbia (Cal.).

GUIDEBOOKS AND LITERATURE

Sierra Whitewater by Charles Martin. 1974. $5.95 plus 50¢ postage and 36¢ sales tax in California. Available from Fiddleneck Press, P.O. Box 114, Sunnyvale, Calif. 94088.

Anybody's Gold: The Story of California's Mining Towns by Joseph Henry Jackson. San Francisco: Chronicle Books, 1970.

California Bureau of Land Management's White Water Use Study by Brad Welton and Dick Harlow. Available from Bureau of Land Management, Folsom District Office, 63 Natoma St., Folsom, Calif. 95630.

Gold Rush Days with Mark Twain by Wm. Robert Gillis. New York: A. & C. Boni, 1930.

Gold Rush Diary by Elisha Douglass Perkins (1832–52). Lexington, Ky.: University of Kentucky Press, 1967. Tells of ventures on the Overland Trail out west to the Pacific. Some entertaining river scenes.

Gold Rush Country: A Guide to California's Mother Lode and Northern Mines by the editors of *Sunset* Magazine. Menlo Park, Calif.: Lane Publishers, 1968.

"Troubled Waters: The Stanislaus," *Oar & Paddle*, vol. 1, no. 1 (May–June, 1974). This is a good magazine for whitewater boaters. Contact *Oar & Paddle*, P.O. Box 621, Idaho Falls, Idaho 83401.

"The Upper Stanislaus Gorge" by Mary Ellen Whitmore. *American Whitewater*, vol. 15, no. 3 (Autumn, 1970).

TUOLUMNE

The Tuolumne (pronounced too WAL ah me) is the most exhilarating and delightful stream in the West. More like a giant creek than a river, it filters down through one rock or boulder garden after another. Steep beyond imagining, plunging this way and that, it moves in patterns that are frolicsome, tangled, and mesmerizing. To dance a lightly loaded 7-man raft through the intricacies of the Tuolumne is to test your skill severely, and, truly, it is to laugh with sheer delight, for here is rafting at its very best.

LOCATION: Western slope of Sierra Nevada Range roughly 120 miles, as the crow flies, west and a bit south of San Francisco. About 15 miles west of the entrance to Yosemite National Park.

PUT-IN AND TAKE-OUT: Lumsden Campground to Ward's Ferry bridge

FAVORABLE SEASON: May to September

DIFFICULTY AT LOW TO MEDIUM WATER (800–2000 CFS): III–IV

DIFFICULTY AT HIGH WATER (2000–4000 CFS): IV–V

DIFFICULTY AT EXTREME HIGH WATER (ABOVE 4000 CFS): V to U

VOLUME: 100–12,000 cfs

GRADIENT: 36 feet per mile

LENGTH: 18 river miles

TIME: A fine 1-, 2-, or 3-day trip

RAFT SIZE: 12 to 17 feet

WEATHER: Variable in spring. Warm to hot in summer.

FISHING: Trout

RIVER TRIP PERMITS: As this is written, trip permits are required of commercial outfitters but not of private rafters. For information concerning the current permit policy, contact U.S. Forest Service, Groveland Ranger Station, Hwy 120, Groveland, Calif. 95321. Phone (209) 962-7825.

WATER CONDITIONS: Hetch Hetchy Dam usually provides an adequate flow year round. Most of the time the volume averages from 700 to 1200 cfs. During spring and early summer, however, the flow averages between 1300 and 2600 cfs and occasionally

spurts to 6000 cfs, 12,000 cfs, or more. Above 4000 cfs the Tuolumne is exceedingly dangerous and probably should not be attempted.

Throughout the year the flow fluctuates somewhat with the
demand for electricity, which is greatest during the week and
lowest on weekends. This fluctuation is of concern to boaters
during late summer, when the volume generally drops to a barely
runnable flow of 600 to 800 cfs on Saturdays and often plummets
to a ridiculous trickle of 100 cfs on Sundays. (Because the Clavey
River bolsters the flow 5 miles below the put-in, it is often possible to continue downriver on Sunday if one has run the first 5
miles on Saturday.) On Monday mornings the flow usually picks
up dramatically between 11 A.M. and noon. For current flow information call Hetch Hetchy Dam, (209) 989-2431.

RIVER HAZARDS: With over 50 major rapids and an extremely
steep gradient, the Tuolumne should be attempted only by vary
experienced and well-equipped boaters. The first 5-mile stretch
from the put-in to the confluence with the Clavey River is the
steepest, with a fall of 40 feet per mile. Scout Clavey Falls, found
just below the mouth of the Clavey; at some water levels this
sheer fall can be run on the left, while at others it must either be
lined, portaged, or run on the right. Below the Clavey there is
a bit more space between rapids, but the rapids continue to be
very tricky. At extremely low water, the last rapid before Ward's
Ferry bridge is the most difficult of the run.

ROAD DIRECTIONS: To reach the Lumsden put-in, turn north from
state route 120 onto Ferreti Road at La Casa Loma Store and
Chevron station located 8 miles east of Groveland. Then turn
right onto the narrow, rutted, dirt road to Lumsden Campground.
The put-in, about 2 miles downstream from Lumsden bridge, is
marked by a wide spot in the road. About 100 yards beyond, or
upstream, from the put-in is the campground, which offers toilets,
tables, and free camping.

The Ward's Ferry bridge take-out is reached by paved road
from Groveland. At the north end of the bridge on the upstream
side, there is a short, steep, dirt road going down to the water's
edge.

LOCAL SHUTTLE DRIVER: Lee Hilarides, who runs La Casa Loma
Store and Chevron station, will shuttle vehicles to Ward's Ferry

for a reasonable fee. Lee also has cabins, trailer spaces, and camp-sites for rent.

MAPS

U.S.G.S. quadrangles: 15′ Tuolumne (Cal.), 15′ Sonora (Cal.).

GUIDEBOOKS AND LITERATURE

Sierra Whitewater by Charles Martin. 1974. $5.95 plus 50¢ postage and 36¢ sales tax in California. Available from Fiddleneck Press, P.O. Box 114, Sunnyvale, Calif. 94088.

"Trouble on the Tuolumne" by Carl Trost, *American White-water*, vol. 16, no. 4 (Winter, 1971), pp. 120–121.

The Tuolumne River: A Report on Conflicting Goals with Em-phasis on the Middle River by Robert Hackamack and the mem-bers of the Tuolumne River Conference. 1970. $2.00. A Sierra Club publication. Available from Sierra Club, Tuolumne River Conference, 5100 Parker Rd., Modesto, Calif. 95350. 82 pp. with map and photographs.

EAST CARSON

Swift yet calm, this little river glides smoothly from high moun-tain meadows to desert canyons. Though its steep gradient sug-gests otherwise, it is an easy stream with only minor rapids. Un-like many rivers, which alternately pool up in calms and crash down in rapids, the East Carson flows fast and steady with few interruptions.

LOCATION: Eastern slope of the Sierra Nevada Range in north-ern California/Nevada about 20 miles southeast of Lake Tahoe

PUT-IN AND TAKE-OUT: Hangman's Bridge near Markleeville, Calif., to abandoned dam near U.S. 395 in Nevada

FAVORABLE SEASON: June

DIFFICULTY: II

VOLUME: 60–2500 cfs

GRADIENT: 27 feet per mile

LENGTH: 20 river miles

TIME: 2 days

RAFT SIZE: 9 to 17 feet

WEATHER: Fair and cool in June; cold nights.

FISHING: Rainbow, cutthroat, and brook trout as well as the primordial Carson River cutthroats, Piute trout. License required.

WATER CONDITIONS: Most of the year, the East Carson ranges between 100 and 500 cfs and is too low to run. During the spring run-off, however, which generally begins mid-May and recedes in early July, the flow usually ranges from 900 to 2000 cfs and is delightfully runnable. On those rare occasions when the flow exceeds 2000 cfs, the river becomes markedly more difficult.

RIVER HAZARDS: Though it is a mild river with relatively easy rapids, the East Carson presents a few special problems. About 1 mile below the put-in, a large fallen tree sprawls across the river's narrow channel, leaving only a tight passage on the far left. Because there are no eddies above this savage snag, which has been the scene of many serious accidents, it is crucial that boaters stop well upstream and scout.

Midway through the run a barbed-wire fence spans the river. Cutting this wire would only raise the ire of the riparian landowners, perhaps spurring them into taking action against future boaters. A better solution is to tie a brightly colored cloth to the wire so as to alert boaters. When passing under wires of this sort, a boat is placed sideways in the current, the members of the crew crouch as low as possible and someone in the center of the boat reaches down stream, grabs the wire, lifts and swings it over the entire raft, and releases it after the raft has passed completely underneath.

WARNING: Be careful not to go over the old dam at the end of the run, where the river plunges 40 feet into a hypnotizing caldron of foam. One can tell he is approaching the dam by the many willows lining the banks just above it, and by the loud roar of the falls.

ROAD DIRECTIONS: The quaint California settlement of Markleeville is best approached from the west via U.S. 50 and then state route 89 and from the east via route 88. An easy put-in is found 1 mile southeast of Markleeville at Hangman's Bridge, located where route 89 crosses the East Carson River. Shuttle to the Nevada take-out up route 89 to Woodfords, northeast on route 88 to Centerville, across to Gardnerville, and southeast 5 miles on U.S. 395 to the take-out turn-off. Finding this turn-off takes attention. Keep an eye on the river as you drive south along U.S. 395. A short distance south of where the river veers sharply westward away from the highway, a dirt road leaves the highway and runs west parallel to but well uphill from the river's southern bank. The take-out is immediately upstream from the abandoned dam, shown on the Mt. Siegel quadrangle map as "pump." As you drive in along the crude road this dam appears as a 40-foot waterfall.

MAPS

U.S.G.S. quadrangles: 15′ Markleeville (Cal.), 15′ Topaz Lake (Cal.), and 15′ Mt. Siegel (Cal./Nev.).

U.S.G.S. "Plan and Profile: Carson River, Nevada-California." Sheets 2 and 3. 75¢ per sheet.

GUIDEBOOKS AND LITERATURE

Sierra Whitewater by Charles Martin. 1974. $5.95 plus 50¢ postage and 36¢ sales tax in California. Available from Fiddleneck Press, P.O. Box 114, Sunnyvale, Calif. 94088.

A Contribution to Geographic and Economic History of Carson, Walker and Mono Basins in California and Nevada by William M. Maule. San Francisco: U.S. Forest Service, California Region, 1938. Plates and maps, reproduced from typed copy.

The Daring Adventures of Kit Carson and Fremont, among Buffaloes, Grizzlies, and Indians . . . Being a spirited diary of the most difficult & wonderful expeditions ever made, opening the great pathway to the Pacific! New York: Hurst & Co., 1885.

Kit Carson's Autobiography, edited by M. M. Quaife. Lincoln, Neb.: University of Nebraska Press, 1966.

Southwestern Rivers

LODORE, WHIRLPOOL, AND SPLIT MOUNTAIN CANYONS OF THE GREEN RIVER

"The Gates of Lodore." Say it aloud; the very sound of the name suggests the awesomeness of the place. At the Gates of Lodore, the Green River leaves the low plain of Brown's Hole to knife with spectacular effect directly into the towering Uinta Mountains. The two halves of the imposing Uintas stand close together like great jaws ready to clamp shut on the audacious river that dares to divide them. But it is the river that is strongest here. Far older than the mountains, the Green resolutely maintained its course for countless centuries as the upstart Uinta Range pushed skyward around it. In the craggy, precipitous canyons that have been created, the river moves alternately through long calms and booming, boulder-cracking rapids. Except for an occasional small green park and a fringe of vegetation along the banks, the canyons are arid and rocky.

When shafts of summer sunlight angle into these narrow, winding canyons, people flock in to risk their lives on the thundering water. So many come that in order to protect the narrow green fringe, campsites with tables, outhouses, and firepits have been established and must be used by all. Fortunately, the whole place is protected as the Dinosaur National Monument. The Monument encompasses not only the Green and its tributary the Yampa but also a dinosaur bone quarry near the take-out at Split Mountain.

PHOTOGRAPH 29   Craggy and precipitous, the Canyon of Lodore knifes through the towering Uinta Mountains.

During the 1890s, Brown's hole just above the Gates of Lodore was the hideout of Butch Cassidy and the Wild Bunch, who, when not loafing around the Hole, passed their time dynamiting trains, heisting banks, and evading lawmen.

In Red Canyon, not far upriver from Brown's Hole, there is an easy 7-mile run good for first-time rafters. The put-in is just below Flaming Gorge Dam, and the take-out is at Little Hole.

LOCATION: Middle Rocky Mountains, Uinta Range, Dinosaur National Monument, northwestern Colorado/northeastern Utah

PUT-IN AND TAKE-OUT: Gates of Lodore to Split Mountain boat ramp

FAVORABLE SEASON: May to September (best month: June)

DIFFICULTY AT NORMAL SUMMER FLOW: IV

DIFFICULTY AT HIGH WATER: V

VOLUME: 700–10,000 cfs

GRADIENT: 12 feet per mile

LENGTH: 44 river miles

TIME: 4 to 6 days

RAFT SIZE: 12 to 33 feet

WEATHER: Can be chilly and wet in May. In summer, the weather is usually dry except for occasional thundershowers, and temperatures fluctuate in the mid 80s by day and in the low 50s at night.

FISHING: Middling catfish and trout in the river. Excellent trout up Jones Creek, which has a fish hatchery on its upper reaches. As there are some endangered species of fish in the river, check with the Monument visitor center before fishing these canyons. A Utah license may be purchased for the duration of your trip.

RIVER TRIP PERMITS: Permits are required. At the time this is written, the Dinosaur National Monument has, aside from the Grand Canyon and Cataract Canyon, the most detailed guidelines governing river boating found anywhere. Trip leaders must have experience on rivers of comparable or greater difficulty. Rafts must be made of heavy material and must be at least 12 feet long and 6 feet wide (7-man size). No motors are allowed. Life preservers, detailed river maps (such as Les Jones's scroll map), a first-aid kit, a full extra set of oars or paddles per boat, an air pump, a repair kit, water containers, extra rope, and emergency food must be carried. Maximum boat loads are spelled out as follows.

		Number of People per Boat	
Boat Size	*Oar raft with supplies*	*Oar raft without supplies (1-day trip)*	*Paddle raft with or without supplies*
13' raft (7-man size)	3	4	4
16' raft (10-man size)	4	6	6
22' pontoon	9	10	Rafts larger
27' pontoon	11	15	than Green
33' pontoon	14	17	River Boats (17') must have oars & frames.

The intention of these regulations is not to discourage rafting but to minimize accidents by keeping inexperienced, ill-prepared boaters and unsafe, overloaded boats off the rivers. If you have a well-rigged raft 7-man size or larger and follow the safety code spelled out in Chapter Two, you should have no trouble obtaining a permit. For full details on boating regulations and application forms for trip permits, write River Ranger, Dinosaur National Monument, P.O. Box 101, Dinosaur, Colo. 81610.

The rivers of Dinosaur are very popular, so it is wise to secure trip permits many months in advance. When you write, ask them also to send you a map of the Monument; the maps they provide make it much easier to find the put-in and take-out.

WATER CONDITIONS: The Green is controlled by Flaming Gorge Dam, which generally releases runnable flows all year round. High flows, usually ranging between 3000 and 6000 cfs, are released in May, June, and July. Low flows of from 700 to 2000 cfs are the norm for the rest of the year. For precise information about current flow conditions, contact Power Operations Office, Colorado River Storage Project, Montrose, Colorado; phone (303) 249-4551. Or contact Flaming Gorge Field Division, Dutch John, Utah; phone (801) 885-3415.

RIVER HAZARDS: This run should be attempted only by experienced people. Scout all major rapids. In the canyons a sign displaying the rapid's name is posted above each major rapid.

Lodore Canyon. In Lodore, the river falls 270 feet in 18 miles for an average gradient of 15 feet per mile. Of the 36 rapids, 6 are medium or major. The most difficult rapids are Upper and Lower Disaster Falls and Hell's Half Mile. Upper and Lower Disaster Falls in low water are rated IV and II, respectively, but in high water they together rate V. Hell's Half Mile rates IV in low and V in high water. The first Powell expedition, in 1869, was terrorized by these three rapids—they lost the *No Name* in Upper Disaster—and named them accordingly. Although they do not entirely live up either to their names or to Powell's descriptions of them in his journal, they should nevertheless be approached with utmost caution. In Upper Disaster the river narrows and accelerates into a broad, massive backroller flanked by large rocks and smaller holes. Just below, in Lower Disaster, the Green charges down an elongated scrub board of holes and wild waves. In the two parts of Disaster Falls, the river drops 35 feet in 0.6 miles. In Hell's Half Mile, where the drop is 30 feet in less than 0.5 miles, the river brushes around some big midstream boulders, speeds through a narrow chute of towering backcurlers, and then splits around two islands into three long, steep, rocky channels. When running Hell's Half Mile, the rafter enters just left of the pointed rock at the head of the rapid, ferries right to line up with the chute, and then, after keeping bow-in through the chute's cresting haystacks, ferries right again to hit the center channel between the islands, where he picks his way down through the rocks and holes.

Whirlpool Canyon. In Whirlpool, the river falls 105 feet in 10 miles for an average drop of 10.5 feet per mile. Whirlpool has 11 rapids, all of which are fairly easy.

Split Mountain Canyon. In this canyon the river falls 145 feet in 7 miles for an average gradient of 21 feet per mile. Of the 13 rapids, 4 are medium and several are sometimes major. Split Mountain Canyon's first and most difficult rapid in Moonshine Rapid. Rated IV, Moonshine consists of a long, fast approach, a riverwide hole with a narrow place in the center, where a raft can sometimes squeeze dryly through, and a long, swift, boulder-dotted runout. One mile below moonshine is S.O.B. Rapid. Rated III–IV, S.O.B. is rough and wild no matter how it is run, but it is usually not dangerous if the bow is kept into the waves. Not far below S.O.B. is Schoolboy Rapid, rated III. Here the current swings tightly against a low cliff on the left; an elementary right ferry handles it with ease.

All the significant rapids in each of the three canyons are covered on Les Jones's scroll map.

ROAD DIRECTIONS: The put-in just above the Gates of Lodore, which sports a concrete boat ramp, an electric outlet for motorized air pumps, water, primitive camping facilities, and toilets, is in the extreme northwestern corner of Colorado. To get there take gravel road #318 northwest from Maybell, on U.S. 40.

The shuttle is a slow 140 miles each way; allow at least 8 hours for a round trip. From the Gates of Lodore, take road #318 back to Maybell, turn right onto U.S. 40, drive west 80 miles, and at Jensen, Utah, turn right onto Route 149, the route to the Dinosaur National Monument quarry area. Once inside the Monument, follow the signs to the Split Mountain campground and boat ramp.

MAPS

Leslie Jones scroll map: "Lodore, Whirlpool, & Split Mountain Canyons of the Green." For information on how to order these scroll maps, see Chapter One.

Dinosaur River Guide. A detailed river map showing rapids and containing a photographic history of the river and surrounding area. Waterproof edition $6.00. Available from: Westwater Books, P.O. Box 365, Boulder City, Nevada 89005.

Overview map: U.S.G.S. Special Map, "Dinosaur National Monument, Utah-Colo." U.S.G.S. note describing this map: "The text printed on the reverse side of this map discusses the history of exploration and mapping of the area and describes the topography, rock formations, and ancient and present-day flora and fauna, with illustrations. Also includes a generalized columnar section of the rocks exposed." Specify contour or relief edition. $1.50.

U.S.G.S. quadrangles: 7½′ Canyon of Lodore North (Colo.), 7½′ Canyon of Lodore South (Colo.), 7½′ Jones Hole (Utah/Colo.), 7½′ Island Park (Utah), 7½′ Split Mountain (Utah), 7½′ Dinosaur Quarry (Utah).

GUIDEBOOKS AND LITERATURE

River Runner's Guide to Dinosaur National Monument and Vicinity by Philip T. Hayes and George C. Simmons. $3.00. Provides thorough, mile-by-mile account of geological features, plus maps and historical information. Covers both the Green and the Yampa. Available from The Powell Society, Ltd., 750 Vine St., Denver, Colo., 80206.

The Exploration of the Colorado River and Its Canyons by John W. Powell. Major Powell's own account of his exploration of the Green and Colorado Rivers. New York: Dover, 1961. 400 pp. Illustrated reprint of 1895 *Canyons of the Colorado*. $3.00.

The Geologic Story of the Uinta Mountains by W. R. Hansen. U.S.G.S. Bull. 1291, 1969. 134 pp. Illustrated.

Geology of Dinosaur National Monument and Vicinity, Utah-Colorado by G. E. and B. R. Unterman. Utah Geological and Mineralogical Survey Bull. 42, 1954. 288 pp. Illustrated. Map.

Guide to Dinosaur Land and the Unique Uinta Country by G. E. and B. R. Unterman. Vernal, Utah. 1972. Illustrated.

The Outlaw Trail; A History of Butch Cassidy and His Wild Bunch by Charles Kelly. New York: Devin-Adair, 1959. 374 pp. Illustrated.

This Is Dinosaur; Echo Park Country and Its Magic Rivers by Wallace E. Stegner. New York: Knopf, 1955. 97 pp. Illustrated.

Wild Rivers of North America by Michel Jenkinson. New York: Dutton, 1973.

For additional information write Dinosaur National Historical Association, P.O. Box 127, Jensen, Utah 84035.

YAMPA

Meandering through a breath-taking canyon of sandstone cliffs, the Yampa offers days of drifting and warm swimming and a bullet-fast ride through one of the West's most lethal rapids. A tributary of the Green and a part of Dinosaur National Monument, the Yampa links up with Whirlpool and Split Mountain Canyons to form an unsurpassed 72-mile river adventureland. Deer, bobcat, coyote, and rabbit roam the Yampa's banks.

LOCATION: Middle Rocky Mountains, Dinosaur National Monument, northwestern Colorado/northeastern Utah

PUT-IN AND TAKE-OUT: Deerlodge Park to Split Mountain boat ramp

FAVORABLE SEASON: Early May to mid-July

DIFFICULTY: IV

VOLUME: 200–7000 cfs

GRADIENT: 12 feet per mile on the Yampa—Deerlodge to Echo Park; 8 feet per mile on the Green—Echo to Split Mountain boat ramp

LENGTH: 72 river miles (46 miles on the Yampa, 26 on the Green)

TIME: 4 to 7 days. Although the run can be done in 4, 6, or 7 days, allow time for loafing and exploring side canyons, particularly the Indian storage cave near Mantel Ranch. (See Les Jones's scroll map for location; the cave is up a little canyon on the left about 34 miles below the put-in.)

RAFT SIZE: 12 to 33 feet

WEATHER: Sometimes chilly and wet in May. In June, the weather is usually dry with occasional thundershowers. June temperatures range in the mid-80s by day and in the low 50s by night.

FISHING: Plenty of catfish, some trout, plus Colorado "salmon" of the whitefish type. See "Lodore, Whirlpool, and Split Mountain" fishing note above.

RIVER TRIP PERMITS: Permits are required. See discussion of Dinosaur National Monument permit requirements in previous section.

WATER CONDITIONS: Run-off on the Yampa begins in April, peaks in late May or early June, and recedes to unrunnable sometime in July. The Yampa is seldom runnable after August 1st and is sometimes too low to run as early as July 1st. The Green is dam controlled and runnable all year.

RIVER HAZARDS: The great hazard on the Yampa is Warm Springs Rapid, a long raceway of mad water pocked with a series of holes along the left, jagged rocks on the right, and an enormous hole dead center at the foot (see Photograph 19). Rated IV, Warm Springs has flipped 33-foot pontoons and has claimed the lives of at least three professional boatmen. Understandably, passengers on most commercial and many private trips are asked to walk around this one. Found 41 miles below Deerlodge Park, Warm Springs lies at the mouth of Warm Springs Draw. Land on the right to scout thoroughly.

The Yampa's other rapids are relatively easy. Only two are noteworthy and perhaps deserve scouting: The first, found 10 miles below Deerlodge Park, is Teepee Rapid, rated II–III, and the second, found 13 miles below Teepee, is Big Joe Rapid, rated II.

For an account of Whirlpool and Split Mountain Canyons on the Green, see the previous section.

ROAD DIRECTIONS: The Deerlodge Park put-in, with its campground outfitted with tables and outhouses but no water or other facilities, lies at the eastern tip of Dinosaur National Monument in the northeastern corner of Colorado. It is reached via a gravel road that runs northwest from U.S. 40 about 15 miles west of Maybell. This road, which passes the town of Lily and then follows the river to Deerlodge, is marked by a small sign that is easy to miss in the dark of night.

For the shuttle, return to U.S. 40, go west to Jensen, then, after turning right onto Route 149, which leads to the Monument's quarry area, follow the signs to the take-out at Split Mountain boat ramp.

MAPS

Leslie Jones scroll map: "Yampa River." (For lower portion of the trip on the Green you will also need the scroll map "Lodore, Whirlpool, & Split Mountain Canyons of the Green.")

Dinosaur River Guide. Contains detailed river map plus a photographic history of the river and surrounding area. Also covers the Green. Waterproof edition $6.00. Available from Westwater Books, P.O. Box 365, Boulder City, Nev. 89005.

Overview map: U.S.G.S. Special Map, "Dinosaur National Monument, Utah-Colo." U.S.G.S. note: "The text printed on the reverse side of this map discusses the history of exploration and mapping of the area and describes the topography, rock formations, and ancient and present-day flora and fauna, with illustrations. Also includes a generalized columnar section of the rocks exposed." Specify either contour or relief edition. $1.50.

U.S.G.S. quadrangles: 7½' Indian Water Canyon (Colo.), 7½' Haystack Rock (Colo.), 7½' Tanks Peak (Colo.), 7½' Hells Canyon (Colo.), 7½' Canyon of Lodore South (Colo.), 7½' Jones Hole (Utah/Colo.), 7½' Island Park (Utah), 7½' Split Mountain (Utah), 7½' Dinosaur Quarry (Utah).

GUIDEBOOKS AND LITERATURE

"Down the Yampa in the Land of Carved Walls" by Harold Gilliam. *San Francisco Chronicle,* "This World" section, Sunday, August 5, 1973.

See also bibliography for Lodore, Whirlpool, and Split Mountain Canyons above. Virtually all the books that apply to them apply to the Yampa.

THE GREEN RIVER WILDERNESS:
DESOLATION AND GRAY CANYONS *

This is a voyage under a big sky through country of stark and desolate beauty. The Canyon of Desolation resembles the Grand Canyon in its majesty and bigness. Shorter Gray Canyon is just downstream. Both canyons are isolated and wild; both inspire awe with countless untrammeled beaches, Indian petroglyphs, and natural arches. They were named by explorer John Wesley Powell, who first descended the Green River in 1869 on his way to the Colorado. Later this stretch of river was frequented by Butch Cassidy and the Wild Bunch; the story of their exploits is told by Pearl Baker in *The Wild Bunch at Robber's Roost.*

Except for a few exciting rapids, this is a run of soothing, mild water. It is a place for the rafter who has deep feelings for rivers and their canyons but is not looking for high adventure.

LOCATION: Eastern Utah about 120 miles southeast of Salt Lake City

---

* Prepared with the assistance of Tim Lawton and Mike Rettie.

PUT-IN AND TAKE-OUT: Sand Wash to foot of Swasey Rapid

FAVORABLE SEASON: June to October (best month: June)

DIFFICULTY AT LOW WATER: IV

DIFFICULTY AT HIGH WATER: III–IV

VOLUME: 2000–20,000 cfs

GRADIENT: 6 feet per mile

LENGTH: 84 river miles

TIME: 5 to 10 days

RAFT SIZE: 7 to 18 feet

WEATHER: Hot

FISHING: Catfish plentiful. Trout in some sidestreams.

RIVER TRIP PERMITS: Permits are not currently required of private groups. However, boaters are asked to check in at the ranger station at Sand Wash. Because permits may be required in the future, it would be wise to write ahead and check on current permit policy. Write to Bureau of Land Management, District Office, P.O. Drawer AB, Price, Utah 84501.

WATER CONDITIONS: Runnable all year. High flows from 8000 to 20,000 cfs occur during May, June, and July. Low flows ranging from 2000 to 4000 cfs are the norm the rest of the year. This run becomes rockier and more difficult when the water level drops below 3000 cfs.

RIVER HAZARDS: Despite its high rating, this is a relatively easy run suitable for intermediates alone or beginners in the company of experienced rafters. Most of the 60 or so rapids are elementary, but a few are difficult and should be scouted. These difficult rapids include McPherson Rapid, rated III, Coal Creek Rapid, rated IV, and Rattlesnake Rapid, rated III—all are covered both on Les Jones's scroll map and in Felix Mutschler's *River Runner's Guide.* Three and one-half miles below the Swasey take-out, there is a dam, rated class IV; so if you continue below Swasey, take care.

ROAD DIRECTIONS: The Sand Wash put-in lies 21 miles as the crow flies or 29 river miles downriver from Ouray. It can be approached from the north via Myton or from the south via Wellington. Both routes involve over 50 miles of rough road, and so should be attempted only by day, never by night; unfamiliar put-ins are always much more difficult—and sometimes impossible—to locate at night.

Coming via Myton. Myton is situated about 100 miles as the crow flies or 140 road miles east of Salt Lake City on U.S. 40. The road to Sand Wash turns south from U.S. 40 a few miles southwest of Myton. Shown on Utah state highway maps, this road runs south and somewhat west through the Bad Land Cliffs until it turns east to follow Minnie Maud Creek (also called Nine Mile Creek) down to the Green River.

Coming via Wellington. Wellington lies on U.S. 50 about 70 miles by air or 81 miles by road southeast of Provo, Utah. The turnoff is 4 miles east of Wellington. The road climbs northward through the Roan or Brown Cliffs and then swings eastward to join the Myton road as it follows Minnie Maud or Nine Mile Creek down to Sand Wash.

Another possible put-in is Ouray. Though more accessible than Sand Wash, the Ouray put-in adds 29 miles of flat water to the trip.

Shuttle. With a Sand Wash put-in, shuttle up Minnie Maud Creek, traverse the Roan or Brown Cliffs, pass Wellington, and take U.S. 50 south to the take-out near the town of Green River. If you put in at Ouray, shuttle around widely to the west, taking U.S. 40 to Duchesne, state route 33 to Castle Gate, and then U.S. 50 to Green River.

The take-out just below Swasey Rapid lies 12 miles upriver from the town of Green River, and is reached by a dirt road running up the east side of the river. Be aware that this road is not passable during or just after heavy rain. It is also possible to take out right at the town of Green River.

MAPS

Leslie Jones scroll map: "Green River: Desolation and Gray Canyons." Includes historic notes and running instructions.

Green River Wilderness: Desolation River Guide by Laura Evans and Buzz Belknap. $3.95. A detailed, mile-by-mile river map showing rapids, side streams, points of interest, etc. Many fine photographs. Available from Westwater Books, P.O. Box 365, Boulder City, Nevada 89005.

U.S.G.S. quadrangles: The run from Sand Wash to Swasey Rapid or the town of Green River is covered by five maps—15′ Nutters Hole (Utah), 15′ Firewater Canyon (Utah), 15′ Flat Canyon (Utah), 15′ Range Creek (Utah), and 15′ Gunnison Butte (Utah). If you put in at Ouray, also get these two maps, 7½′ Ouray (Utah) and 7½′ Uteland (Utah).

GUIDEBOOKS AND LITERATURE

River Runner's Guide to the Canyons of the Green and Colorado Rivers with Emphasis on Geologic Features. Vol. 4, "Desolation and Gray Canyons," by Felix E. Mutschler. $3.00. A mile-by-mile description of rapids, history, and geological features. Available from The Powell Society Ltd., 750 Vine St., Denver, Colo. 80206.

The Exploration of the Colorado River and Its Canyons by John Wesley Powell. New York: Dover, 1961. $3.00.

Massacre: The Tragedy of White River by Marshall Sprague. Boston: Little, Brown, 1957. Gripping and historically accurate. Some reference to Green River. Conjures the atmosphere of the place.

The Sun Dance Religion: Power for the Powerless by Joseph G. Jorgensen. Chicago: University of Chicago Press, 1972. Ute/ Shoshoni sun dancing.

The Utes: A Forgotten People by Wilson Rockwell. Denver: Sage Books, 1956.

The Wild Bunch at Robber's Roost by Pearl Baker. Los Angeles: Westernlore Press, 1965.

WESTWATER CANYON OF THE COLORADO *

Compress the mighty Colorado into the narrow width of a Cali-

---

* Prepared with the assistance of Tim Lawton and Mike Rettie.

fornia river, and you have the wild millrace that is Westwater Canyon, also called Granite Canyon. Short but very tough, this stretch of river speeds between sheer sandstone cliffs and sculpted black schist of Pre-Cambrian origin. Once you have begun, the canyon permits no turning back, no escape. In the fast sections bailing must be constant, and rowing must be strong and precise.

LOCATION: Eastern Utah 190 miles south of Salt Lake City and 5 miles west of the Utah-Colorado border

PUT-IN AND TAKE-OUT: Westwater Ranch to Rose Ranch near Cisco

FAVORABLE SEASON: July to September

DIFFICULTY AT 2000–12,000 CFS: IV

DIFFICULTY AT 12,000–25,000 CFS: V

DIFFICULTY ABOVE 25,000 CFS: U

GRADIENT: 10 feet per mile

LENGTH: 17 river miles

TIME: 2 days

RAFT SIZE: Rafts 16 to 37 feet long are commonly used. Under 6000 cfs, 12-foot rafts may be all right. Above 12,000 cfs, only pontoons have a prayer in Westwater.

WEATHER: Generally hot. Up to 110° in June. Occasional thundershowers.

FISHING: Colorado River salmon, that is, bony squawfish; also, lots of small catfish.

RIVER TRIP PERMITS: Permits are required for private trips through Westwater. Permits for small groups are free, but a $10 fee is charged for permits for groups of 25 people or more. Though small groups can often obtain permits on short notice, it is essential that large groups request permits at least 80 days in advance of their proposed trips. During the rafting season, a Bureau of Land Management ranger lives in a trailer at the Westwater Ranch put-in. This friendly individual is prepared to issue permits for private parties, provide information and assistance, and check permits for all river runners. If he is not in when you happen by, sign the visitor register. Naturally, the Bureau of Land Management people strongly recommend that everyone attempting Westwater have full and proper equipment plus considerable previous rafting experience on rivers of comparable difficulty. To obtain permit application forms and further information, write well ahead to Bureau of Land Management, P.O. Box 1327, Monticello, Utah 84535. Or call (801) 587-2247.

WATER CONDITIONS: This is a free-flowing river with a widely fluctuating water level. During May, June, and sometimes part of July, spring floods of up to 50,000 cfs transform Westwater into a heaving maelstrom. Above 12,000 cfs the rocks submerge and the individual rapids merge into a single, continuous blast of raging spume. Under these conditions just keeping a raft off the canyon walls demands enormous effort and skill. The boat is spun, one buoyancy tube after another is forever being sucked down, people get flushed out—the scene is crazy and unpredictable. Only pontoons should attempt the canyon above 12,000 cfs, and even they should stay home when flows mount over 25,000 cfs. Flows below 12,000 cfs, on the other hand, are manageable for 10-man boats, and levels below 6000 cfs are all right for 7-mans. During most of the year when the river is not in flood, flows generally range between 2000 and 7000 cfs. Current flow information may be obtained from the Bureau of Land Management people mentioned above.

RIVER HAZARDS: This is a run for veteran rafters preferably in the company of others who have made the run before. The country is open and the river relaxed at the Westwater Ranch put-in. But a few miles downstream, the canyon's limestone cliffs begin to muscle up and in, making campsites scarce and forcing the river into a faster pace. There is, though, a good campsite at the mouth of the Little Dolores River, 7 miles below the put-in. A half-mile walk up the Little Dolores brings one to a good swimming hole at the foot of a waterfall.

Two miles below this camp is Funnel Falls, rated II (Photograph 30). Here the channel pinches to a fraction of its width

PHOTOGRAPH 30   Funnel Falls in the narrow, lunar defile that is Westwater Canyon. (*Bob Krips Photo, courtesy of the American River Touring Association.*)

and the river drops suddenly, creating a broad cresting wave. Like many big waves, this one alternately rounds off and crests back in an unpredictable manner. If you are lucky, your raft sweeps through dry; if you are not, it takes on much water. From Funnel Falls to horrendous Skull Rapid, the river is a millrace.

Skull Rapid, class IV, presents the rafter unfamiliar with it with an insoluble dilemma: It should be scouted, but to scout it is to render impossible the optimum run. In Skull the river narrows and accelerates through a zone of haystacks and holes and then pounds against the righthand cliff which juts into the river and dramatically divides the current into a whirlpool (merely an inescapable eddy at low water) gouging into the cliff on the right and a surging runout on the left. The best run, generally, is to approach right of center and pick up momentum ferrying left through the narrow entrance and maintain this earnest ferry left to avoid not only the whirlpool on the right but also the great cleaving edge of cliff dividing the current dead center. But here's the problem: To scout Skull the rafter must pull into a small eddy just above its brink on the left (no small feat in itself), and this rules out any possibility of entering right of center and gathering momentum left through the entrance. Solution? None. But if it's any comfort, the cleaving cliff edge does have an ample eddy cushion which, if you can pull at least somewhat left in the turbulent approach, will tend to spill your raft safely off to the left.

Below Skull there is a short calm. Then the water again picks up speed to whip through Little Cisco (also called Sock It to Me), rated II, Last Chance, also a II, and other rapids on its way to the end of the canyon not far downstream.

ROAD DIRECTIONS: The road to Westwater Ranch may be hard to find. First drive to the junction of Interstate 70 and U.S. 50 and U.S. 6, which is 8 miles west of the Utah/Colorado border. Take the road that goes south to Westwater. When the road forks after crossing the creek, go left. There is a Bureau of Land Management ranger station at the put-in near Westwater Ranch.

Where U.S. 50 turns north just east of Cisco, the little road running east leads to the take-out at the old pump house near Rose Ranch. If necessary, ask in Cisco for directions.

MAPS

Leslie Jones scroll map: "Westwater Canyon."

Canyonlands River Guide by Bill and Buzz Belknap. $3.95. A mile-by-mile river map showing rapids, points of interest, access points, etc. With historic photographs. Available from Westchester Books, P.O. Box 365, Boulder City, Nevada 89005.

CATARACT CANYON OF THE COLORADO *

Moving through the Land of Standing Rock, Cataract Canyon not only offers striking scenery and deep isolation but also has some of the most challenging big water in North America. This is a three-phase voyage: At the outset there are 51 miles of calm river, then come 16 miles of exploding rapids, and last come 27 miles of still water on the upper reaches of Lake Powell.

LOCATION: Southeastern Utah upriver from Lake Powell

---

* Prepared with the assistance of Tim Lawton and Mike Rettie.

PUT-IN AND TAKE-OUT: Potash Mine near Moab to Hite marina on Lake Powell. It is also possible to put in on the Green River at the town of Green River, Utah, or at Mineral Canyon, about 65 miles downstream from the town of Green River. The Green, which is larger than the Colorado at the confluence, crawls 117 miles through Labyrinth and Stillwater Canyons to join the Colorado just above Cataract Canyon.

FAVORABLE SEASON: May to September (*Warning:* During wet years Cataract can be too high for small boats, that is, anything under 28 feet, in May and June.)

DIFFICULTY: IV–V

VOLUME: 4000–60,000 cfs

GRADIENT: Overall is 5 feet per mile. For the 16 miles of rapids in Cataract, the slope is 15 feet per mile. In Big Drop the slope is 29 feet per mile for 3 miles.

LENGTH: 94 miles

TIME: 5 to 8 days

RAFT SIZE: Boats of 16-foot size up to pontoons are commonly used. The upper limit for boats under 20 feet is about 25,000 cfs. Escorted 12-foot boats may be all right under 5000 cfs.

EQUIPMENT NOTE: A small outboard motor is needed to cross the upper reaches of Lake Powell at the end of the trip.

WEATHER: Hot

FISHING: Colorado River salmon and catfish; the latter go wild for Bisquik balls.

RIVER TRIP PERMITS: Permits are required. Permit requirements are similar to those for the Grand Canyon (see discussion of Grand Canyon permits below). For information and application forms, write well ahead to Superintendent, Canyonlands National Park, 446 South Main, Moab, Utah 84532.

WATER CONDITIONS: Because Cataract Canyon drains an even

broader area of the Southwest than Westwater and because the nearest dam is quite far off, Cataract's flow fluctuates enormously. Most of the year the flow ranges between 6000 and 12,000 cfs. But during May, June, and part of July, the flow often climbs to 40,000 cfs and occasionally soars over 100,000 cfs. In the spring of 1966, for instance, the volume skyrocketed to 115,000 cfs; Georgie White ran the canyon then and reported 50-foot waves. During dry years, however, the spring run-off does not climb much over 10,000 cfs.

Between 11,000 and 14,000 cfs Cataract is very tough. Some of the rapids are a bit easier at 20,000 cfs. But as the volume rises above 25,000 cfs, the rapids begin to flow together and the run becomes exceedingly difficult.

RIVER HAZARDS: In its short 16-mile length, Cataract Canyon has about 32 rapids, give or take a few depending on the level of Lake Powell. Approach each with caution, scouting often.

The toughest section is the 3-mile stretch near the end of the run with a drop of 29 feet per mile, a staggering drop for a river this size. Within the space of these 3 miles, two huge rapids occur, Mile Long and Big Drop. Both these rapids are conglomerates made up of several individual rapids each. When flows exceed 40,000 cfs, these individual rapids combine into single, continuous maelstroms, but at lower water levels they separate into distinct, abrupt drops. The following chart from Les Jones' scroll map shows how various water levels affect Big Drop. The ratings are on the Western (1-to-10) Scale:

Flow	Description	Difficulty Rating
4000–8000 cfs	Big Drop is three abrupt, rocky drops.	(3) (6) (7)
8000–12,000 cfs	Big Drop is three abrupt, rocky drops.	(4) (6) (7)
12,000–24,000 cfs	Three rapids tend to but don't combine.	(3) (5) (6)
40,000–60,000 cfs	Three rapids combine.	(4) (8) (9)
60,000 cfs–flood		(10+)

Big Drop, foremost among Cataract's rapids, is exceedingly difficult *at almost all water levels* because it demands precise maneuvering in extremely heavy water. Unlike most of the big rapids of the Grand Canyon, which, though enormous, generally require little technical maneuvering (in many cases one just keeps the bow into the waves and hangs on), Big Drop demands that the rafter ferry with accuracy in the midst of towering waves, any one of which could flip his boat should it broach. (While the rapids of the Grand Canyon are caused by rock fanning out into the river from side canyons, Cataract's rapids are caused by the giant rubble of talus slopes constricting the river.) The three rapids that make up Big Drop should be run one at a time. Stop above each and scout *with total thoroughness*. Study each rock and wave until you know the rapid blind. The names of Big Drop's three rapids are Teapot (or Big Drop One), Satan's Seat (sometimes called Kolb), and Satan's Gut.

ROAD DIRECTIONS: The Potash Mine put-in lies on the north bank about 17 miles downriver from Moab. It is reached by Scenic Hwy 279, which runs down along the north side of the river from U.S. 160. Shuttle around to the north through Green River and Hanksville to the take-out at Hite. On the south side of Lake Powell where state route 95 crosses the lake, Hite is a barebones little marina with cold beer and boat ramps.

INTRIGUING LOCAL SPOT: Arches National Park, with more than 100 natural stone arches, is just upriver from the Potash put-in.

MAPS

Leslie Jones scroll map: "Cataract Canyon."

Canyonlands River Guide by Bill and Buzz Belknap. $3.95. A mile-by-mile river map showing rapids, points of interest, access points, etc. With historic photographs. Also covers Westwater Canyon. Available from Westwater Books, P.O. Box 365, Boulder City, Nevada 89005.

Overview map: U.S.G.S. Special Map, "Canyonlands National Park and Vicinity, Utah."

U.S.G.S. quadrangles: Entire run covered by 6 maps of the 15′ series—15′ Hatch Point (Utah), 15′ Upheaval Dome (Utah), 15′ The Needles (Utah), 15′ Orange Cliffs (Utah), 15′ Mouth of Dark Canyon (Utah), 15′ Browns Rim (Utah). For greater detail, the run is covered by 13 maps of the 7½′ series—7½′ Carlisle 1 NW (Utah), 7½′ Carlisle 2 NE (Utah), 7½′ Carlisle 1 SW (Utah), 7½′ Carlisle 2 SE (Utah), 7½′ Carlisle 3 NE (Utah), 7½′ Carlisle 3 NW (Utah), 7½′ Carlisle 3 SW (Utah), 7½′ Orange Cliffs 4 SE

(Utah), 7½′ White Canyon 1 NE (Utah), 7½′ Orange Cliffs 4 SW (Utah), 7½′ White Canyon 1 NW (Utah), 7½′ White Canyon 2 NE (Utah), 7½′ White Canyon 2 NW (Utah.).

GUIDEBOOKS AND LITERATURE

River Runner's Guide to the Canyons of the Green and Colorado Rivers. Vol. 2, "Labyrinth, Stillwater, and Cataract Canyons" by Felix E. Mutschler. Denver: The Powell Society, Ltd. $3.00.

Archaeological Remains in the Whitewater District, Eastern Arizona by Frank Roberts. Washington, D.C.: U.S. Government Printing Office. Technical but excellent.

The Exploration of the Colorado River and Its Canyons by John Wesley Powell. New York: Dover, 1961. $3.00.

Prehistoric Indians of the Southwest by Hannah Marie Wormington. Denver: Denver Museum of Natural History, 1970. $2.00.

The Pueblos: A Camera Chronicle by Laura Gilpin. New York: Hastings House, 1941. Excellent photographs of riverside cliff dwellings.

Standing Up Country; the Canyonlands of Utah and Arizona by Gregory Crampton. New York: Knopf, 1965. $17.00.

All the above books, except Roberts, are available for the prices indicated from Canyonlands Natural History Association, 72 South Main, Moab, Utah 84532. This source also has many other books that treat the surrounding area; a complete list will be sent on request.

THE GRAND CANYON

The Colorado of the Grand Canyon is a river apart. Fashioned on an immense scale, and moving with cosmic rhythm, it pools up in lengthy calms, some 10 miles long, and crashes down in great, sudden drops of incredible violence. The canyon is a swirling maze of blazing stone, here cream white, there glaring red, elsewhere jet black. Written on the mile-high walls is the story of the earth from its earliest hour; the Pre-Cambrian schist of the inner gorge hardened when the infant earth's crust first cooled. Stacked above the schist in horizontal belts of variegated stone are the ages, the eons of time. Men, take women. Women, take men. The main danger down here is climbing the walls—I mean—you need each other.

To voyage through the Grand Canyon is to do more than grip

PHOTOGRAPH 31 Marble Gorge on the Grand Canyon run as seen from a cave high in the canyon wall. (*Bob Krips Photo, courtesy of the American River Touring Association.*)

stone, see time, and brave big whitewater. It is also to thirstily chug drink in a desert canyon dotted in places with towering ocotillo and barrel cactus; to play with intimate friends in cool glens like Vasey's Paradise and Elves Chasm where waterfalls enter the river, and to gaze in silence at Red Wall Cavern, a hole in the wall of Marble Gorge said to be large enough to seat 50,000 people.

Some of the Grand Canyon's most singular offerings are hidden up its side canyons. For instance, a 3-mile hike up Tapeats Creek followed by a scramble up Thunder River brings one to a stunning waterfall where Thunder River gushes out of a limestone cave. Half a day's climb (12 miles) along Havasu Creek takes one up past spectacular waterfalls to heavenly Supai, an oasis village where the Havasupai Indians still dwell as they have for centuries. (It is possible to arrange to stay overnight with the Indians. Write to Havasupai Tourist Information, Havasupai Tourist Enterprise, Supai, Ariz. 86435.)

LOCATION: Colorado Plateau in northwestern Arizona

PUT-IN AND TAKE-OUT: Lee's Ferry to Diamond Creek or Lake Mead

FAVORABLE SEASON: April through October

DIFFICULTY: V

VOLUME: 6000–20,000 cfs

GRADIENT: 8 feet per mile

LENGTH: 225 river miles to Diamond Creek; 280 to Pierce Ferry on Lake Mead

TIME: 14 to 21 days

RAFT SIZE: Boats 16 to 37 feet long are commonly used. Well-rigged 12-foot rafts may be all right if escorted and expertly manned.

FISHING: Some catfish in the river; use doughballs or prepared catfish bait. The larger cats weigh up to 14 pounds and put up a strong fight. There are also trout and black bass in some side-streams. Arizona license required.

WEATHER: A desert climate prevails in the canyon. Daytime heat is commonly over 100° F, and nights are rarely below 65°. Despite the predominant dryness, however, sudden, brief, after-noon thundershowers are very common; so keep ponchos accessible by day. The water at Lee's Ferry, having been just released from the icy depths of Lake Powell, is a dangerously chill 56° F, but as it moves through the canyon it gradually warms, gaining roughly 1 degree every twenty miles, until, when it enters Lake Mead, it is a simmering 70° to 75°.

During the heat of the day, which commences the instant the sun is up, the shores are like ovens. Fortunately, though, things are noticeably cooler out on the river. Protection from the sun is essential at least some of the time: everyone should have at least one long-sleeved shirt, a pair of long pants, and a number of wide-brimmed hats with straps. Despite all precautions these hats are always getting washed overboard; so take plenty.

PHOTOGRAPH 32   Camped on the moving earth. (*Bob Krips Photo.*)

During the warm nights only the lightest of sleeping bags is necessary. A good combination is a light bag plus a sheet. For the first, warmer half of the night, stretch out on top of the bag and cover yourself with the sheet. Later, as temperatures drop, crawl into the bag.

RIVER TRIP PERMITS: Trip permits are required and the requirements are many: Trip leaders must have had either previous experience in the canyon or considerable experience on other whitewater rivers. Rafts must be at least 16 feet long (10-man size) and, except in rare cases, must travel in groups of two or more. Rafts down to 12 feet long may be used if piloted by people of adequate experience and escorted by rafts of at least 16 feet.

Gear must include lifejackets for each crew member plus at least one extra jacket per boat (on large boats, one spare jacket for every 10 people), a full set of spare oars or paddles per boat, a complete first-aid kit, detailed river maps, a patch kit, an air pump, extra ropes, and an emergency signalling mirror or flares. Also, sturdy garbage bags, water containers, biodegradable soap, water purification supplies (Clorox or Purex), and either a fire pan or a fire blanket must be carried. In addition, some form of portable toilet is required; small rafts can generally get by with a wide-mouthed, tight-lidded, plastic bottle for carrying waste until it can be buried in a proper location. All this gear is carefully checked out by the National Park Service ranger at the Lee's Ferry put-in, so make sure your gear is in good condition, *especially those lifejackets.*

At the time this is written, the environmental impact of boaters on the inner canyon is being studied. While this study is pending, the Park Service is holding use to the 1972 level. It is clear that we must protect the canyon from overuse and permanently preserve it in its natural state so that future generations may experience it just as we do now. But the unfortunate and blatantly unfair aspect of this present policy is that the Park Service is allotting a meager 7 percent of the user days to private and an overwhelming 93 percent to commercial rafters. This is done simply because this was the ratio of private to commercial boaters in 1972. Today and in the future, as more and more people run rivers on their own, it is obvious that private rafters deserve greater access to the Grand Canyon. We all look forward to seeing the Park Service, which has always been fair in the past, correct this injustice.

Because Grand Canyon permits are much in demand and are issued on a first-come, first-served basis, it is wise to request your permit a full 9 months before you plan to take your trip. Request full, current details on requirements and application forms for private trip permits from Inner Canyon Unit Office, Grand Canyon National Park, P.O. Box 129, Grand Canyon, Ariz. 86023.

WATER CONDITIONS: Water flow through the Grand Canyon is controlled by Glen Canyon Dam, which is located just upstream from Lee's Ferry. Generally, runnable flows are released all year round, with slightly higher average discharges occurring during April, May, and June.

In response to the demand for electricity in Phoenix, these flows usually fluctuate daily between 6000 and 20,000 cfs. The resulting daily 12-foot tides create uncanny conditions in the canyon. For one thing, the rafter can actually choose the water level he wants for a run through a particular rapid; if the flow at a given time does not suit his fancy, he just waits half a day for a completely altered water level. (For information about how various water

levels affect the difficulty of the rapids, see "River hazards" below.) Boaters must also moor their rafts in deep pools beside steep
beaches at night lest they find their boats stranded high and dry
the next morning. Because the peak flows tend to overtake the
low flows, the amount of fluctuation gradually diminishes as one
moves downstream. Below Lava Falls, at mile 179 as measured
down from Lee's Ferry, the tides even out and are no longer of
concern to the boater. When you put in at Lee's Ferry, ask the
National Park Service ranger about current flow conditions.

RIVER HAZARDS: The Grand Canyon is extremely difficult and
dangerous but definitely runnable. It should be regarded as a
high-level test of whitewater skill and approached with sustained
caution and vigilance.

Of the 113 rapids, roughly 60 are rated and require thorough
scouting. Most of these rated rapids are uniquely steep and appear from upstream as horizon lines across the river. Although
some call for adept maneuvering, the majority consist mainly of
towering waves and, when entered correctly, demand only that
the bow be kept into the waves. Rafts 16 feet or longer may often
choose between sneaking down the side and running the big
water down the middle; rafts shorter than 16 feet probably should
sneak whenever possible. Holes large enough to flip pontoons are
common and, more often than rocks, are the major obstacles. Small
boats 16 feet or less should expect to flip once or twice in the
course of a run through the canyon.

The difficulty of Grand Canyon rapids alters dramatically with
changing water levels. As flow increases, some rapids become
much more difficult, while others become much easier. The following table, with difficulty ratings on the Western Scale by Les
Jones and Doc Marston, shows how different water levels affect
the difficulty of the canyon's toughest rapids.

Mile *	Rapid	Difficulty	
		Low (7000 to 12,000 cfs)	High (18,000 cfs)
8	Badger	7	5
11	Soap Ck.	8	9
17	House Rk.	7	4
24½	M.24 ½ R.	7	5

* Mileage in the canyon is measured from Lee's Ferry.

Mile	Rapid	Difficulty	
		Low (7000 to 12,000 cfs)	*High* (18,000 cfs)
72	Unkar	10	5
76½	Hance	9	9
78½	Sockdolager	6	8
81	Grapevine	10	9
90	Horn Ck.	10	9
93½	Granite	9	8
95	Hermit	9	9
98½	Crystal	4	5
150	Upset	7	8
179	Lava	10	10

Because current discharges from Glen Canyon Dam generally range between 6000 and 20,000 cfs, the above ratings will usually apply. However, a more complete chart of this type, showing ratings for all the major rapids at flows from 4000 to 118,000 cfs can be found on Les Jones's invaluable scroll map of the canyon. Below 5000 cfs, a large number of the canyon's rapids become very rocky and exceedingly hazardous.

In my opinion, the three most difficult rapids are Hance, Crystal, and Lava Falls. Hance is a long, broad nightmare of rocks, holes, and jumbled waves with no clear passage. In Crystal the river narrows and accelerates into a long chute of enormous back-curling waves that press against the lefthand cliff. In order to avoid these waves, a raft must tuck under an inconveniently placed rock and scoot across the lip of one of the biggest holes in the river. This hole has chewed and swallowed countless pontoons and smaller boats.

Lava Falls is a steep, riverwide no-man's-land of gargantuan holes, exploding foam, and airborne waves. Like Hance, it should be scouted from both banks. There is a relatively calm route down the left side that is used by some oar boats, but to hit this route a boat must, in speeding water, ferry across the current between two rocks little more than 10 feet apart; and to miss this side gate is to hit the biggest, meanest, deadliest hole in the canyon. A somewhat safer but wildly tumultuous course runs down the other side about a quarter of the way out from the right bank. This route involves hitting a miniscule slick through the first broad backroller, dropping down a chaotic foam-filled washboard of medium-sized holes, getting flushed up onto a big slanty piece of lava, getting sucked off the lava into a washing machine of huge, frenzied, leaping waves, and finally nosing through a series of towering but orderly haystacks that gradually diminish into calm. A merry ride.

Two other tricky rapids, Sockdolager and Gravevine, are rendered even more perilous by the fact that they are unscoutable.

In the Lower Granite Gorge below Diamond Creek, there is a rapid thought by many to be one of the two or three most difficult in the entire canyon. Called Mile 234 Rapid, this savage raceway has utterly demolished whole rafts. A mind-boggling hole at its head blocks off the entire left side of the river, while on the right the water speeds over a precipitous but smooth drop, blasts down a runway of big haystacks, and crashes resoundingly into a gnarled, many-clawed rock jutting out from the righthand cliff. A staunch Avon was once ripped in two here. A boater's only hope is to shave closely past the enormous hole and then ferry left with total effort, keeping the bow in just enough to prevent the boat from being flipped in the high standing waves. There is a substantial pillow on the upstream side of the claw rock, but unless you pull well left, this will offer no protection.

A different sort of hazard in the canyon is presented by scorpions. Shake out shoes before putting them on in the morning and roll out sleeping bags just as you bed down. But do not be spooked by the presence of these little beasties in the canyon; their stings are almost never fatal.

A SPECIAL NOTE ON TAKE-OUTS: Most oar-powered trips pull out at Diamond Creek at mile 225, because in so doing they miss only 15 miles of river and avoid 40 miles of still water on Lake Mead. The Hualapai Indians own the road leading to the Diamond Creek take-out and charge for its use. Currently, the charge is $5.00 per person plus $5.00 per raft. Because Diamond Creek is occasionally inundated by flash floods that may wash out the road (this road is best suited to four-wheel-drive vehicles when in *good* condition), it is wise to leave vehicles in Peach Springs rather than down at the mouth of the creek. Arrangements may be made in advance with the Hualapai Wildlife and Outdoor Recreation Department to park your vehicle behind their office in Peach Springs and to have one of their rangers drive it down to the river on the day of your take-out ($10 fee). Contact Director, Hualapai Wildlife and Outdoor Recreation Department, P.O. Box 216, Peach Springs, Ariz. 86434. Phone (602) 769-2227.

Going on to Pierce Ferry on Lake Mead requires either a motor or a hellish row across 40 miles of torrid flat water. After descending from Lee's Ferry in the rig pictured in Photograph 1, three companions and I spent an entire night and much of the next day rowing from Separation Rapid, the final rapid, to Pierce Ferry. Pushing on through the night to escape the heat, we spelled one another at the oars and caught what sleep we could between times. A slight current helped us for the first 20 miles, but after that it was all dead water and, when the sun rose, brain-frying heat. No wind stirred. Lake Mead was like a vast, slick bathtub of simmering sweat. During the night, with the dark shadows of cliffs moving against the backdrop of stars, each of us had rowed far beyond his allotted watch, but in the oven of day we eyed the clock strapped to the right-hand oar and rowed not a minute over our 2-hour stint. But not rowing was probably worse than rowing, for at least with the continual swing and heave of the oars one did not concentrate on his own sticky agony.

The Pierce Ferry take-out is usable only when Lake Mead is high, above, say, the 1050-foot contour. When the lake is low, a broad, bottomless mud flat blocks off all passage to the Pierce Ferry beach. At such times, take out on the far, western, side of the Pierce Ferry peninsula at South Cove. To approach South Cove by land, follow one of the routes toward Pierce Ferry mentioned below, and, as you near the lake, follow the signs to South Cove rather than to Pierce Ferry.

ROAD DIRECTIONS: The put-in at Lee's Ferry lies just south of the Utah-Arizona border and is reached via U.S. Alternate 89. A bit north of where Alternate 89 crosses the Colorado over Navajo Bridge, a well-marked, paved spur road angles northeast along the river to sun-baked Lee's Ferry, which consists of a trailer cafe-store, a ranger station, a campground, and a broad, sloping launch site. Rafters may camp right at the launch site. As the put-in for the world's most renowned whitewater run, Lee's Ferry has a resort atmosphere: River-struck, would-be boatmen wander around trying to get hired onto the big pontoons, bus loads of awkward-looking passengers, secretly called "turkeys" by the boatmen, strut around the river beach brandishing cameras, and everywhere there is the clamor of massive pontoons preparing and pushing off. The few private rafters (currently only a single private launching is allowed per day) feel rather out of place; but we look for this to change as access to the river is more fairly distributed.

Shuttle around to the south. In taking U.S. 89 south and Route 66 west, either go through Flagstaff or, for a view of the Grand Canyon from the rim, swing along state highway 64.

The Diamond Creek take-out is on the Hualapai Indian Reservation at the end of a rough road that runs northwest from Route 66 just west of Peach Springs. If you plan to take out here, see the special note above.

The Pierce Ferry take-out on Lake Mead may be approached by two roads. One, called the Hackberry-Lake Mead Road, breaks away from Route 66 just west of the Hackberry motel and gas station. The other, which is marked by a sign saying "Pierce Ferry," leaves U.S. 93 halfway between Kingman, Arizona, and Boulder City, Nevada. Both routes involve over 50 miles of gravel road and both, after joining together, pass through Meadview, a desolate gas station/cafe on the cactus-studded ridge over Pierce Ferry.

MAPS

Leslie Jones scroll map: "Grand Canyon." All who raft the canyon on their own should have several copies.

Grand Canyon River Guide by Buzz Belknap. Based on U.S.G.S. maps, this excellent map shows rapids and their ratings and includes excerpts from Powell's log and historic photographs. Waterproof edition $5.95. Available from Canyonlands Press, P.O. Box O, Kanab, Utah 84741.

Pictorial Color Map of the Grand Canyon by Jack Curry. A colorful, waterproof map of the river with photos and mile-by-mile notes covering geology, history, points of interest, and rapids. $8.95. Available from River Map, P.O. Box 6339, Salt Lake City, Utah 84106.

Overview maps: These two striking, enormous U.S.G.S. special maps cover a large portion of the run. "Grand Canyon National Park and Vicinity, Arizona," 38 by 60 inches, $1.50. "Grand Canyon National Monument, Arizona," 33 by 42 inches, $1.00.

U.S.G.S. quadrangles: The run from Lee's Ferry to Diamond Creek is covered by 18 maps—15′ Lee's Ferry (Ariz.), 15′ Tanner Wash (Ariz.), 15′ Emmett Wash (Ariz.), 15′ Nankoweap (Ariz.), 15′ Vishnu Temple (Ariz.), 15′ Bright Angel (S) (Ariz.) (This special map includes a brief geologic history of the canyon. Specify either contour or relief edition. Price is 75¢, same as other quadrangles.), 15′ Havasupai Point (Ariz.), 15′ Supai

(Ariz.), 15′ Kanab Point (Ariz.), 15′ Powell Plateau (Ariz.), 15′ Tuckup Canyon (Ariz.), 15′ National Canyon (Ariz.), 7½′ Vulcan's Throne (Ariz.), 7½′ Whitmore Rapids (Ariz.), 7½′ Vulcan's Throne SW (Ariz.), 7½′ Whitmore Point SE (Ariz.), 7½′ Granite Park (Ariz.), and 7½′ Diamond Peak (Ariz.). If you continue below Diamond Creek to Lake Mead, get 7½′ Travertine Rapids (Ariz.), 7½′ Separation Canyon (Ariz.), 7½′ Spencer Canyon (Ariz.), and 7½′ Devils Slide Rapids (Ariz.). The final stretch to Pierce Ferry has not yet been mapped by the U.S.G.S.

GUIDEBOOKS AND LITERATURE

All these books, except those by Kolb and Jenkinson, are available for the prices indicated from Canyonlands Press, P.O. Box O, Kanab, Utah 84741. The bibliographical notations are from the Canyonlands Press brochure, which includes many other books treating the Grand Canyon.

Rim, River, and Trail Guides

Colorado River Guidebook by Troy L. Pewe. $4.45. Arizona State University Press. Geology, geography, and maps of Marble Canyon and Grand Canyon from Lee's Ferry to Bright Angel Creek.

Grand Canyon National Park, edited by Robert Scharff. David McKay Co. Covers briefly the scenery, rock formations, rims, inner canyon, plant-life, wildlife, Indians, history, place names, accommodations, and even Park regulations. $2.25.

Grand Canyon Perspectives by W. Kenneth Hamblin and Joseph Murphy. Brigham Young University Press. A unique guide to Canyon scenery, geology, and wildlife through interpretive panoramas. $3.80.

Guidebook to the Colorado River by W. Kenneth Hamblin and J. Keith Rigby. Brigham Young University Press. Geology studies of Marble Canyon and Grand Canyon illustrated with aerial and ground photographs. Part 1: "Lee's Ferry to Bright Angel Creek." $2.80. Part 2: "Bright Angel Creek to Lake Mead." $3.30.

River Runner's Guide to the Canyons of the Green and Colorado Rivers. Vol. 3, "Marble Gorge and Grand Canyon" by George C. Simmons and David L. Gaskill. Published by The Powell Society, Ltd. Northland Press. A mile-by-mile description, mainly of geologic features. $4.30.

The Age of Dinosaurs in Northern Arizona by William J. Breed. Museum of Northern Arizona. Illustrated account of Mesozoic life and times. $1.20.

Ancient Landscapes of the Grand Canyon Region by Edwin D. McKee. Classic popular booklet on Grand Canyon geology. In its 26th edition. 70¢.

Grand Canyon: The Story Behind the Scenery by Merrill D. Beal. Grand Canyon Natural History Association. Grand Canyon geology explained clearly and concisely. 50 color photographs, 15 diagrams, and a fold-out aerial map of the Canyon. $1.20.

Story of the Grand Canyon of Arizona, How It Was Made by N. H. Darton. Fred Harvey Co. Professor Darton's booklet, in its 40th edition, explains the forces that created the Canyon—and are still shaping it. $1.20.

History

Exploration of the Colorado River and Its Canyons by John Wesley Powell. Dover. Major Powell's own account of his explorations in the West including the historic 1869 Grand Canyon voyage. $3.30.

A Canyon Voyage by Frederick S. Dellenbaugh. Yale University Press. On-the-spot account of the second Powell expedition 1871-72. $2.25.

Beyond the Hundredth Meridian by Wallace Stegner. Houghton Mifflin. A biography of John Wesley Powell—adventurer, scientist, public servant, and prophet of the American West. $2.95.

Down the Colorado by Robert Brewster Stanton, edited by Dwight L. Smith. University of Oklahoma Press. The tragic story of Stanton's 1889-90 expeditions to survey a railroad through the Colorado River canyons. $5.50.

Grand Canyon Place Names by Byrd H. Granger. University of Arizona Press. Indians, Spaniards, American explorers, pioneer ranchers, miners, and railroaders all contributed to the Canyon's intriguing place names gathered here. $1.70.

The Grand Colorado by T. H. Watkins and other contributors. American West Publishing Co. The story of a river and its canyons. Wallace Stegner notes in his foreword, "The whole river is literally here, as I think it has been in no single book heretofore." Color photography by Philip Hyde. $15.50.

The Story of Man at the Grand Canyon by J. Donald Hughes. Grand Canyon Natural History Association. The fascinating story of four centuries of man's association with the Grand Canyon—

explorers, prospectors, scientists, artists, would-be exploiters, and appreciative admirers. $3.30.

Trail on the Water by Pearl Baker. Pruett Press. Biography of Bert Loper, canyon country character whose experiences on the rivers spanned the first half of the 20th century. $7.45.

Through the Grand Canyon from Wyoming to Mexico by Ellsworth L. Kolb. Macmillan. Kolb's account of his early voyage down the Green and Colorado Rivers.

Grand Canyon: Today and All Its Yesterdays by Joseph Wood Krutch. William Sloane and Associates. A comprehensive introduction to the Grand Canyon by a distinguished naturalist. $2.25.

General

The Colorado by Frank Waters. "Rivers of America" series. Holt, Rinehart & Winston. $4.95.

Desert Solitaire by Edward Abbey. McGraw-Hill. A penetrating look at the canyon country by a philosopher who knows it well. $6.45.

Grand Canyon of the Living Colorado, edited by Roderick Nash for the Sierra Club. Ballantine Books. The backpacker's Canyon, the boatman's Canyon and the people's Canyon, all explored in words and color photography by Ernest Braun, David Brower, Colin Fletcher, Jeffrey Ingram, Martin Litton, Allen Malmquist, Roderick Nash, and Stewart Udall. $4.25.

The Man Who Walked Through Time by Colin Fletcher. Knopf. The author of *The Thousand Mile Summer* observes the Grand Canyon and himself during a long solo hike. $6.45.

Time and the River Flowing: Grand Canyon by Francois Leydet. Ballantine Books. The Sierra Club's exquisite Grand Canyon book with color photographs by many noted cameramen. $4.25.

Wild Rivers of North America by Michael Jenkinson. Dutton. An intriguing glance at some of our finest wilderness rivers, including the Colorado of the Grand Canyon. Photography by Karl Kernberger.

Common Wildflowers of the Grand Canyon by John and Joanne Stockert. Wheelwright Press. Color photographs and descriptions of 75 frequently seen Grand Canyon wildflowers. $1.45.

Wilderness and the American Mind by Roderick Nash. Yale University Press. The wilderness concept is traced from its earliest beginnings in this carefully researched, absorbing book. $2.25.

APPENDIX I

Equipment Checklist

Rafts
Repair kit
(For list of repair-kit contents, see Chapter One.)
Oars or paddles
(Two full sets per raft. Oars must have clips or rubbers affixed plus safety lines.)
Frames with tie-down straps (Optional depending on rig.)
Poop decks with tie-down straps (Optional depending on rig.)
Tarp to cover gear on frame or poop
Carabiners and clips for securing gear to frame or raft
Bailing buckets

Lines:
Bow line
Stern line
200 feet of extra line
Heaving line with monkey fist
Emergency beaching line on spool board with rubber mounting straps (for solo rafts on violent rivers)
Gear tie-down line
Spare coil for cutting short lengths
100-200 feet of parachute cord
Lifejackets
(One per person plus one extra per raft.)
Air pump

Waterproof containers
  Black bags, large & small
  Ammo boxes, large & small
  Wooden boxes, etc.
Air-mattress floors (optional)
Preserver cushions (optional)
Heavy canvas bags
  (Four or more for garbage,
  cans, cold cans, and loose
  gear.)
Shovel
Crash helmets for rocky rivers
Wet suits or long woollies for
  extremely cold water
Ice chest (optional)
Kitchen box
  (For list of kitchen box con-
  tents, see Chapter One.)
Fire pan or fireproof blanket
Sleeping bags
Air mattresses for sleeping
  (may be same as above)
Ponchos
Tents
Clothes and personal things
  (For a list of standard and
  optional personal gear, see
  Chapter One.)
Books

Ditty bag
  Sun cream
  Chapstick
  Tissues
  Sunglasses
  Toilet paper
Emergency and survival gear
  Winch (or block and tackle)
  Compass
  Folding belt knife
  Dextrose
  Extra food
  Aerial flares
  Signal mirror

*For expeditions into ex-
  tremely remote areas:*

Radio transceiver
Personal survival kits sewn
  to lifejackets
Medical kit
  (For a list of medical kit
  contents, see Chapter Four.)
Maps
Tire chains (if muddy or snow-
  covered roads must be ne-
  gotiated)

APPENDIX II

Whitewater Rafting Equipment: A List of Suppliers

This is a guide to sources of specialized whitewater rafting gear such as rafts designed for whitewater, rugged, oversized oars, high-volume, low-pressure pumps, rowing frames, floating rope, patching fabric and glue, and waterproof bags and boxes. Although I have tried to make this list as complete as possible, some suppliers may have been overlooked. I hope that suppliers who have been omitted will contact me, so that future editions of this book will be made more complete.

Alaska Marine & Equipment Inc.
P.O. Box 6208 Annex
Anchorage, Alaska
(907) 272-1428

Alaskan distributor of Avon rafts. Write for a list of dealers. In addition to Avons, dealers carry pumps, glue, patching fabric, and coatings.

American Safety Equipment
  Corp.
7652 Burnet Ave.
Van Nuys, Calif. 91405
(213) 989-2940

Makes a new raft called the Rivermaster.

Avon rafts: See the separate listings for the four U.S. distributors: Seagull Marine in California; Inland Marine in Pennsylvania; Imtra Corp. in Massachusetts; and Alaska Marine & Equipment. Write the distributor nearest you for a list of the dealers in your area.

Barrings Belt and Chain
729 East Buckeye
Phoenix, Ariz. 85034

Glue, patching materials

Bell-Toptex Inc.
2850 East 29th St.
Long Beach, Calif. 90806

Helmets

Campways
12915 So. Spring St.
Los Angeles, Calif. 90061
(213) 532-0910

Imports a new line of rugged Hypalon rafts with thick skins, upturned bows and sterns, and good valves. Also offers frames, repair kits, pumps, waterproof bags, etc.

Canoe California
P.O. Box 61
Kentfield, Calif. 94904
(415) 461-1750

Makes a large line of waterproof bags.

Carboline Co.
350 Hanley Industrial Court
St. Louis, Mo. 63144
(314) 644-1000

Makes an excellent glue for neoprene and Hypalon rafts called Carboline neoprene adhesive F-1.

Duncan Coldwell
4373 69th St.
Sacramento, Calif. 95820
(916) 457-8395

Makes aluminum frames.

The Confluence
P.O. Box 76
Vallecito, Calif. 95251

A shop specializing in whitewater gear, offering Avon rafts, frames, oar clips, patching supplies, etc.

Elliott River Tours, Inc.
1014 Jackson St.
Oakland, Calif. 94607
(415) 465-9355

Makes a fine low-pressure, high-volume pump, plus frames and oars of welded conduit.

Gaco Western, Inc.
P.O. Box 88698
Seattle, Wash. 98188
(206) 246-7744

Makes neoprene glue, aluminum neoprene coating, color Hypalon coatings, and trowelling compound.

High Adventure Headquarters
3925 East Indian School Rd.
Phoenix, Ariz. 85018
(602) 955-3391

Carries a variety of lightweight items for the river boater, including waterproof bags, ammo boxes, etc.

Holcombe Industries
1602 Tacoma Way
Redwood City, Calif. 94063
(415) 364-1770

Makes the Havasu raft and whitewater life jackets.

Imtra Corporation
151 Mystic Ave.
Medford, Mass. 02155
(617) 391-5660

Distributes Avon rafts. Write for a list of dealers in your area. Dealers carry not only Avon rafts, but also pumps, glue, patching fabric, and coatings.

Inflatable Boats Unlimited
P.O. Box O
Kanab, Utah 84741
(801) 644-2691

Exclusive distributor for Rubber Fabricator products in the western United States and Canada. Handles a complete line of neoprene rafts ranging from 6-mans to 37-foot pontoons. Also has pumps, D-rings attached to neoprene patches, patching fabric, valves, oars, life preservers, individual tubes (sponsons), and Sportyaks.

Inland Marine Co.
79 East Jackson St.
Wilkes-Barre, Pa. 18701
(717) 822-7185

Distributor of Avon rafts. Send for list of dealers. In addition to Avon rafts, dealers carry pumps, glue, etc.

Vladimir Kovalik
1342 Jewell Ave.
Pacific Grove, Calif. 93950
(408) 373-5882

Makes fiberglass rowing frames.

Leisure Imports, Inc.
104 Arlington Ave.
St. James, N.Y. 11780

Imports Pyrawa inflatable kayaks.

Marine Wholesale, Inc.
130 S.E. Water Ave.
Portland, Oreg. 97214
(503) 233-8771

Carries superb ash oars in lengths ranging from 6 to 16 feet. The 10-, 12-, and 16-foot lengths have exceptionally strong shafts and are unsurpassed for whitewater use.

Mountain Waterways/Hide &
  Sole Mountaineering
171 North Washington St.
Sonora, Calif. 95370
(209) 532-5621

A shop carrying rafts, water-proof bags, lifejackets, oars, paddles, helmets, ammo boxes, repair kits, frames, and oarlocks.

The Newman Company
8461 Warner Drive
Culver City, Calif. 90230
(213) 871-0300

Imports a line of rafts from Taiwan.

Northwest River Supplies
P.O. Box 3195
Moscow, Idaho 83843
(208) 882-2383

An outfit supplying rafts, inflatable kayaks, lifejackets, waterproof bags and boxes, oars, paddles, wet suits, neoprene fabric, adhesives, oarlocks, dutch ovens, pumps, etc.

Outdoor Adventures
688 Sutter St.
San Francisco, Calif. 94102
(415) 776-3004

A shop specializing in inflatable boats and accessories. Carries Avons, Taiwan imports, inflatable kayaks, and a variety of other rafts, plus pumps, river guidebooks, oars, black bags, ammo boxes, etc. Also books trips with whitewater schools and outfitters.

R.A.F.T., Inc.
440 North First St.
San Jose, Calif. 95112
(209) 795-2828

Makes pumps and rowing frames.

River Gear/Whitewater
  Expeditions
1811 Tulare St.
Richmond, Calif. 94805

This is the author's own outfit. We make rowing frames, poop decks, oar clips, oar rubbers, easy-rower plastic washers, frame tie-down straps, watertight wooden boxes with lift-out trays, and fire pans with fold-down grills. Also, for people who build their own frames, we provide capped thole pins, whitewater thole-pin mounts, and angle-iron brackets.

Rubatex Corp.
Bedford, Va. 24523

Nylon-neoprene fabric

Rubber Fabricators, Inc.

Makes an elaborate line of neoprene inflatable boats which range from dinghies to pontoons. See the separate listings for the two U.S. distributors: Inflatable Boats Unlimited is the sole representative west of the Mississippi, and Wilderness Voyageurs handles everything in the East.

Samson Cordage Works
470 Atlantic Ave.
Boston, Mass. 02210
(617) 426-6550

Makes a number of multifilament polypropylene, solid-braid, floating ropes which are excellent for use as bow and stern lines, heaving lines, etc. Foremost among these ropes, for the rafter, are Samson Supreme MFP and Samson Spot Cord.

Seagull Marine
1851 McGaw Ave.
Irvine, Calif. 92705
(714) 979-6161

Distributor of Avon inflatable boats and accessories. Write for a list of dealers in your area. Dealers carry not only Avon rafts, but also glue, patching fabric, coatings, and pumps (including one that hooks up to your car battery).

A. E. Staley Manufacturing Co.
320 Schuyler Ave.
Kearney, N.J. 07032
(201) 997-1500

Makes one of the finest glues available: N151B Adhesive with N151A Catalyst/Accelerator.

Stearns Manufacturing Co.
Division St. at 30th
St. Cloud, Minn. 56031

Lifejackets

Swanson Boat Oar Factory
Albion, Pa. 16401

Oars and paddles

Voyageur Enterprises
P.O. Box 512
Shawnee Mission, Kan. 66201
(913) 649-1085

Waterproof bags, paddles

Weeks-Howe-Emerson Co.
645 Howard St.
San Francisco, Calif. 94105
(415) 392-2681

Oars, lifejackets, emergency rations

White Stag
5100 S.E. Harney Dr.
Portland, Oreg. 97206

Wet suits

Whitewater Sports, Ltd.
P.O. Box 9406
Denver, Colo. 80209
(303) 572-3840

Waterproof bags, helmets, pardles

Whitewater West
727 South 33rd St.
Richmond, Calif. 94804
(415) 236-1828

Waterproof bags, lifejackets, helmets, paddles, wet suits, inflatable kayaks, and some small rafts

Bryce Whitmore/Wilderness
  Water Ways
33 Canyon Lake Drive
Port Costa, Calif. 94569
(415) 787-2820

Offers the Huck Finn and the Cataraft.

Wilderness Voyageurs
P.O. Box 97
Ohiopyle, Pa. 15470
(412) 329-4752

Eastern distributor of Rubber Fabricator products. Offers a complete line of neoprene rafts ranging from tiny dinghies to mammoth pontoons, plus various accessories.

Wildwater Designs
c/o Walbridge
Penllyn, Pa. 19422

Wet suits, life vests

APPENDIX III

Knots

Whether it be to tie up a raft, lash down a load, line a rapid, rescue a wrapped raft, put up a sauna tent, or bind up a berserk companion, knots are an integral part of life on the river. In general parlance, any method of tying a rope is called a knot. But to the insiders of the art there is a more precise language: A *knot* ties up a bundle, joins the ends of two very small cords, and makes a loop, a noose, or a knob in a rope. A *bend* ties the ends of two ropes together. And a *hitch* ties a rope to a ring, spar, tree trunk, or other object.

DRAWING 68   BOWLINE (KNOT)

The BOWLINE (pronounced BOW lĭn) is used to make a strong, secure loop that will not slip or jam at the end of a rope. This is a basic knot with a wide range of uses. To tie it, first form a loop, then run the free end through, around the standing part, and back through the loop as shown.

DRAWING 69   SHEET BEND

The SHEET BEND is used to join two ropes of different sizes or materials. *Note:* The free ends must be on the same side, for this bend can slip when they are on opposite sides. Because the sheet bend can jam under great load, it is best to use the carrick bend, below, for heavy tension.

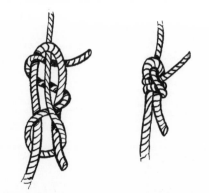

DRAWING 70   DOUBLE SHEET BEND

The DOUBLE SHEET BEND is more secure than the single sheet bend, and is used when the ropes are of greatly differing sizes.

DRAWING 71   CARRICK BEND

Strong, secure, and utterly jam-proof, the CARRICK BEND is used to join two lines which will be subject to heavy pull, as in winching. To tie it, form a loop with one rope and then, with the other rope, form the interlaced pattern as shown. When pulled tight, the carrick bend upsets into the form shown on the right. As there is considerable slippage during the upset, the ends should be longer than those shown. *Note:* For a strong and secure carrick bend, the free ends must be on opposite sides and the under-and-over pattern must be made exactly as shown.

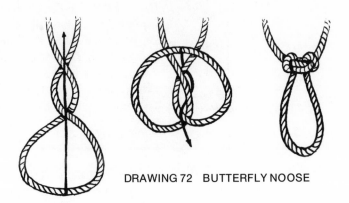

DRAWING 72   BUTTERFLY NOOSE

The BUTTERFLY NOOSE is a loop in the middle of a rope. Secure and jam-proof, it will accommodate a load in any direction. When spaced out along a line, butterfly loops provide purchase points for a winch or strong handholds for several people hauling on the line. To tie it, twist a loop in the bight. Then fold up the lower part of the loop and push it through the center opening as shown.

The DOUBLE HALF HITCH provides a quick, temporary means of securing a line to a post, hook, ring, or branch.

DRAWING 73   DOUBLE HALF HITCH

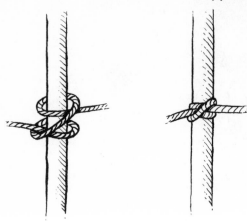

The CLOVE HITCH provides a quick and fairly secure method for attaching a line to a smooth spar or timber, such as a frame or oar. If it is used at the end of a line, take a half hitch with the free end around the standing part.

DRAWING 74   CLOVE HITCH

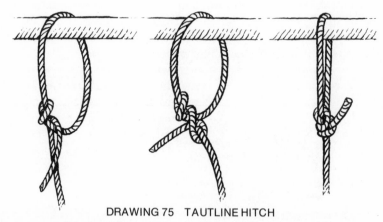

DRAWING 75   TAUTLINE HITCH

The TAUTLINE HITCH, also called a rolling hitch, is a slip hitch which will not slip under tension. It is particularly useful on tent guy ropes. To tie it, take a half hitch around the standing part, bringing the free end around inside the first turn. The second turn wedged inside the first is the crux of this hitch, for it causes the hitch to bind, thus preventing slippage, under tension. The tautline is completed with a half hitch around the standing part. The sketch on the right shows the tautline under strain.

The TRUCKER'S HITCH is used to cinch a line tight when loading.

DRAWING 76   TRUCKER'S HITCH

APPENDIX IV

Photography on Raft Trips

BY RICHARD NORGAARD*

About half the people on raft trips bring cameras. Only a few of the other half bring water colors and easel or even notebook and pencil, thus most of the records of a trip are captured by photography. The camera can interpret as well as record, and raft trips offer forms and color unseen on trips with other modes of travel. Raft trips can increase your perspective.

You should be familiar with both your camera and film before the trip. If you are buying a camera † or if you have not used your present camera for some time, take at least two but preferably three or four rolls of pictures in order to acquaint yourself with its mechanical operation as well as creative possibilities during the weeks preceding the trip. Similarly, experiment with different films before, rather than during, the trip.

The faster, but not the fastest, color films now on the market can capture the action of waves and happy people with little loss of color intensity when directed at rich scenery. Kodachrome X, Ektachrome X, Ektachrome Professional, Agfachrome, and

---

* Richard Norgaard's photographs are published in the Sierra Club *Grand Canyon* book. This article is reprinted with permission of the American River Touring Association.

† For those who plan to do a great deal of whitewater photography, an underwater camera such as the Nikonos can be very useful, for it is designed to get wet.

Ansco 50 are in this class of film. Familiarity with what the film can and cannot do is much more important than type used. Most all of the black-and-white films are suitable for raft trips.

An Army surplus ammunition case will keep your camera dry on the roughest rivers, for they are absolutely watertight. These cases come in two sizes: The smaller is about 3½ × 7 × 10 inches and the larger is about 7 × 7 × 10 inches. One or the other or a combination of these boxes is suitable for any camera outfit. Camera, lenses, and light meter are safer if the case is lined with a thin layer of stiff foam such as that from which skin divers' wet suits are made. An additional but not necessary precaution, except in wet western Canada and the humid tropics, is a small container of desiccant packed in the ammunition case which will absorb any rain, spray, or splash which does get into the case. This combination is the ultimate in protection. It is suitable for the protection of expensive equipment on the roughest, wettest rivers.

There are other ways to keep your camera dry, but they are generally less convenient or more expensive. Do not be fooled by the beautiful new aluminum cases available at atrocious prices; they are not watertight. Surplus stores occasionally carry rubber generator bags which are just as watertight as the ammunition boxes, but it is more difficult to get articles in and out. Both the ammunition boxes and the generator bags are easily tied to the raft, and with a normal load, each floats if it does get loose. Plastic bags are suitable only as protection from splash and spray while the camera is around your neck. Plastic-bag–lined gadget bags never keep a camera dry on a rough river and are a nuisance on a calmer trip. Once on shore, the camera should be taken out of the waterproof container and the container should be left open in order to dry any water which might have entered. If the camera has gotten wet, it should be opened up and aired in the sun. Camera insurance is a good investment.

Less wet trips or less valuable cameras do not demand so much care. On calm rivers your regular camera bag, if packed high on the load when not on your shoulder, is quite suitable. I am most happy with a small but rugged rucksack with outside pockets for film and small accessories on these calmer trips, for it is easily carried on side excursions.

If you are even half serious about taking pictures, you must bring a lot of film. I am somewhat humorously disturbed by people who bring a $200.00 camera outfit and $5.00 worth of film which they ration stringently, thinking they are using it wisely. Using film wisely often means shooting one picture three or four different ways, snapping many action shots of which only a few will not be blurred, or taking many people shots in order to get one with just the right expressions. Rationing beyond the point of using your film to best advantage is a waste, for good pictures are valuable, much more so than unused film. Breaking the rationing barrier is an extravagant experience that often pays off.

Now that you have enough film, you should not be afraid to take the pictures you never took before. The instructions packed with film often recommend taking pictures between 10 A.M. and 3 P.M. because the lighting is best at this time. It is best only in the sense that it is most even. Even lighting eliminates shadows, reflections, backlighting, side lighting, and reflected lighting. Since these are the elements that make pictures interesting, the camera should be used more in the morning and late afternoon that during the mid-day. Look for the interesting lighting effects and try to compare them. High canyon walls so common on river trips often have interesting highlights and deep shadows. Do not be afraid to experiment a little.

The best pictures are usually taken on shore because of the motion of the raft. Passengers often walk around the roughest rapids and waterfalls, and this is the time to get the best rough-water action pictures. The stability of terra firma with its possibilities for using a tripod produces the sharpest pictures. On the shore there is usually more time to prepare for and produce the desired results with little chance of losing equipment. On calmer raft trips and the calm stretches of the rougher rivers, good pictures can be taken while on the rafts—pictures of scenery, wildlife, and people.

The most important phase of taking pictures is the last phase, picking out the ones to be shown to other people. Half an hour of color slides or fifteen minutes of black-and-whites is the limit for most audiences, even friends. Showing the pictures faster is not a solution. One must evaluate each picture and how it relates to other pictures and the interests of the audience in order to get the maximum effect in the limited amount of time. At trip reunions where many people bring their slides and pictures, a limit is often set at 10 or 12 pictures per person. Editing under these conditions is immeasurably harder.

APPENDIX V

Saving Our Last Free Rivers

BY BILL PAINTER*

America is losing one of the most precious of its natural resources —its free-flowing wild and scenic rivers and streams. Already tens of thousands of miles of our most beautiful riverways have been destroyed by damming, ditching, diversion, or pollution. Many more miles of riverscape are threatened by these and other assaults, such as uncontrolled land development, strip mining, and poor lumbering practices. These forces of destruction are depriving Americans of many opportunities to enjoy the pleasures of fishing, whitewater boating, swimming, hunting, nature study, and other forms of recreation, as well as obliterating productive and valuable ecosystems. Yet there are means available to prevent much of the devastation that is planned for the future, if citizens are willing to work for the preservation of their beloved rivers and streams.

The primary agents of destruction are familiar foes to conserva-

* Bill Painter is director of the American Rivers Conservation Council, a national citizens organization dedicated to the preservation of America's remaining wild and scenic rivers. The group publishes a newsletter and lobbies on river issues. They are located at 324 C St. S.E., Wash., D.C. 20003.

tionists—the Federal government and big industry. Perhaps the former is most disturbing, as it is our money, our tax dollars, that pay for the projects of the U.S. Army Corps of Engineers, the U.S. Bureau of Reclamation and the U.S. Soil Conservation Service. Of course, these agencies and their allies in Congress claim that the dams and ditches will provide needed public benefits such as flood control, water supply, power generation, and recreation. In some cases, this has been true, but too often it is a small group of individuals or businesses that profits most from these schemes. Furthermore, on many occasions the water developments fail to accomplish the goals for which they were designed, and in some cases they have made conditions worse.

The flood-control programs of the Army Corps provide outstanding examples of the flaws and fallacies that are often involved in water-resources projects. First, the dams, levees, and ditches that have been built for this purpose have to date cost the Federal taxpayers over $7 billion, yet the annual damages from flooding nationwide continue to climb. The Corps points to figures that estimate the damage that would have occurred if these structures were not in place, but fails to show that much of the impact is attributed to the flooding of homes and businesses that were built *after* the projects were constructed. So, they are taking credit for protecting buildings that would never have been located in the flood-prone area if it weren't assured that flooding would be prevented by the Corps' project. In the proposed Falmouth Dam in Kentucky and the Days Creek Dam in Oregon, more than two-thirds of the flood-control benefits come from the promoting and underwriting of future development in the flood plain.

The above is an example of how such projects are often of most benefit to a few; in this case, it is land speculators who profit from the increased development potential of lands rendered more safe for habitation by the Federal project. There are also instances of the construction of a dam or levee mainly for the benefit of a single industrial facility. Should not those who stand to profit from these projects pay a large share of the costs?

The floodworks on the Mississippi River show how attempts at controlling floods with structures can actually increase flooding problems. In the 1973 flood, the crest at St. Louis was the highest ever, yet the flow of the river was only two-thirds that of the record. This is due largely to constriction of the river by many miles of flood-control levees.

Flood-control projects are not the only example of Federal

monies going to benefit a small sector of the public. The many barge canals and channels dug by the Federal government are a direct subsidy to the barge industry, which could probably not survive in direct, unsubsidized competition with the railroads.

The subsidy of the barge industry also has indirect financial effects on other sectors of the economy. Approximately 30 percent of the increase in intensity of the 1973 Mississippi River floods can be attributed to the wing dikes built by the Corps to constrict the river channel for navigation purposes.

Still another example of tragic devastation of riverways for wasteful purposes is the irrigation programs of the Bureau of Reclamation, spelled Wrecklamation by some of its antagonists. Here we find the Federal government spending hundreds of millions of dollars to dam and divert the waters of rivers so that marginal lands can be brought under cultivation, while at the same time the government is paying farmers to keep lands out of production to help stabilize farm prices.

So, the agents of destruction are hard at work on our rivers, tearing them apart in the name of "progress"; and they have plenty of plans for the future. For instance, the Soil Conservation Service, which has already ditched over 6000 miles of streams, rendering them virtually useless for fishing and other forms of recreation, figures there are a total of 150,000 miles of waterway that should be channelized. What kinds of programs are there that are aimed at *protection* of our rivers?

First, there is the National Wild and Scenic Rivers System. Established by Congress in 1968, the System now consists of 10 rivers totaling over 1000 miles of riverway. These rivers are protected from any water-resources development which would diminish their scenic, historic, fish and wildlife, geologic, recreational, or scientific value. In addition, the administering agency usually purchases lands or interests in land consisting of a strip along the river averaging ¼ mile back from each bank. This protects the shoreline from adverse residential and commercial development. When necessary, the agencies establish regulations to prevent overuse of the river.

Several states have enacted some form of river protection statute. Most of these just protect the designated rivers from damage by water-resources development. Others go even further, attempting to prevent adverse land uses along the rivers. The most successful of these programs involve some form of state zoning, although the purchase of land or scenic easements is also being used to some degree. Shoreline management laws have also been of help in some states. Among the leading states in the field of river protection are Michigan, Minnesota, Ohio, Tennessee, and Wisconsin.

Another legislative measure which offers partial protection to rivers is flood-plain management. First, it can limit intensive development along those stretches of rivers that are prone to flooding. Second, by preventing unwise building on flood-prone land, the demand for dams and levees to protect such foolish development can be eliminated.

Several states have some form of flood-plain management program, but perhaps the most important flood-plain law is the Federal Flood Insurance Act. Recent amendments to this Act have made it an important tool for river conservationists. Basically, it provides low-cost, subsidized flood-damage insurance to those who have already made the mistake of locating in flood-prone areas, but it requires that local communities which include flood-prone lands pass ordinances to prevent further construction that would be subject to a high risk of flooding.

Another key piece of legislation is the National Environmental Policy Act of 1969. This requires that a detailed Environmental Impact Statement must be prepared for each action by the Federal government that would have a significant impact on the environment. The statement must describe all the adverse environmental effects of the proposed project and outline all of the alternatives to the proposal. This has brought many of the faulty planning procedures of the Army Corps, Bureau of Reclamation, Soil Conservation Service, and Tennessee Valley Authority into the open, providing good evidence for those opposed to wasteful and destructive projects.

Action through government channels is not the only means available for river conservation. Numerous local clubs have undertaken projects to clean up and otherwise improve a stream. One very promising river-protection method involves scenic easements. Under such an easement, a landowner sells or donates certain development rights on his property to a unit of government or a nonprofit conservation trust. By so doing, he retains the ownership of the land and any improvements on the land, but gives up the right to subdivide or otherwise develop the property. If all the residents along a scenic river can band together and agree to sign scenic easements, they can assure themselves that the area will remain as it is. In addition, landowners can get a tax deduction for the estimated value of the development rights they have lost, if they donate the easement.

What can each of us do to help protect our remaining wild and scenic rivers? First, become informed. Join a local conservation organization that stays on top of the various projects planned for your area. If time allows, become an active member of such a group. By becoming involved in an actual campaign to protect a river, one will gain essential knowledge and skills, including working familiarity with water-related legislation and the capacity to be successful at the political level. This may lead one to become a leader against an unwanted dam or ditch or for designation of a local river under a wild and scenic rivers system.

APPENDIX VI

Conservation Organizations

American Rivers Conservation Council
234 C St., S.E.
Washington, D.C. 20003

American River Touring Association
1016 Jackson St.
Oakland, Calif. 94607

American Forestry Association
919 17th St., N.W.
Washington, D.C. 20016

Appalachian Mountain Club
5 Joy Street
Boston, Mass. 02108

Environmental Defense Fund
2728 Durant
Berkeley, Calif. 94704

Friends of the Earth
230 Park Ave.
New York, N.Y. 10017

Sierra Club
1050 Mills Tower
San Francisco, Calif. 94104

Wilderness Society
5850 Jewell Ave.
Denver, Colo. 80222

Wildlife Society
Suite S 176, 3900 Wisconsin Ave., N.W.
Washington, D.C. 20016

APPENDIX VII

Whitewater Schools

Whitewater schools provide an excellent and relatively safe introduction to rafting. Some of the outfits mentioned below offer a brief taste of the sport, while others provide a full course in it. Those that offer only 1-day trips are generally not, in a strict sense, schools. But they do instruct participants in the do's and don't's and in raft control—and then off you go with your guides to spend the day maneuvering the rafts through the rapids. The other outfits offer extended, intensive instructional courses lasting from a few days to a month. Many of the longer courses rove from river to river, beginning on moderate and working up to fierce water. Some of these longer courses are designed to prepare the individual to become a professional river guide, and the material covered includes all the myriad skills involved in rafting, from camp cooking to oar and paddle technique to equipment repair to reading the water to emergency procedures and beyond.*

---

* I hope these schools (and any I have overlooked) will keep me informed concerning any changes in their offerings, so that future editions of this book can be kept current.

IN THE EAST

Blue Ridge Enterprises, Inc., 3412 Porter St. N.W., Washington, D.C., 20016. One-day paddle raft trips on the Shenandoah Staircase near Harper's Ferry.

Mountain Streams & Trails Outfitters. Address in season: Box 106, Ohiopyle, Pa. 15470. Phone (412) 329-8810. Winter address: 2420 Saunders Station Rd., Monroeville, Pa. 15146. Phone (412) 372-6254. One-day paddle trips in rafts and inflatable kayaks on the Cheat and Youghiogheny Rivers.

Smokey Mountain River Expeditions, Box 252, Hot Springs, N.C. 28743. One-day paddle raft trips on the French Broad River of western North Carolina.

Wilderness Voyageurs, Inc., Box 97, Ohiopyle, Pa. 15470. Phone (412) 329-4752. One-day paddle raft trips on the Youghiogheny River.

Wildwater Expeditions Unlimited, Inc., Box 55, Thurmond, W.Va. 25936. Phone (304) 469-2551. One- and two-day paddle raft voyages on the New and Gauley Rivers of West Virginia.

Wildwater Ltd. Address in season: Long Creek, S.C. 29658. Phone (803) 647-5336. Winter address: (Sept. 15 to May 30) c/o James C. Greiner, 154 Marshall Terrace, Danville, Va. 24541. Phone (703) 792-0807. One-day paddle raft trips on the Chatooga.

IN THE WEST

Adventures Unlimited, P.O. Box 363, Columbia, Calif. 95310. Phone (209) 532-6363. Offers one-day paddle trips for beginners in rafts and inflatable kayaks on the lower Stanislaus.

American Guides Association, Box B, Woodland, Calif. 95695. Phones: (916) 662-6824 or (916) 662-3168. Offers comprehensive 10-day (5 weekend) and 7-day (pre-Easter week) boatman's training courses during February and March on California's Sierra rivers.

American Whitewater School (sponsored by the American River Touring Association), 1016 Jackson St., Oakland, Calif. 94607. Phone (415) 465-9355. Offers a variety of courses including a comprehensive, 33-day professional river-guide course which begins on the Rogue and then moves to the Middle and Main Forks of the Salmon; a 23-day whitewater workshop which begins on the Green River of Dinosaur National Monument and then also moves to the Middle and Main Forks of the Salmon; a 19-day Grand Canyon paddle experience; and 2-day river classrooms on the South Fork of the American. The two longer courses cover oar and paddle raft technique, kayaking, shore camping techniques, etc. Also, on many of ARTA's regular trips on rivers all over the West, passengers are offered a paddle option.

Canyoneers River Oarsmanship Workshops, Box 2997, Flagstaff, Ariz. 86001 or Box 2554, Grand Junction, Colo. 81501. With Gaylord Staveley. Offers a comprehensive series of 2-day and 5-day oarsmanship courses on rivers in Colorado, Utah, and Texas.

Grand Canyon Youth Expeditions, Inc., R.Rte. 2, Box 755, Flagstaff, Ariz. 86001. Phone (602) 774-8176. Three-week rowing expeditions through the Grand Canyon.

Meander Tours Whitewater Workshop, P.O. Box 511, Pinedale, Calif. 93650. Offers 5-day whitewater rafting workshops and noncommercial, shared-expense trips on rivers in California and the West. Also offers paddle option on regular one- and two-day trips on the Kings River in California.

Orange Torpedo Trips, Box 1111, Grants Pass, Oreg. 97526. Phone (503) 479-5061. Paddle trips in inflatable kayaks on the Klamath, the Rogue, and the Deschutes.

Parklands Whitewater School (sponsored by Parklands Expeditions), Box 371, Jackson Hole, Wyo. 83001. Ten-day boatman training courses in rafts and Sportyaks on rivers in the Jackson Hole area.

River and Forest Skills School (sponsored by R.A.F.T., Inc.), 440 North 1st St., San Jose, Calif. 95112. Phone (209) 795-2828. Offers a one-week sampler course which includes mountain climbing, kayaking, and rafting. Also offers other courses in rafts and inflatable kayaks on rivers around the West.

Travel Institute, 714 9th Ave., Salt Lake City, Utah 84103. Paddle option on trips in the Utah area.

Wilderness World, 1342 Jewell Ave., Pacific Grove, Calif. 93950; Phone (408) 373-5882. Offers comprehensive, 6-day, boatman's training courses on the Rogue River.

Whitewater Expeditions—River Explorations, 1811 Tulare St., Richmond, Calif. 94805. This is the author's outfit. Each season we conduct a few purely instructional trips on western rivers in the course of which trip members learn the full range of rafting skills including rowing and paddling technique and everything from emergency procedures to camp cooking. Also, each year we guide oar-powered expeditions down new, sometimes unexplored rivers in the wilds of British Columbia, Alaska, Mexico, Central and South America, and beyond. On these trips the group (all of our groups are small) pulls together to cope with strange lands, unknown water, and, often, exotic cultures along the river. Although each person is thoroughly schooled in water dynamics, emergency procedures, camp cooking, and so on, and, while everyone who so desires gains some experience at the oars, the amount of rowing participants do depends heavily on the nature of the river we are exploring.

Whitewater Guide Trips, 12120 S.W. Douglas, Portland, Oreg. 97225. Phone (503) 646-8849. Whitewater youth camp for boys aged 12 through 17.

Wild Rivers—Idaho/Wilderness Encounters, Inc., P.O. Box 232, Cambridge, Idaho 83610. Phone (208) 257-3410. Paddle trips on the Main Salmon in inflatable kayaks and, possibly by the time this book is released, Sportyaks.

Zephyr Whitewater School, Box 529, Columbia, Calif. 95310. Phone (209) 532-6249. Offers a 5-day course in whitewater rafting plus a paddle option on daily trips on the Stanislaus and American Rivers in California.

APPENDIX VIII

Rafting Outfitters

The outfitters listed here offer raft trips on rivers throughout the western United States and Canada and also in foreign lands. On the majority of these trips, passengers take little part in guiding the rafts, and they are waited on in camp, often with considerable style. Those who seek greater participation in their encounter with the river would do well to go instead with friends or with a whitewater school. But for some, these trips are made to order. Most of these outfits also hire boatmen and boatwomen from time to time.

Adventure Bound, Inc., 6179 South Adams Drive, Littleton, Colo. 80121

Adventures Unlimited, P.O. Box 363, Columbia, Calif. 95310

Alaska Wilderness River Trips, Inc., Box 1143, Eagle River, Alaska 99577

Al Beam Floats, Box 354, Ketchum-Sun Valley, Idaho 83340

American Guides Association, Inc., Box B, Woodland, Calif. 95695

American River Touring Association (ARTA), 1016 Jackson St., Oakland, Calif. 94607

Arizona River Runners, Inc., P.O. Box 2021, Marble Canyon, Ariz. 86036

B. A. Hanten, Morrison's Lodge, Merlin, Oreg. 97532

Barker-Ewing Float Trips, Box 1243, Jackson, Wyo. 83001

Canadian River Expeditions Limited, 1412 Sandhurst Place, West Vancouver, B.C., Canada

Canyoneers, Inc., Box 957, Flagstaff, Ariz. 86001

Cascade Raft Expeditions Ltd., P.O. Box 46441, Vancouver 8, B.C., Canada

Colorado River and Trail Expeditions, Inc., 1449 E. 30th South, Salt Lake City, Utah 84106

Cross Tours and Expeditions, Inc., 274 West 1400 South, Orem, Utah 84057

Echo, The Wilderness Company, 2424 Russell St., Berkeley, Calif. 94705

Eldon Handy's Salmon River Expeditions, Inc., Box 15, Jerome, Idaho 83338

Erickson's Adventures, P.O. Box 2067, Scottsdale, Ariz. 85251

Etcetera, P.O. Box 131, Vallecito, Calif. 95251

Flagg Float Trips, P.O. Box 269, Wilson, Wyo. 83014

Fort Jackson Corporation, Jackson, Wyo. 83001

Fort Lee Co., Box 2103, Marble Canyon, Ariz. 86036

Georgie's Royal River Rats, P.O. Box 12489, Las Vegas, Nev. 89112

Grand Canyon/Canyonlands Expeditions, P.O. Box O, Kanab, Utah 84741

Grand Canyon Dories, Inc., Box 5585, Stanford, Calif. 94305

Harris Boat Trips, 250 N. 500 E., Box 776, Centerville, Utah 84014

Hatch River Expeditions Co., Inc., 411 East 2nd North, Vernal, Utah 84078. (In addition to regular trips over the West, the Hatch brothers will arrange paddle trips on request.)

Headwater Float Trips, P.O. Box 1300, Jackson, Wyo. 83001

Holiday River Expeditions, Inc., 519 Malibu Drive, Salt Lake City, Utah 84107

Kent Frost Canyonlands Tours, Inc., 295 Blue Mt. Drive, Monticello, Utah 84535

Meander Tours, P.O. Box 511, Pinedale, Calif. 93650

Missouri River Cruises, Box 1212, Fort Benton, Mont. 59442

Moki Mac River Expeditions, 6829 Bella Vista Drive, Salt Lake City, Utah 84121

Mother Lode, 581 Continental Dr., San Jose, Calif. 95111

Mountain River Guides, 3325 Fowler Ave., Ogden, Utah 84403

Nicholson's Salmon River Float Trips, Route 3, Twin Falls, Idaho 83301

North American River Expeditions, 570 N. Main, Moab, Utah 84532

O.A.R.S., Inc., P.O. Box 67, Angels Camp, Calif. 95222

"Old Timer" Float Trips, Inc., Box 1074, Jackson, Wyo. 83001

Outdoors Unlimited, 2500 Fifth Ave., Sacramento, Calif. 95818

Parklands Expeditions, P.O. Box 371, Jackson Hole, Wyo. 83001

Primitive Area Float Trips, Box 585, Salmon, Idaho 83467

R.A.F.T., Inc., 440 North 1st St., San Jose, Calif. 95112

River Adventures West, P.O. Box 801, 17901 Castellamare Drive, Pacific Palisades, Calif. 90272

Rogue River Raft Trips, Morrison's Lodge, 8500 Galice Rd., Merlin, Oreg. 97532

Salmon River Boat Tours, Box 1185, North Fork, Idaho 83466

Sanderson Bros.' Expeditions, P.O. Box 1535, Page, Ariz. 86040

Slickrock River Co., Box 10543, Denver, Colo. 80210

Snake River Float Trips, Moran, Wyo. 83013

Snake River Outfitters, 811 Snake River Avenue, Lewiston, Idaho 83501

SOBEK Expeditions (specializes in daring raft expeditions in far-off, exotic places), P.O. Box 67, Angels Camp, Calif. 95222

Solitude Float Trips, Box 112, Moose, Wyo. 83012

Tag-A-Long Tours, 452 N. Main St., Box 1206, Moab, Utah 84532

Teton Expeditions, Inc., 427 E. 13th St., Idaho Falls, Idaho 83401

Tex's Tour Center, P.O. Box 67, Moab, Utah 84532

Tour West, P.O. Box 333, Orem, Utah 84057

Travel Institute, 714 9th Ave., Salt Lake City, Utah 84103

Upper Missouri Wilderness Waterway Cruise Co., Box 724, Fort Benton, Mont. 59442

Western River Expeditions, Inc., Box 6339, Salt Lake City, Utah 84106

Whitewater Expeditions/River Exploration/River Gear, 1811 Tulare St., Richmond, Calif. 94805

Whitewater Guide Trips, 12120 S.W. Douglas, Portland, Oreg. 97225

White Water River Expeditions, Box 1249, Turlock, Calif. 95380

Wilderness Encounters Inc., Box 232, Cambridge, Idaho 83610

Wilderness River Outfitters and Trail Expeditions, P.O. Box 871A, Salmon, Idaho 83467

Wilderness Water Ways (Bryce Whitmore), 33 Canyon Lake Dr., Port Costa, Calif. 94569

Wilderness Waterways, Inc., Box 2700, Idaho Falls, Idaho 83401

Wilderness World, 1342 Jewell Ave., Pacific Grove, Calif. 93950

Wonderland Expeditions, P.O. Box 338, Green River, Utah 84525

World Wide River Expeditions, Inc., 2982 Metropolitan Way, Salt Lake City, Utah 84109

Zephyr River Expeditions, P.O. Box 529, Columbia, Calif. 95310

A Glossary of
River and Rafting Terms

ABOVE

Upriver from.

ALLUVIAL

Pertaining to material carried or laid down by running water. Alluvium is the material deposited by streams. It includes gravel, sand, silt, and clay.

BACK PIVOT

Turning the raft from a ferry angle to a stern-downstream position. Used in tight places to recover from an extreme ferry angle, this maneuver narrows the passing space of the boat and allows it to slide closely past obstructions.

BACKROLLER

A broad reversal, such as that found below a dam or ledge.

BAR

An accumulation of sand, gravel, or rock in the river channel or along the banks.

BASKET BOAT	A 10-man size, military-surplus raft constructed of an upper and a lower buoyancy tube; the upper tube flares outward, giving the boat a bowl- or basketlike appearance.
BEAM	The width of a raft at its widest point.
BELAY	To wrap a line around a rock or tree so as to slow or stop slippage. This technique allows one man to hold a line under great pull.
BELOW	Downriver from.
BIG WATER	Large volume, fast current, big waves, often accompanied by huge reversals and extreme general turbulence. The terms big water and heavy water are closely similar, but big water carries stronger suggestions of immense volume and extreme violence.
BOAT	Raft. These words are interchangeable.
BOIL	A water current upwelling into a convex mound.
BOULDER FAN	A sloping, fan-shaped mass of boulders deposited by a tributary stream where it enters into the main canyon. These often constrict the river, causing rapids.
BOULDER GARDEN	A rapid densely strewn with boulders that necessitate intricate maneuvering.
BOW	Front of a boat. See Galloway Position.
BOW-IN	With bow pointed forward.

BROACH

To turn a boat broadside to the current. Usually spells certain upset in heavy water.

CARTWHEELING

Technique of spinning a raft just before a collision with a rock so as to rotate the raft off and around the rock.

CFS

Cubic feet per second. Sometimes referred to as second feet. A unit of water flow used to indicate the volume of water flowing per second past any given point along a river.

CHANNEL

A raftable route through a section of river.

CHUTE

A clear channel between obstructions, steeper and faster than the surrounding water.

CONFLUENCE

The point where two or more rivers meet.

CURLER

A high, steep wave that curls or falls back onto its own upstream face. Considered by most to be a form of reversal. See Reversal.

DOUBLE-OAR TURN

Rowing technique used to turn (or to prevent the turning of) a raft. Consists of simultaneously pulling on one oar while pushing on the other.

DRAW STROKE

Paddling technique of moving the boat sideways toward the paddle. Effective only with small, light rafts.

D-RING

Metal, D-shaped ring attached to a raft and used to secure frames, lines, rope thwarts, etc.

DROP

An abrupt descent in a river. A pitch.

EASY-ROWER WASHER — Large plastic, rubber, or metal washer placed between the oar and frame to reduce friction.

EDDY — A place where the current either stops or turns to head upstream. Usually found below obstructions and on the inside of bends.

EDDY CUSHION — The layer of slack or billowing water that pads the upstream face of rocks and other obstructions. See Pillow.

EDDY FENCE — The sharp boundary at the edge of an eddy between two currents of different velocity or direction. Usually marked by swirling water and bubbles. Also called an eddy line and an eddy wall.

FALLS — A drop over which the water falls free at least part of the way.

FERRY — A maneuver for moving a boat laterally across a current. Usually accomplished by rowing or paddling upstream at an angle. See also Reverse Ferry.

FLOOD PLAIN — That portion of a river valley, adjacent to the river channel, which is built of sediments deposited by the river and which is covered with water when the river overflows its banks at flood stages.

FOUR-MAN RAFT — A boat 4½ by 9 feet that will, on small rivers, accommodate one or two people. Only those 4-mans with inflated tube diameters of at least 16 inches are suitable for river use. These little boats handle best when loaded with only one person and fitted with frame and 6- or 7-foot oars.

FREEBOARD

The distance from the water line to the top of the buoyancy tube.

GALLOWAY POSITION

Basic position for oar boats; the oarsman faces the bow, which is pointed downstream.

GATE

Narrow, short passage between two obstacles.

GRADIENT

The slope of a river expressed in feet per mile.

GREEN RIVER BOAT

A raft 8 by 17 feet made by Rubber Fabricators that can accommodate five or six people.

G-RIG

Three pontoons lashed together side by side. Invented by and named for Georgie White, this floating island is suitable only for enormous rivers like the Frazer River in British Columbia or the Colorado of Cataract Canyon and the Grand Canyon.

GRIP

The extreme upper end of a single-bladed paddle, shaped for holding with the palm over the top.

HAIR

Fast, extremely turbulent water covered with white, aerated foam.

HANGING TRIBUTARY

A tributary stream that enters a main canyon over a waterfall. The tributary canyon mouth is on the wall of the main canyon rather than at river level.

HAYSTACK

A large standing wave caused by deceleration of current.

HEAVY WATER

Fast current, large waves, usually associated with holes, boulders, and general turbulence. See Big Water.

HOLE	A reversal. This term is generally applied to reversals of less than riverwide width. See Souse Hole.
HOUSE BOULDER	A house-sized boulder.
HUNG UP	Said of a raft that is caught on but not wrapped around a rock or other obstacle.
HYDRAULIC	A reversal. This is a general term for reversals, eddy fences, and other places where there is a hydraulic gap, a powerful current differential. Sometimes used in the plural to refer to the whole phenomenon of big water, where massive waves, violent currents, and large holes are the obstacles, rather than rocks.
HYPOTHERMIA	A serious physical condition caused by a lowering of the core body temperature. Symptoms include lack of coordination, thickness of speech, irrationality, blueness of skin, dilation of pupils, decrease in heart and respiratory rate, extreme weakness, and uncontrolled shivering. Victims often become unconscious and sometimes die. *First aid:* Quickly strip off wet clothes and surround victim skin-to-skin in a bare-body sandwich; administer hot drink, etc.
J-RIG	A pontoon-sized raft formed by joining several giant snout-nosed sponsons.
JUMP TO!	Jump to the downstream side of the raft, fast! This command is used just before collisions with rocks and other obstructions. If a crew is quick, the raft's upstream side is

	lifted up in time to let the current slide under, rather than into, the raft. This action often prevents the raft from becoming wrapped.
KEEPER	A reversal capable of trapping a raft for long periods. Similar to but more powerful than a stopper.
LEDGE	The exposed edge of a rock stratum that acts as a low natural dam or as a series of such dams.
LEFT BANK	Left side of the river when facing downstream.
LINING	The use of ropes to work a boat down through a rapid from shore.
LOGJAM	A strainer dam of logs across a river. This dangerous phenomenon is common on small streams in wooded country.
MEANDER	A looplike bend in the course of a river.
"NICE LOOKING RUBBER"	One of the higher compliments that can be paid a raft.
OAR CLIP	A piece of resilient metal in the shape of a pinched U that is used to hold an oar to the thole pin.
OAR FRAME	Same as rowing frame.
OAR RUBBER	Piece of thick rubber used to hold an oar to the thole pin.
OUTFIT	The articles and methods used to fit out, or rig, a raft for river running. For example, the outfit of an oar raft includes a rowing frame, oars, the method of securing the frame to the raft, the method of securing the gear to the frame, etc. The outfit of a paddle raft includes

paddles, rope thwarts, perhaps a frame or poop deck, and so on. The term may also be used to refer to any commercial company, especially one engaged in outfitting trips down rivers.

PAINTER

A line, usually about 20 feet long, attached to the bow of paddle rafts and the stern of oar rafts. Not to be confused with the much longer bow and stern lines.

PANCAKING

In a threesome raft, when the bow boat flips back onto the middle boat.

PARK

In a generally steep-walled canyon, a wide, level place adjacent to the river with grass and trees, often found at the mouths of tributaries.

PILLOW

The layer of slack water that pads the upstream face of rocks and other obstructions. The broader the upstream face, the more ample the pillow. Also called an eddy cushion.

PITCH

A section of a rapid steeper than the surrounding portions; a drop.

PIVOT

Turning the raft from a ferry angle to a bow-downstream position. This narrows the passing space of the boat, allowing it to slide closely past obstructions. Sometimes called a front pivot.

PONTOON

An inflatable boat 22 feet long or larger. These mammoth rafts usually have 3-foot tubes and 9-foot beams and range in length from 22 to 37 feet.

POOL

A deep and quiet stretch of river.

PORTEGEE

Rowing technique of moving a boat forward by pushing on the oars.

PRY STROKE

Paddling technique of moving a boat sideways away from the paddle. Effective only with small, light rafts.

RAPID

A fast, turbulent stretch of river, often with obstructions, but usually without an actual waterfall. Contrary to common misconception, only the plural takes an "s."

REVERSAL

A place where the current swings upward and revolves back on itself, forming a treacherous meeting of currents that can drown swimmers and slow, swamp, trap, or flip rafts. Some reversals take the form of flat, foamy, surface backflows immediately below large obstructions just under the surface, while others consist of steep waves that curl heavily back onto their own upstream faces. Reversals are also called hydraulics, stoppers, keepers, white eddies, roller waves, backrollers, curlers, sidecurlers, souse holes, and, most frequently, holes. Although some of these terms are used loosely to refer to any sort of reversal, others carry more precise shades of meaning and refer to certain types of reversals. Each of these terms is discussed separately in this glossary.

REVERSE FERRY

A rowing technique whereby the oarsman rows diagonally downstream for a short distance so as to power stern first into an eddy. With a heavy raft, this technique sometimes provides the *only* means of entering a small eddy.

RIFFLE	A shallow rapid with very small waves, often over a sand or gravel bottom. Does not rate a grade on either the Western or the International scale of difficulty.
RIGHT BANK	Right side of the river when facing downstream.
ROCK GARDEN	A rapid thickly strewn with exposed or partially covered rocks that demand intricate maneuvering.
ROLLER WAVE	A reversal. This term is used variously to mean curler and back-roller.
ROPE THWARTS	In paddle rafts, taut ropes or straps running crossways from tube to tube and often positioned just forward of cross tubes. When paddlers wedge their knees under these rope thwarts, they are able to deliver stronger strokes and are less likely to be washed overboard. Rope thwarts should in no way entangle or hamper a paddler coming free from an overturned raft; this tragedy occurs all too often.
ROWING FRAME	A rigid frame that provides a seat for the oarsman and allows the raft to be controlled by large oars. It often also serves as a rack for gear. Also called an oar frame.
SANDPAPER	Small choppy waves over shallows.
SCOUT	To examine a rapid from shore.
SECTION	A portion of river located between two points; a stretch.
SEVEN-MAN RAFT	A boat 6½ by 12 feet that will accommodate three or four people. This is a fine all-around raft.

SHORTY PONTOON

A 22- to 25-foot pontoon. See Pontoon.

SHUTTLE

The process of moving vehicles from the put-in to the take-out or trip members in the reverse direction. This can be accomplished by driving at least two vehicles to the take-out and one back to the put-in, by hiring local drivers, or by using a charter flight service if you can afford it. Or you can hitchhike with a sign reading: RIVER RAFTING —NEED RIDE UPRIVER.

SIDECURLER

A reversal parallel to the main current, formed by a side current passing over a rock as it enters the main channel.

SIX-MAN RAFT

A boat 5½ by 12 feet that will accommodate one to three people. The cheaper varieties, if used at all, should be fitted with frame and 8-foot oars and should carry only one person.

SLEEPER

Submerged rock or boulder just below the surface, usually marked by little or no surface disturbance.

SMOKER

An extremely violent rapid; hair.

SNEAK

To take an easy route around a difficult spot. Often takes the form of maneuvering down one side of a big rapid in order to avoid the turbulence in the center.

SOUSE HOLE

A hole found below an underwater obstruction, such as a boulder. This term usually refers to holes of narrow or moderate width that have water pouring in not only from the upstream and downstream directions but also from the sides.

SPONSONS

Enormous inflatable tubes mounted alongside pontoons for added stability.

SPORTYAK

A one-man, 7-foot rowboat of rigid plastic with spray shields jutting up from bow and stern.

STAGE MARKER

A gauge placed along a river shoreline that is calibrated in feet or fractions thereof starting from an arbitrary zero point. With appropriate conversion information, these readings may be converted into cfs or, more important, raftability ratings.

STAIRCASE

A stretch of river where the water pours over a series of drops that resemble a staircase.

STANDING WAVE

A wave caused by the deceleration of current that occurs when fast-moving water slams into slower-moving water. Unlike ocean waves, which sweep forward while the water in them remains relatively still, merely rising and falling in place, these waves stand in a fixed position while the water rushes through them. The height of these waves is measured vertically from the trough to the crest.

STERN

Rear of a boat.

STOPPER

A reversal powerful enough to stop a raft momentarily. Also called a stopper wave. See Keeper.

STRAINER

Brush, fallen trees, bridge pilings, or anything else that allows the cur-

	rent to sweep through but pins boats and boaters. These are lethal.
STRETCH	A portion of river located between two points; a section.
SWEEP OAR	A large oar extending over the bow or stern, commonly with the blade angled at the throat.
TEN-MAN RAFT	A boat 8 by 16 feet that will accommodate four to six people. This is an excellent all-around boat.
THOLE PIN	An upright steel pin on a rowing frame that serves as a fulcrum, or pivot point, for the oar. Uncapped pins are used with oar rubbers, while capped pins, which are far safer, are used with oar clips.
THREESOME RAFT	Three rafts lashed together side by side. See G-rig.
THROAT	On an oar or paddle, the point where the shaft meets the blade.
TONGUE	The smooth V of fast water found at the head of rapids.
TRIM	The angle to the water at which a boat rides. The crew and gear should be positioned so that the boat is level from side to side, and slightly heavier in the bow than in the stern.
TRIPLE-RIG	Same as Threesome Raft.
WET SUIT	A close-fitting garment of neoprene foam that provides thermal insulation in cold water.
WHITE EDDY	A reversal below a ledge or other underwater obstruction characterized by a foamy backflow at the surface.

WRAPPED   Said of a raft pinned flat around a rock or other obstruction by the current.

A Selected Bibliography

This bibliography applies mainly to Part I. For bibliographies pertaining to individual rivers, see the river listings in Part II.

American National Red Cross. *Advanced First Aid and Emergency Care*. Garden City, N.Y.: Doubleday & Co., Inc., 1973. 318 pp.

American National Red Cross. *Canoeing*. Garden City, N.Y.: Doubleday & Co., Inc., 1956. 445 pp.

American National Red Cross. *Standard First Aid and Personal Safety*. Garden City, N.Y.: Doubleday & Co., Inc., 1973. 268 pp.

Angier, Bradford. *How To Stay Alive in the Woods*. New York: Collier Books, 1962. 285 pp. (Originally published by Stackpole Books in 1956 as *Living Off the Country*.)

Appalachian Mountain Club. *A.M.C. New Englnand Canoeing Guide*. Boston: Appalachian Mountain Club, 1971. 600 pp.

Ashley, Clifford W. *The Ashley Book of Knots*. Garden City, N.Y.: Doubleday, Doran & Co., Inc., 1944. 620 pp.

Blackadar, Dr. Walt. "I Dig Hair—Big, Not Long." *American Whitewater*, vol. 16, no. 4 (Winter, 1971), pp. 132-136. (In order to subscribe to this whitewater magazine, contact AWA Journal, P.O. Box 1584, San Bruno, Calif. 94066.)

Blosser, Dr. John. "Wilderness Medicine." *Emergency Medicine* (July, 1972), pp. 21-45.

Braun, Ernest, and David Cavagnaro. *Living Water*. Palo Alto, Calif.: American West Publishing Co., 1971. 184 pp. "An exploration with stunning color photographs and text of the vital, varied role that water plays in sustaining both man and nature."

Brower, David, ed. *The Sierra Club Wilderness Handbook*. New York: Ballantine Books, 1967. 272 pp.

Burrell, Bob, and Paul Davidson. *Wildwater West Virginia*. Parsons, W. Va.: McClain Printing Co., 1972. 159 pp.

Carter, Randy. *Canoeing Whitewater River Guide*. Oakton, Va.: Appalachian Books, 1967, rev. ed. 1974. 195 pp.

Elliott, Bob. "A Manual for White-Water Rafting." Oakland, Calif.: American River Touring Association, 1971. 8 pp.

"First Aid for a Raft." *Oar & Paddle*, vol. 1, no. 2 (July-August, 1974), pp. 28-29.

Kauffman, John M. *Flow East: A Look at Our North Atlantic Rivers*. New York: McGraw-Hill, 1973. 284 pp.

Kodet, Dr. E. Russel, and Bradford Angier. *Being Your Own Wilderness Doctor*. New York: Pocket Books, 1972. 173 pp. (Originally published in 1968 by Stackpole Books.)

Miracle, Leonard, with Maurice H. Decker. *Complete Book of Camping*. New York: Outdoor Life/Harper & Row, 1961. 594 pp.

Palzer, Bob, and Jody Palzer. *Whitewater; Quietwater*. Two Rivers, Wis.: Evergreen Paddleways, 1973. 156 pp.

Pringle, Laurence. *Wild River*. Philadelphia: J. B. Lippincott Co., 1972. 128 pp., illus.

"Public Health Standards: Colorado River. Grand Canyon." Grand Canyon National Park, 1972. 10 pp.

Schwenk, Theodore. *Sensitive Chaos*. London: Rudolf Steiner Press, 1965. 145 pp. "The creation of flowing forms in water and air—an in depth study of water as the unifying element of organic wholeness as expressed in art as well as natural forms."

Shakespeare, William. *Shakespeare: The Complete Works*. Edited by G. B. Harrison. Harcourt, Brace & World, Inc., 1948. 1668 pp. A true guide to survival.

Sindelar, Jim, and Walt Harvest. "Souse Holes—the Ins and Outs." *American Whitewater*, vol. 16, no. 1 (Spring, 1971), pp. 5-7.

Thomas, Eben. *Hot Blood and Wet Paddles*. Hallowell, Maine: Hallowell Printing Co., 1974. 188 pp.

Trost, Carl. "Life Jackets?" *American Whitewater*, vol. 17, no. 1 (Spring, 1972), pp. 12-25.

Underhill, J. E. "Bear!" British Columbia Department of Recreation and Conservation, Parks Branch, 1971. 4 pp.

United States Department of Agriculture. *First Aid Guide for USDA Employees*. Washington, D.C.: U.S. Government Printing Office, 1962. 64 pp.

Urban, John T. *A Whitewater Handbook for Canoe and Kayak.* Boston: Appalachian Mountain Club, 1965. 76 pp.

Whitney, Peter Dwight. *White-Water Sport: Running Rapids in Kayak and Canoe.* New York: The Ronald Press, 1960. 120 pp.

Wilson, Donald H., M.D. "Head Injury in Whitewater." *American Whitewater*, vol. 18, no. 1 (Spring, 1973), pp. 14-15.

Winn, Pete, with Bob Elliott, Bob Melville, Dan Marshall, David Kay, and ARTA's Grand Canyon staff. *River Guides' Manual.* Oakland, Calif.: American River Touring Association, 1973. 50 pp.

Index